Gerald T. Sheppard

Wisdom as a Hermeneutical Construct

Gerald T. Sheppard

Wisdom as a Hermeneutical Construct

A Study in the Sapientializing of the Old Testament

Walter de Gruyter · Berlin · New York
1980

Beiheft zur Zeitschrift für die alttestamentliche Wissenschaft

Herausgegeben von Georg Fohrer

151

Library of Congress Cataloging in Publication Data

Sheppard, Gerald T 1946–
Wisdom as a hermeneutical construct.

(Beiheft zur Zeitschrift für die alttestamentliche Wissenschaft; 151)
Bibliography: p. 161

1. Wisdom literature–Criticism, interpretation, etc. 2. Bible. O.T. Apocrypha. Ecclesiasticus–Criticism, interpretation, etc. 3. Bible. O.T. Apocrypha. Baruch–Criticism, interpretation, etc. 4. Bible. O.T.–Criticism, interpretation, etc. I. Title. II. Series: Zeitschrift für die alttestamentliche Wissenschaft : Beiheft ; 151.

BS410.Z5 vol. 151 [BS1455] 221'.08s 79-13156
ISBN 3-11-007504-0 [229'.4'06]

CIP-Kurztitelaufnahme der Deutschen Bibliothek

Sheppard, Gerald T.:

Wisdom as a hermeneutical construct : a study in the sapientializing of the old testament / Gerald T. Sheppard. – Berlin, New York : de Gruyter, 1980.
(Zeitschrift für die alttestamentliche Wissenschaft : Beih. ; 151)
ISBN 3-11-007504-0

Printed in Germany

Satz und Druck: Hubert & Co., Göttingen
Bindearbeiten: Lüderitz & Bauer, Berlin 61

To my parents,
Emma and Thomas I. Sheppard

Foreword

I wish to express my gratitude most of all to Professor Brevard S. Childs of Yale University for his persistent interest, suggestions, and encouragement on this project. The best of this research should be viewed as a tribute to him. I am also indebted to the copious criticisms and suggestions of Professor Sid Z. Leiman, S. Dean McBride, and Robert R. Wilson. Likewise, for various stages of typing and proofreading, I thank Samuel Huestis, Ann Salinas, Erma Frodsham, Ron Hock, Leslie Wolff, and Karen Lanier. My wife, Marilyn, deserves much credit for this effort. Not only did she give sacrificially of her time to allow me to pursue the research, but she also proofread parts of the manuscript and helped prepare the bibliography.

I am grateful to the Layne Foundation for tuition grants and to Yale University for stipends, without which graduate study would not have been possible. Union Theological Seminary in New York, through the offices of President Donald W. Shriver and Dean Milton McC. Gatch, generously provided the subvention fee for publication. Finally, I want to thank Professor Georg Fohrer for his acceptance of this work in the BZAW Monograph series.

This book is dedicated to my parents, Thomas and Emma Sheppard, who tirelessly supported and encouraged my work. They always read the Scriptures in the present tense, as a guide to the obedient life. I have sought in this monograph to understand something about how they and the generations of the faithful before them found contemporary wisdom in such ancient religious traditions.

Gerald T. Sheppard

Table of Contents

Abbreviations

AK	*Antike Kunst*
Aq.	Aquila
Ara.	Aramaic
B	LXX, Codex Vaticanus (= II, Holmes)
BA	*Biblical Archaeologist*
BBB	*Bonner biblische Beiträge*
Bib	*Biblica*
BVC	*Bible et vie chrétienne*
BZAW	*Beihefte zur Zeitschrift für die alttestamentliche Wissenschaft*
CBQ	*Catholic Biblical Quarterly*
CBQMS	*Catholic Biblical Quarterly–Monograph Series*
Eth. Enoch	Ethiopic Enoch
EvTh	*Evangelische Theologie*
G	Greek texts of Sirach or Baruch
HTR	*Harvard Theological Review*
IDB	G. A. Buttrick (ed.), *Interpreter's Dictionary of the Bible*
Inter.	*Interpretation*
JBL	*Journal of Biblical Literature*
JBR	*Journal of Bible and Religion*
JQR	*Jewish Quarterly Review*
JSS	*Journal of Semitic Studies*
JThS	*Journal of Theological Studies*
KerDo	*Kerygma und Dogma*
L	Latin texts of Sirach and Baruch
LCL	Loeb Classical Library
LXX	The Septuagint
MsA, MsB, MsC, MsD	Hebrew fragments of Sirach as distinguished by the Vattioni Polyglot Edition (Naples, 1968)
MT	Masoretic Text
n.	footnote
NT	New Testament
OLZ	*Orientalische Literaturzeitung*
OT	Old Testament
OTS	*Oudtestamentische Studiën*
OTSt	*Old Testament Studies*
RB	*Revue biblique*
RSV	Revised Standard Version
S	Syriac texts of Sirach or Baruch
SVT	*Supplements to Vetus Testamentum*
Symm.	Symmachus

Syr. Bar. Apoc.	Syriac Apocalypse of Baruch
Syroh.	Syrohexapla
TDig.	*Theology Digest*
Theod.	Theodotion
ThLZ	*Theologische Literaturzeitung*
ThR	*Theologische Rundschau*
TRev	*Theologische Revue*
TPQ	*Theologisch-Praktische Quartalschrift*
TUGAL	*Texte und Untersuchungen zur Geschichte der altchristlichen Literatur*
VT	*Vetus Testamentum*
WMANT	*Wissenschaftliche Monographien zum Alten und Neuen Testament*
WZKM	*Wiener Zeitschrift für die Kunde des Morgenlandes*
ZAW	*Zeitschrift für die alttestamentliche Wissenschaft*

Chapter I

Introduction

Biblical wisdom research, in the last few decades, has shifted from the detached examination of a few isolated wisdom books to a vigorous search for wisdom influence throughout the entire corpus of Scripture. In the spirit of this renewed appreciation for the genuine significance of wisdom in the life and literature of Israel, this monograph is a probe into a literary and theological function of wisdom in the exilic and post-exilic periods. More specifically, it is, first, an investigation into the way certain early post-exilic literature interpreted the Torah as a guide to wisdom and, second, an application of that information to illuminate certain corresponding redactional features of Old Testament books. Because the particular choice of method arises as an attempt to circumvent some persistent problems in the current "wisdom influence" discussion, a consideration of that discussion must precede the full statement of our approach to the subject.

The Problem of Wisdom in Recent Critical Scholarship

In the period since the end of World War II, one of the most exciting and fruitful areas of critical biblical research has been the study of wisdom literature in the OT. Whereas in the period of the 20's and 30's publication was limited to several learned and judicious studies, e.g., Fichtner, Duesberg, Rankin, beginning with the late 40's a veritable flood of monographs and articles have appeared in the field of wisdom.[1]

The reasons for the new interest are clear enough. The epoch-making article of Erman comparing Egyptian material with Proverbs launched an international debate over the place of Israel's wisdom traditions in the

[1] For bibliography on the earlier period see W. Baumgartner, "Die israelitische Weisheitsliteratur," *ThR*, 5 (1933): 259–61. For the later discussion, see R. B. Y. Scott, "The Study of the Wisdom Literature," *Inter*, 24 (1970): 20–45, and J. L. Crenshaw, "Prolegomenon" in *Studies in Ancient Israelite Wisdom* (New York: KTAV Publishing House, 1976), pp. 1–21.

ancient world.[2] This new investigation opened up the possibility of recovering ancient roots to the phenomenon of biblical wisdom and allowed scholars to break out of the narrow historical boundaries to which OT wisdom had been confined. Moreover, this expanded possibility for wisdom evoked a fresh literary critical search for it in Scripture. Baumgartner's early form critical essay demonstrated that Gunkel's method could also be successfully applied in this area as well.[3] On the basis of the older documentary analysis, R.H. Pfeiffer even posited an Edomite wisdom source for the core of Gen. 1–11.[4] There were other factors as well which played a role. Undoubtedly the growing interest in the "secular" side of Israel's life, which reacted against the overemphasis on the "kerygmatic" approach to OT, entered into the picture.[5]

After World War II these initial probes into wisdom continued to inspire scholarly interest in the subject. The new contributions, however, reflected a quite different fascination with the presence and significance of "wisdom elements" in non-wisdom literature. In 1944 von Rad had pointed up wisdom elements in the Succession Narrative, but Fichtner's pioneering study of Isaiah in 1949 was the first to explore such isolated features as a key to the background and message of a biblical author.[6] Similarly, in 1953 von Rad wrote a brilliant essay on the form and function of the Joseph Story which found in the Story's concentration on the "anthropological factor" a concern for novelistic instruction in wisdom.[7] Once the detection of isolated wisdom elements proved a basis for assessing the background and interpretation of biblical literature in general,

---

[2] Cf. A. Erman, "Das Weisheitsbuch des Amen-em-ope," *OLZ*, 27 (1924): 241–52. For bibliography concerning these events, see Scott, op. cit., p. 23 and Crenshaw, op. cit., p. 32, n. 32.

[3] W. Baumgartner, "Die literarischen Gattungen in der Weisheit des Jesus Sirach," *ZAW*, 34 (1914): 169–98.

[4] R.H. Pfeiffer, "Edomite Wisdom," *ZAW*, 3 (1926): 13–25; "A Non-Israelite Source of the Book of Genesis," *ZAW*, 48 (1930): 66–73; and "Wisdom and Vision in the Old Testament," *ZAW*, 52 (1943): 93–102.

[5] J.E. Priest attributes to Gunkel the earliest contemporary stress on wisdom's secular nature; see his "Where is Wisdom to be Placed?" *JBR*, 31 (1963): 726. For J. Coert Rylaarsdam, early wisdom, likewise, lacked a transcendental reference; see his *Revelation in Jewish Wisdom Literature* (Chicago: University of Chicago Press, 1946), p. 57.

[6] G. von Rad, "Der Anfang der Geschichtsschreibung im alten Israel," *AK*, 32 (1944): 1–42; J. Fichtner, "Jesaja unter den Weisen," *ThLZ*, 74 (1949): 75–80.

[7] G. von Rad, "The Joseph Narrative and Ancient Wisdom" in *The Problem of the Hexateuch and Other Essays* (London: Oliver E. Boyd, 1965), pp. 281–300.

the search for wisdom escalated quickly into a major scholarly debate characterized by the current "wisdom influence" studies.[8]

But with this new impetus came a whole series of confusing problems which for the most part have remained unresolved. A brief review of some of the major areas of debate and the representative positions of the protagonists can serve to illustrate the present impasse.

Definition of wisdom. Just what is wisdom? Is it an appropriate biblical category? Does its definition derive from form critical, or historical, or material evidence? Is it a distinct social movement, a secular stance on life, a literary convention, or merely the presence of intellectual tradition in Israel? The obvious lack of consensus in both the method of inquiry and the conclusions about wisdom are reflected in the spectrum of scholarly opinion.

On the one hand, scholars have sought to define the phenomenon of wisdom very narrowly. W. McKane is a good representative of this approach. Distinguishing between a so-called "old wisdom" and a later development, he defined wisdom in its earlier manifestations as "primarily a disciplined empiricism engaged with the problems of government and administration."[9] Since piety is irrelevant to statescraft, McKane rejected any assumption that beyond its strict utilitarianism there lay a religious base.[10] In spite of the consistency and forcefulness of McKane's description, few scholars have been convinced that the term can be limited in this manner. McKane has been criticized for introducing much later philosophical categories, such as the use of the concept "empirical" to describe the epistemology of wisdom. Moreover, his preference for historical and archaeological, to the exclusion of form critical or literary arguments for wisdom, meant that his definition was constricted to lines of close continuity between the limited Palestinian evidence and the better Egyptian and Mesopotamian materials.

On the other hand, there were scholars like J. McKenzie who defined wisdom in such a broad, general way as to represent the other end of the spectrum. In his definition wise men were simply "convinced of experience and they know that wisdom arose from reflection on experience."[11] By

---

[8] The term "wisdom influence" became popular in the middle of the debate, particularly once the significance of such evidence was less than certain. Cf. J. L. Crenshaw, "Method in Determining Wisdom Influence Upon 'Historical' Literature," *JBL*, 88 (1969): 129–42.

[9] W. McKane, *Prophets and Wise Men* (Naperville: Alec R. Allenson, 1965), p. 53.

[10] Ibid., pp. 48–52.

[11] John McKenzie, "Reflections on Wisdom," *JBL*, 86 (1967): 5.

viewing the faith of wise men as a product of the collective experience of Israel and her ancestors, McKenzie identified the wise men "with the historian(s), and thus effectively designated the historical books as wisdom literature."[12] With such a broad, inclusive definition, one wonders if most of the OT has not been included within the definition in a way that vitiates its real historical and theological significance.

Of course, in between these two extremes are a host of other attempts at definition. Probably the most ambitious is the approach presented by von Rad. In his *Old Testament Theology*, von Rad saw a development from "old wisdom" to "theological," and finally, to "apocalyptic wisdom."[13]

The earliest of these manifestations of wisdom in Israel, von Rad called "old wisdom." Originating under the influence of Egyptian models, it found classical expression in the Israelite schools which flourished during the time of the "Solomonic Enlightement."[14] The discipline of old wisdom was a combination of an empirical assessment of reality, the function of teaching the product of such inquiry, and a deep piety which led the wise men to limit their observations to those areas not approached through the eye of faith. Nevertheless, wisdom and theology represented two different "forms of the apperception of truth for mankind–one systematic (philosophical and theological) and one empirical and gnomic."[15] The phenomenon of old wisdom in ancient Israel is exemplified in Prov. 10ff., Qoheleth, and the Joseph Story.

In plotting the later historical typology, von Rad postulates that during the exilic and post-exilic periods, Israel experienced a revolution in her concept of wisdom, from old wisdom to "theological wisdom." From a study of Prov. 1–9 and early Jewish wisdom literature he found that "the realm which the older human and empirical teaching had excluded with such a clear recognition of its limits was precisely that into which the theological wisdom entered, claimed, and filled."[16] Still later, this theological wisdom fell into a stultifying scepticism which blunted its confessional *a priori* and subsequently produced a new literature, namely, that of apocalyptic. In this final "apocalyptic wisdom," the scribal wise

---

[12] Ibid., p. 8.

[13] G. von Rad, *Old Testament Theology* (New York: Harper & Row, 1965), Vol. I, pp. 418–59.

[14] Ibid., p. 425 and von Rad, "The Joseph Narrative," op. cit., pp. 292–300.

[15] Von Rad, *Old Testament Theology*, op. cit., p. 421. Also, see his "Die ältere Weisheit Israels," *KerDo*, 2 (1956): 54–72.

[16] Ibid., p. 441.

men moved away from the more complex historical models of the past and reduced their perception of reality to a dangerously oversimplified "deterministic" pattern.[17]

In spite of the brilliance of the description, von Rad's distinctions labor under a number of vague historical assumptions and depend on modern philosophical categories which introduce an alien precision to the literature's own terms of definition. Solomonic Enlightenment, the characterization of wisdom as "international," "eudaemonic," and "empirical," the late dating Prov. 1–9, and the transformation of wisdom into apocalyptic, have all come under heavy criticism.[18] Admitting weaknesses in his formulation, von Rad produced an entirely new and equally impressive volume, *Weisheit in Israel.* Although he left the structure of wisdom's development in Israel essentially the same, von Rad refined or changed his use of the primary sources (esp. Prov. 1–9).[19] This kind of uncertainty accounts for the failure of scholars to reach an agreement on even the definition of wisdom and pinpoints at the outset the confusion within the discipline.

Forms and provenance of wisdom. It is hardly surprising that in the post World War II period the form critical questions dominated the study of wisdom. Earlier research had established the peculiarities of certain idioms, cliches and stylistic features in the traditional wisdom books of Proverbs, Job, and Qoheleth. But in what sense could one speak of wisdom forms? Several excellent form critical studies appeared. In his well-known article, R. B. Y. Scott was able to summarize some of the results.[20] But what was troubling was that the discovery of forms did not seem to provide a bridge to a provenance *(Sitz im Leben)* in the same way the method had done with the narrative and prophetic material.

Again various proposals were put forward as a possible setting for wisdom literature which offered a form critical rationale. McKane argued for the training of diplomats as the origin of old wisdom, Kayatz posited a school system and Duesberg located old wisdom in the courts.[21] In the early 60's Gerstenberger caused a great stir by positing a setting for wisdom in

[17] Ibid., pp. 303 ff. Cf. Klaus Koch, *The Rediscovery of Apocalyptic* (London: S. C. M. Press, 1973), pp. 43–44, in which Koch reviews the changes from edition to edition of von Rad's *Theology* in the course of a negative assessment of von Rad's position.

[18] See Crenshaw, "Prolegomenon," op. cit., p. 4.

[19] G. von Rad, *Wisdom in Israel* (Nashville: Abingdon Press, 1972), pp. 65 ff.

[20] Scott, loc. cit.

[21] Cf. Christa Bauer-Kayatz, *Studien zu Proverbien 1–9, WMANT*, 22 (1966): 147 ff. and H. Duesberg and I. Fransen, *Les Scribes Inspirés* (Maredsous, Belgium: Éditions de Maredsous, 1937), Vol. 1, pp. 129 ff.

the "family ethos" as "rules for social conduct."[22] Finally, Whybray sought to overcome the problem of locating a single setting for wisdom by postulating a general "intellectual tradition" which permeated every dimension of Israel's social strata.[23]

In his scholarly assessment of wisdom influence studies, Crenshaw criticized his colleague's methods of detecting wisdom in as much as their conclusions often depended merely on so-called wisdom vocabulary and themes.[24] Although he proposed as a corrective a more rigorous application of form critical method, Crenshaw did not adequately express why the method had failed in the past.[25] As an example of one such limitation, R. Murphy observed the tendency of wisdom proverbs to float freely throughout the widest range of differing life settings.[26] Likewise, Fichtner noted that the method itself frequently failed to distinguish "between the original meaning of a wisdom genre and the way in which it is utilized, that is, between form and function."[27] As a consequence, despite some explanations, it still remained a puzzlement why the form critical method did not seem to offer the insights expected. The material seems to have a dynamic which was not fully understood by the application of the older methods.

The relation of old to later wisdom. The complexities within the phenomena of wisdom had long been recognized. Very early the theory was proposed that wisdom had undergone a transformation from Israel's conceiving it as a practical skill to her seeing it as a form of philosophical reflection which culminated in a concept of hypostatization. How then was one to understand the forces that led to a development from the pragmatic to the theologically abstract, from mundane advice to Wisdom's recital of her participation in Israel's traditions (cf. Prov. 8 and Sir. 24)? By and large, the inability to join the two alleged stages of development within wisdom is reflected in the tendency of scholars to deal with only one stage to the exclusion of the other. Thus, Eichrodt in his *Theology* focused

---

[22] E. Gerstenberger, "Convenant and Commandment," *JBL*, 15 (1965): 38ff. See his *Wesen und Herkunft des sogenannten "Apodictischen Rechts,"* WMANT, 20 (1961): 70ff.

[23] R.N. Whybray, *The Intellectual Tradition in Israel, BZAW*, 27 (1974): 75ff. His proposal is vulnerable to the criticism of circular reasoning, because it depends at the outset on a "terminology of the intellectual tradition" which is "characteristic of Proverbs, Job, and Ecclesiastes" (p. 75).

[24] Crenshaw, "Methods in Determining Wisdom Influence," op. cit., pp. 132–33.

[25] Ibid., p. 142.

[26] R. Murphy, "Assumptions and Problems in Old Testament Wisdom Research," *CBQ*, 29 (1967): 407–18.

[27] G. Fohrer, "Remarks on Modern Interpretation of the Prophets," *JBL*, 80 (1961): 315.

almost entirely on the so-called "theological wisdom," whereas McKane and Whybray found only the earlier stage of great importance.[28]

The problem was intensified by the work of Kayatz. By means of a careful comparison of datable Egyptian parallels with Prov. 1–9, Kayatz successfully destroyed the critical distinction between an early and later stage.[29] The effect of this study was to erode seriously the whole concept of early and later wisdom. While von Rad's *Theology* found Prov. 1–9 to exemplify late theological wisdom, his subsequent work, *Wisdom in Israel,* assigned these chapters to pre-exilic Israel and made the phrase "the fear of God"–a characteristic slogan for wisdom in Prov. 1–9–the summarizing rubric for all wisdom whether early or late.[30] Moreover, the lack of evidence for a comparable development of wisdom in the wisdom literature of Egypt and Mesopotamia eliminated the possibility of specific extra-biblical control in the question. Obviously, without an adequate measure of the historical typology of wisdom in Israel, the more subtle questions of "wisdom influence" have no solid ground on which to stand.

Wisdom influence. Surely the most widespread and characteristic feature of the modern debate focused on the issue of so-called "wisdom influences."[31] From the outset the vagueness of the term and the different applications of the concept constituted a major problem.

In spite of the early articles which adumbrated the approach, certainly it was the ingenious article of von Rad in 1953 which popularized the

---

[28] Conversely, Eichrodt devoted only twelve pages of his two-volume *Theology* to wisdom in the sense of old wisdom. See his *Theology of the Old Testament* (Philadelphia: Westminster Press, 1961), Vol. II, pp. 80–92. The topic is introduced pejoratively, "For Israel's central concerns, however, the fullness of divine self-communication in spirit and word were far more important than wisdom" (p. 81). Positively, its universalistic orientation compensated for the tendency of Israel to think that she had absolutely captured the market on truth (p. 82). Wisdom, also, was a bridge to the pagan world (p. 87) and a channel to satisfy "a vital need of the Israelite aspiration after knowledge" (p. 92), lest it run aground in error. The moral emphasis based on the mundane wisdom (p. 339) together with the fact that it *finally* avoided an ethic based on expedience (p. 375) were its more commendable features. Unfortunately, the move to hypostatization reflected the work of sages "who wished to rate their own authority no less highly than that enjoyed by the prophets, who appealed to the Word and Spirit of God" (p. 86; also, see pp. 84, 160) and whose misjudgement led detrimentally to a "dogmatic explanation of the world quite divorced from reality." This latter tendency culminated in the doctrine of "mechanical retribution" (pp. 87–88). Job and Qoheleth were a reaction to the "self-conceit" of this "autonomous wisdom" (p. 88).

[29] Kayatz, loc. cit.

[30] Von Rad, *Wisdom in Israel*, op. cit., pp. 53 ff.

[31] For the most recent critique of these studies, see Crenshaw, "Prolegomenon," op. cit., pp. 9–13.

approach and initiated a new phase of the discussion. Von Rad argued that the Joseph Story is not like the other cycles of sagas in Genesis linked together under the rubric of divine promise.[32] He argued that it shared the interests of international wisdom in its novelistic concern with subtle psychological details, its meticulous recollection of the customs and the social order of a distant government, and its concentration on the "anthropological factor" in human experience. In addition, von Rad sought to show that Joseph is portrayed as a model of the educational ideal of a wisdom-trained aspirant to the Egyptian royal court and that Joseph's activity in the narrative conforms to the dictum of wisdom sayings in Proverbs. Since von Rad found in the Joseph Story the same theological outlook as that of old wisdom (cf. Prov. 10ff.), he concluded that this narrative arose in court circles during the Solomonic Enlightenment and functioned similar to its Egyptian counterparts as didactic instruction in official conduct.[33]

Von Rad's article was immediately attractive because of his ability to illuminate a variety of problems in a remarkably fresh way. Yet, the vagueness of the method was troubling and left his proposal open to a number of serious criticisms. His insight into the material seemed intuitive, while the support mounted to confirm his position was eclectic and circumstantial. Crenshaw attacked not only the circularity of von Rad's evidence for wisdom themes, but pointed up theological elements in the narrative that exceeded von Rad's own definition of old wisdom.[34] The lack of hard historical evidence, the ambiguity of wisdom's definition, and the absence of any rigorous proof for the existence of the political novel as a didactic *Gattung* diminished the strength of von Rad's hypothesis.[35]

Nevertheless, the impact of von Rad's approach became apparent in the host of articles which applied a similar method to other narrative literature seeking "wisdom influence."[36] The most direct result of von Rad's study was Whybray's analysis of the Succession Narrative and

---

[32] Von Rad, "The Joseph Narrative," op. cit., p. 281.

[33] Ibid., pp. 290–91. For a recent criticism of von Rad's method and conclusions, see D. B. Redford, "A Study of the Biblical Story of Joseph," *SVT*, 20 (1970): 100–5.

[34] Crenshaw, "Methods in Determining Wisdom Influence," op. cit., pp. 135–37.

[35] For an attempt to strengthen the argument for the political novel as a common literary genre, see R. N. Whybray, *The Succession Narratives: A Study of II Samuel 9–20; I Kings 1 and 2* (Naperville: Alec R. Allenson, 1968), pp. 96–116.

[36] For example, on Gen. 1–11 see Charles C. Forman, "Koheleth's Use of Genesis," *JSS*, 5 (1960): 256–63; J. Pedersen, "Wisdom and Immortality (Gen. 1–3)," *SVT*, 3 (1955): 238–46; W. Malcolm Clark, "A Legal Background to the Yahwist's Use of 'Good and Evil' in Genesis 2–3," *JBL*, 88 (1969): 266ff.; and L. Alonso-Schökel, "Sapiential and

S. Talmon's investigation of the book of Esther.[37] Both attempted to build on von Rad's theory which assumed a literary *Gattung* of the didactic political novel. These were two of the more impressive studies in the discussion, and a synopsis of one of them will suffice to illustrate this method of research.

Talmon described Esther as a "historicized wisdom-tale" designed "to portray wisdom."[38] As in the Ahiqar novel, the portrayal of leading characters and their interaction demonstrates the enactment of wisdom advice like that found in Proverbs and Qoheleth. Trained by the quiet counsel of Mordecai, Esther overpowered Haman with her mastery of court wisdom. Individual wisdom features include the relationship between Esther and Mordecai (following the wisdom theme of the "adoption by a wise man"), the typological antithesis between good and evil persons, and consistent, one-dimensional detail of character activity.[39] Likewise, no attention is given to theological dogmatics; God is only implicit in the orders of reality for which Esther shows her knowledge and respect. Talmon concludes that the author of the book Esther borrowed directly from the Joseph story in the process of writing a novelistic narrative of the same literary wisdom type.[40]

Like the studies of von Rad and of Whybray, the success of Talmon's essay depended on his accumulating an impressive quantity of evidence by a variety of means in support of the thesis. However, this very selectivity in means and evidence inevitably biased the assessment of the literature. The argument for a specialized literary genre of the political novel that primarily teaches wisdom has not been established distinct from the general tendency of ancient literature which depicts characters stereotypically in wise and foolish activity. Such stereotypical wisdom depiction would hardly suggest a formal didactic wisdom genre. The fact that this literature could and did function in an historical context in connection with the feast of Purim suggests that other forces besides simply instruction in wisdom were probably at work in its composition.

Beyond the confines of narrative literature, the general method of wisdom influence studies was also applied to legal and prophetic mate-

---

Covenant Themes in Genesis 2–3," *TDig*, 13 (1965): 3–10. On Exodus, see R.C. Denton, "The Literary Affinities of Exodus 34,6f.," *VT*, 13 (1963): 34–51.

[37] R.N. Whybray, *The Succession Narrative*, op.cit., p. 1ff. and S. Talmon, "Wisdom in the Book of Esther," *VT*, 13 (1963): 419–55.

[38] Talmon, op.cit., pp. 426–27.

[39] Ibid., pp. 426–53.

[40] Ibid., pp. 454–55.

rials.[41] Moshe Weinfeld offered one of the most elaborate arguments for wisdom influence upon the legal and hortatory speeches of Deuteronomy. He proposed that only an origin from a circle of scribal sages could successfully account for the range of different literary resources found in Deuteronomy.[42] This hypothesis alone, he argued, explains both its composition as a literary imitation of a suzerain-vassal treaty,[43] and its wisdom style, vocabulary, and doctrines.[44] The didactic idioms, the pedagogical presentation of the deuteronomic historiography on the pattern of reward and punishment, and the concern with concepts like the good life, didacticism, humanism, and theodicy all offer conspicuous evidence for wisdom.[45] Consequently, Weinfeld surmised, "The means which the deuteronomic circle used to foster its aims are identical with those employed by Israelite wisdom teachers and by wisdom teachers of other ancient Near Eastern peoples.[46]

Although Weinfeld constructed an attractive case for wisdom influence of some kind, he does not show convincingly why these same features would be intolerable to other origins for the book. Moreover, even his own dating of the composition of Deuteronomy depended chiefly on its connection with the treaty formulary. Therefore, at the center of the discussion one finds already a competing sphere of influence other than wisdom which Weinfeld did not fully integrate into this thesis.[47] Lack of

---

[41] For examples of studies in Deuteronomy, see J. l'Hour, "Les Interdits To'ebah dans le Deuternome," *RB*, 71 (1964): 481–503; J. Malfroy, "Sagesse et Loi dans le Dtn. Études," *VT*, 15 (1965): 144–47; C. Scheol, "Die 32 wunderbaren Wege der Weisheit und das Buch Deuteronomium," *TPQ*, 116 (1968): 229–37; J. R. Boston, "The Wisdom Influence Upon the Song of Moses," *JBL*, 87 (1968): 198–202; J. W. McKay, "Man's Love for God in Deuteronomy and the Father/Teacher–Son/Pupil Relationship," *VT*, 22 (1972): 426–35; and Calum M. Carmichael, *The Laws of Deuteronomy* (Ithaca: Cornell University Press, 1974). For examples of literature on the prophets, see n. 48.

[42] Moshe Weinfeld, *Deuteronomy and the Deuteronomic School* (Oxford: Clarendon Press, 1972): pp. 9, 55–56.

[43] Ibid., p. 57.

[44] Ibid., pp. 158–78; 244–319.

[45] Ibid., pp. 244–319.

[46] Moshe Weinfeld, "Deuteronomy–The Present State of Inquiry," *JBL*, 86 (1967): 256. See also his "The Dependence of Deuteronomy upon Wisdom Literature" (hb) in the *Y. Kaufmann Jubilee Volume* (1960), pp. 89–109.

[47] I can only find one place where he speaks directly to this issue, under the sub-title "Didacticism": "Deuteronomy as a 'Book of the Covenant' followed the treaty model in its educational imagery as in other features. Indeed, as we shall see, it is sometimes hard to say which is the origin of a certain education motif: the covenant or wisdom. We must therefore take into account influences from both spheres, though that of wisdom appears to have been the stronger. It seems that in order to strengthen the Israelite loyalty to the

information about wisdom schools or their politics further weakens his argument. Finally, in the cumulative presentation of features like "humanism" and "didacticism" Weinfeld assumed a strict ideological control over wisdom in Israel which has yet to be established.

The prophetic literature of the OT has also received considerable attention. After Fichtner's essay, "Jesaja unter den Weisen" (1949), numerous investigations of wisdom influence upon Isaiah, as well as upon the other prophets, appeared.[48] At the height of the discussion, W. Whedbee viewed Isaiah's message in relation to court wisdom. Contrary to a purely secularistic empiricism, such wisdom recognized "the mysterious interplay of Jahweh's counsel (ʿēṣā) and man's" (cf. Is. 28:23ff.; 29:15–16).[49] The counselors of the court likewise regarded God to be the Creator and sustainer of all world order, the underlying principle to all wisdom.[50] For that reason, Isaiah did not repudiate the wise men or their wisdom, but he sought to call them back to their own first principles which have been forfeited in the heat of a political crisis.[51] Even Isaiah's emphasis on a divine "plan" depended on the technical vocabulary of court wisdom.[52] Whedbee generalized his method for detecting the various adaptations of wisdom by the prophet:

> If therefore the speech contains terms and themes indigenous to wisdom, it is appropriately called wisdom in origin. In short, if a definite wisdom orientation can be shown to be a constitutive feature of the speech, it is a safe bet that the prophet is employing wisdom materials.[53]

Despite the sophistication and genuine contribution of Whedbee's analysis, the ambiguity of what constitutes "terms and themes indigenous to wisdom" limited his attempt either to prove "a definite wisdom orientation" or to circumscribe its significance for understanding Isaiah. The strength of the form critical method, however, lay in its ability to delineate non-wisdom literary types that had been blurred by the introduction of

---

covenant the author of Deuteronomy not only relied on covenant typology, but also employed modes of expression and imagery taken from the sapiential sphere" (*Deuteronomy and the Deuteronomic School*, op.cit., p.298). Surely, this matter requires much more discussion than simply to say that "wisdom appears to be the stronger."

[48] Fichtner, loc.cit. For additional bibliography, see Crenshaw, "Methods in Determining Wisdom Influence," op.cit., p.129. An important recent work is that of J. Jensen, *The Use of Tôrâ by Isaiah*, *CBQMS*, 3 (1973).

[49] William J. Whedbee, *Isaiah and Wisdom* (New York: Abingdon Press, 1971), p.125.

[50] Ibid., pp.118–20.

[51] Ibid., pp.121, 125.

[52] Ibid., p.147.

[53] Ibid., p.25.

wisdom features foreign to the original setting. Still a problem persists in determining which so-called "wisdom features" are indeed foreign to the literary content within an essentially non-wisdom genre.

Similarly, there has been little agreement since Gunkel first assessed the presence of certain "wisdom psalms" in the Psalter. For Gunkel these psalms lacked the consistent formal characteristics that distinguished psalms of other literary types. Wisdom psalms probably include Ps. 49, 1, 91, 112, 128, 37 and 73.[54] S. Mowinckel sought to give wisdom psalms a specific life setting in sage circles as instruction in prayer and piety.[55] More recently, Roland E. Murphy attempted a summary of the evidence for a distinct literary type based on isolated wisdom features in style and content.[56] Nevertheless, the problems that plagued the other studies continued to weaken this inquiry as well. The failure of wisdom psalms to conform to distinct literary patterns of composition debilitated the usual form critical means for locating a particular life setting for these psalms. Naturally, the ambiguity of wisdom's definition continued to dull the edge of the argument for a wisdom provenance.

In sum, the present wisdom influence discussion labors under a lack of sufficient historical information and control. Even the rhetorical function of alleged wisdom features often remains unassessed when, in fact, a feature sapiential in origin may prove to be non-sapiential in intended function, and *vice versa*. Crenshaw, well-recognized for his scholarly assessment of the current discussion, bluntly concluded that "wisdom scholarship is in dire need of methodological precision."[57] Although Crenshaw's own alternative suggestion has lost its earlier excitement, he has at least succeeded in calling attention to the serious problems which threaten to relativize the value of the past wisdom research.

A New Approach

In the light of this impasse it is the intention of this investigation to offer a new approach to the problem of OT wisdom. The aim of the thesis is obviously not to resolve all the problems outlined. Such a goal is both

[54] This list of Gunkel's wisdom psalms follows the estimate of Roland E. Murphy, "A Consideration of the Classification, 'Wisdom Psalms,'" *SVT*, 9 (1963): 205. For a different estimate see A. Descamps, "Pour un classement littéraire des psaumes," *Mélanges Bibliques Rédigés en L'honneur de André Robert* (Paris: Bloud & Gay, 1957), pp. 187–96.

[55] S. Mowinckel, "Psalms and Wisdom," *SVT*, 3 (1955): 205 ff., esp. pp. 208, 211.

[56] Murphy, op. cit., pp. 207 ff.

[57] Crenshaw, "Prolegomenon," op. cit., p. 9.

presumptuous and unrealistic. The intent is much more modest and will seek to establish a new direction for one area of the problem. Of course, if successful, it is hoped that the approach will ultimately have wider implications for problems not treated in this study.

The writer will attempt to defend the thesis that at a certain period in the development of OT literature, wisdom became a theological category associated with an understanding of canon which formed a perspective from which to interpret Torah and prophetic traditions. In this sense wisdom became a hermeneutical construct for interpreting sacred Scripture. Although several scholars have observed this phenomenon in the second-century book of Sirach, no one has yet sought either to sketch the contours of such interpretation or to explore the possibility of a similar perspective at points in the late redaction history of the OT.[58] Likewise, Bar. 3:9–4:4 will be shown to supply additional evidence that the phenomenon in Sirach was not unusual in post-exilic times and that it may have roots in an even earlier period.

Hence, the approach of this present work will depart from the usual methods of starting from the earliest period and working forward. Instead, it will begin with literature in the later Hellenistic period, namely, Sirach and Baruch. Certain advantages accrue by beginning this study of wisdom with sources from the Hellenistic period. A historical control on the perennial problem of historical development within wisdom is immediately established. Only in this period does wisdom emerge clearly as a theological concept that can be used to interpret canonically distinct parts of Scripture; for example, the Torah and the prophetic literature.

Furthermore, the Jewish-Hellenistic sources are well suited for relatively objective criteria in determining the nature of Israel's later wisdom reading of earlier traditions. With both Sirach and Baruch one frequently has at hand an ancient author interpreting fixed texts that are still pre-

---

[58] For a discussion of wisdom as a "theological idiom" in early Jewish literature, see Harvey H. Guthrie, *Wisdom and Canon: Meanings of the Law and the Prophets* (Seabury: Seabury-Western Theological Seminary, 1966). An interesting instance of similar interpretation is found in Yalkut Shimeoni Tehillim 702 in which the author addresses the same question to three different canonical divisions of Scripture–Wisdom, Prophets, and Torah–with three different responses based on verse citations. The response of wisdom recalls Prov. 13:21. Abridged parallels to this type of three-fold, canonical interpretation occur in J. Makkoth 31d and פסיקתא דבר כהנא, ed. Buber, p. 158b, cf. S. Liebermann, שקיעין, p. 76. See Sid Z. Leiman, *The Canonization of Hebrew Scripture* (Hamden, Connecticut: Archon Books, 1976), p. 70; n. 305. For scholars that find in Sirach the interpretation of the Torah as a source of wisdom like that of the biblical wisdom books, see n. 68.

served separately in the OT for the modern scholar. One can often measure quite tangibly how that author conforms parts or the whole of a non-wisdom biblical text into a redaction-like representation of it in a new context concerning wisdom. Thus the particular interpretive activity can be followed in a way rarely available to a historical critical study of the OT itself. In addition, the sources are divergent enough to afford a fairly representative sampling of the full range of options actually employed in the period.

Since one of the weakest areas in the past wisdom discussion obviously has been the determination of wisdom's definition, the matter of definition is crucial to the success of the present investigation. Although Sirach makes reference to all of the books of the later *MT* canon (with the probable exception of Ruth, Song of Songs, Esther, and Daniel), as well as to the division of the Torah and to a prophetic collection including "The Twelve," there is little evidence of wisdom as a precise canonical collection.[59] Nevertheless, because there is a sufficient distinction between the

[59] For bibliography on the books cited by Ben Sira, see Leiman, op. cit., p. 29 and n. 134. Sir. 49:10 expressly mentions "The Twelve" as a separate division of Scripture. The identification of wisdom with "the book of the covenant," i.e., "the Torah," in Sir. 24:23 and with "the book of the commandments" in Bar. 4:1 assumes more than simply the legal core of Mosaic injunctions. Evidence that the five books of Moses stand behind this reference to the Torah in Sir. 24:23 lies both in the lack of attention given to legal material and in the limitation of the autobiographical history of wisdom to the narratives of the Pentateuch. The identification of the Torah with wisdom in Sir. 24:23 is, therefore, confirmed by the exegetical demonstration in the Wisdom Song that precedes it. Wisdom concludes her autobiography with the deuteronomic command and fulfillment that she find one place in the promised land, i.e., Zion, in which to set her tent and conduct worship (e.g., Dt. 12:15, 18, 21, 26). There is no interest in the events of conquest, the activity of judges, or the rise of the monarchy.
The status of wisdom books in Ben Sira's Scripture is a more difficult problem. With the exception of Moshe Segal [ספר בן סירא השלם (Jerusalem: Bialit Institute, 1953), p. 258] and Leiman (op. cit., pp. 150–51, n. 135), the majority of Sirach scholars find in Sir. 39:1 an explicit reference to the Torah, Prophets, and Wisdom as canonical collections which provide the primary resources of sagacious reflection. In his "Aspects der Alttestamentliche Kanonbildung," *VT*, 18 (1968): 173–89, J. C. H. Lebram even proposes a bias for *Heilsgeschichte* in the order of the canonical collections in Sir. 39:1. In any case, if Leiman has some reservation about the existence by the time of Ben Sira of wisdom as a canonical collection (op. cit., pp. 71–72, esp. n. 317), he does not doubt that Proverbs and Qoheleth are probably "inspired canonical books" for Ben Sira (ibid., pp. 28, 131). Within a generation Ben Sira's grandson wrote in a preface that his grandfather had mastered "the Torah, the Prophets, and the other writings."
In addition, there is evidence in Sirach that Proverbs was regarded as a Solomonic book, if not clearly a part of a larger Solomonic collection. In Sir. 47:17, which is part of the eulogy to Solomon, we read that he amazed the people בשיר משל חידה מליצה (MsB). The

Torah, which is a canonical division, and wisdom, which is a theological concept, both Sir. 24 and Bar. 3:9–4:4 must construct an elaborate proof to demonstrate a close connection between them.[60] Consequently, this writer is convinced that the key to understanding these post-exilic examples of wisdom interpretations lies in their use of canon.[61] Moreover, the requisite definition of a "wisdom interpretation" for this investigation does not consist in an abstract formulation but in the minimal evidence of a consistent shift of non-wisdom material from the Torah and the Prophets to a new context and concern for wisdom like that of Proverbs and perhaps Qoheleth. Both of these books were well known to Sirach and since the author of Sirach particularly depends on Proverbs in order to produce his own book of "wise instruction and apt proverbs" (Sir. 50:27) one can

---

last three expressions recall Prov. 1:6 in which the goal of wisdom is to discern similarly משל ומליצה דברי חכמים וחידתם. Only here in Proverbs does this same epitomization occur in these terms. The phrase דברי חכמים has apparently been dropped, perhaps because of its lack of viability for the author as a *nomen technicus* for the wisdom literary types. Instaed שיר is added and may be an allusion to the same designation at the beginning of the Song of Songs which is likewise attributed to him. Otherwise, it may function to account for the inclusion of traditional hymnic material in the corpus of Ben Sira's book. The early recognition of Proverbs and Qoheleth as wisdom books from Solomon is attested in Talmud and Midrash, e.g., Sifre on Dt. 1:1; Tosefta Yadayim 2:14; Shir Ha-Shirim Rabah 1:1, 6, and Berakhoth 57b.

[60] There were undoubtedly oral traditions of wisdom available to the writer of Sirach which are no longer extant. These traditions, like the ones before them, preserved the role of wisdom as a means of religious discourse distinct from the word of a prophet or a priest (cf. Jer. 18:18; Ezek. 7:26). Concerning the problem of oral and literary resources that are probably lost to the present inquiry, see J. G. Snaith, "Biblical Quotations in the Hebrew of Ecclesiasticus," *JTS*, 18 (1967): 1–12.

[61] Albert C. Sundberg has argued recently against using the term "canon" for anything short of a list of received books. See, for example, his "The Old Testament of the Early Church: A Study in Canon," *HTR*, 51 (1958): 205–26. Likewise, the term "canon" can be shown to be late and Christian in its application to an ordered body of sacred Scripture. Nevertheless, the most recent study by Sid Z. Leiman demonstrates once more the value of the concept to describe the formation of the Hebrew Bible (op. cit., pp. 110ff.). Leiman defines "canon" as books "accepted by Jews as authoritative for religious practice and/or doctrine, and whose authority is binding upon Jewish people for all generations" (ibid., p. 14). He rejects the notion of Sundberg that there was no limited Jewish canon of Scripture prior to the first century of the Christian era (ibid., pp. 38–39, 129–30). Moreover, Leiman regards both the Torah and the Prophets to be closed collections of inspired canonical books by ca. 450 (ibid., p. 29; cf. D. N. Freedman, "The Law and The Prophets," *SVT*, 9 (1962): 250–65). He postulates the closing of the Hagiographa shortly after the death of Antiochus IV, ca. 164/163 B. C. (ibid., p. 30). Despite problems in his dating, Leiman has demonstrated the validity of the concept of "canon" to describe the function of some parts of Scripture in the period of Ben Sira and before.

argue that Proverbs represents at least *part* of a literary definition for wisdom in the mind of the post-exilic author.

The self-conscious link between the wisdom of Sirach and that of Proverbs has already been expressed by scholars in a variety of ways. After examining Ben Sira's use of OT, J.K. Gasser concluded succintly, "Die Proverbien hat er nachgeahmt."[62] The classic study of Duesberg devoted an entire chapter to "Le Ben Sira Commentateur des Proverbs" in which Ben Sira is shown to glean and to assemble wealth of the sacred Scriptures after the style of Proverbs.[63] Ben Sira's purpose was to venerate Proverbs as an inspired book and to explicate its doctrine by means of other Scripture.[64] According to Th. Middendorp, Ben Sira consciously related himself as a successor or continuator ("Nachfolger") of Proverbs and the wisdom tradition which it represents.[65] In E.G. Bauckmann's comparison of Proverbs and Sirach, he contrasts the different functions of the Law in each book.[66] Despite the common tradition which Sirach overtly shares with Proverbs, Ben Sira breaks with the older wisdom by making the Law "zum eigentlich wesentlichen Inhalt seiner Weisheitslehre."[67] That is to say, only with Sirach "ist das alte Ziel der Weisheitslehre das neue Ziel des Gesetzes geworden."[68] Therefore, this investigation seeks to build on this current inquiry into Sirach and to advance that discussion by examining the techniques by which non-wisdom traditions of the Torah have been conformed to teach wisdom like that of the biblical wisdom tradition. Bar. 3:9–4:4 will be shown to illustrate the same type of wisdom interpretation of sacred tradition as that found in Sirach.

---

[62] J.K. Gasser, *Das althebräische Spruchbuch und die Sprüche Jesu Ben Sira* (Gütersloh: C. Bertelsmann, 1903), p. 254. Also, see pp. 241 ff.

[63] H. Duesberg, op. cit., rev. ed., 1966, p. 706. At one place (p. 702), Duesberg describes the genre of Sirach as in the style of Pirque Aboth.

[64] Ibid., p. 706 ff.

[65] Th. Middendorp, *Die Stellung Jesu Ben Siras zwischen Judentum und Hellenismus* (Leiden: E. J. Brill, 1973), p. 78.

[66] E.G. Bauckmann, "Die Proverbien und die Sprüche des Jesus Sirach," *ZAW*, 72 (1960): 33–63.

[67] Ibid., p. 55.

[68] Ibid. Among the many similar assessments, see H. Ludin Jansen, *Die Spätjüdische Psalmendichtung, ihr Entstehungskreis und ihr 'Sitz im Leben'* (Oslo: Kimmisjon hos Jacob Dybwad, 1937), p. 114, and Joseph Haspecker, *Gottesfurcht bei Jesus Sirach* (Rome: Päpstliches Bibelinstitute, 1967), pp. 167, 176. Some scholars speak of this synthesis of wisdom and Torah in Sirach as "gesetzliche Weisheitslehre." For example, J. Fichtner, *Die altorientalische Weisheit in ihrer isr.-jüd. Ausprägung, BZAW*, 62 (1933), p. 97; Bauckmann, op. cit., p. 56; and J. Marböck, *Weisheit im Wandel: Untersuchungen zur Weisheitstheologie bei Ben Sira, BBB*, 37 (1971): 89.

Two criteria have determined the selection of the particular texts to be investigated. First, passages were chosen from Sirach and Baruch which recall earlier OT texts, particularly texts found in the biblical epic literature seen originally in a non-wisdom context. Second, the selected passages were from larger literary units in which wisdom interpretations of the OT are likely to occur: a Wisdom Song (Sir. 24), a paranesis on the way of wisdom (Bar. 3:9–4:4), and an instruction about creation and the giving of the Law (Sir. 16:29–17:10). The investigation itself will focus on the way these selected texts make reference to the OT, whether by means of direct citation, paraphrase, or vague allusion. Since the biblical references are not cited formally, but edited into an interpretive prose, the purpose of this investigation is to describe the "redactional shape" which these Hellenistic writers have given the older material.[69]

By carefully comparing the original non-wisdom context of an OT passage with its new role in the context of wisdom, one can draw a fairly objective picture of a wisdom interpretation. This can be done because a shift in context often allows for rather exact terms of measurement. For instance, the Hellenistic author may strategically omit integral parts of the original context to which he alludes, or he may reveal a pattern of selecting only a certain type or sequence of images for wisdom from non-wisdom material. Sometimes the subject depicted or the person portrayed will be

---

The close relationship between wisdom and the Torah is further demonstrated in the description of the ideal sage in 39:1–3. The sage studies "the Law of the Most High," together with "the wisdom of all the ancients" and "the prophets of old" (v. 1). Although this language probably recalls the Torah, if not the Prophets and Wisdom, as canonical collections, the subsequent descriptions of the scholarly task (39:2–3) are clearly reminiscent of the prologue to Proverbs (1:3, 6):

G of Sir. 39:2–3	LXX of Prov. 1:3, 6
2b στροφαῖς παραβολῶν	3 στροφὰς λόγων
3a ἀπόκρυφα παροιμιῶν	6a σκοτεινὸν λόγον·
3b αἰνίγασιν παραβολῶν	6b αἰνίγματα
	(cf. παραβολὴν, v. 6a)

That is, Scripture is a proper object of wisdom study by which one exercises the skill of the sage as found in Prov. 1:3–6 (cf. Sir. 47:17). It is little wonder that the product of such inquiry includes a wisdom assessment of contextually non-wisdom texts.

[69] Similarly, NT studies frequently characterize the Gospel writers as "collectors" or "transmitters" of traditional resources, which include the OT. Joachim Rohde describes the process of redaction, "Besides the grouping of the material under definite points of view and in definite contexts, it was a matter of selection, omission, and inclusion of traditional material, and modifications of it which, although slight, were yet very characteristic." See his *Rediscovering the Teaching of the Evangelists* (Philadelphia: Westminster Press, 1968), p. 9.

altered radically in moving from text to interpretation. Just as conspicuous is the use of vocabulary distinctive of wisdom literature (e.g., Proverbs) which is introduced in a manner that transforms entirely the original meaning of the fixed texts. Thus, by concentrating on the oblique manner in which the Hellenistic authors have refracted non-wisdom texts, such as narrative in the Torah, the writer hopes to gain a minimal insight into the anatomy of post-exilic wisdom interpretation.

Because not all of the oral and literary wisdom resources of post-exilic Palestine are available to the modern scholar, this investigation cannot do complete justice to the place accorded the wisdom literature of Sirach and Baruch in its own time. Moreover, this investigation neither assumes that every use of OT in this literature is a wisdom interpretation nor does it purport to provide an exhaustive portrait of post-exilic wisdom exegesis. At best, the conclusions from the analyses of selected passages are limited by the priority of control over what constitutes a measurable wisdom interpretation of fixed OT texts. Conversely, the narrow focus of such controlled analyses offers an unusually precise insight into the wisdom reading of past traditions.

Once the form and function of wisdom interpretation in these later sources has been described and summarized, the writer will return to the OT with this newly-won information and determine to what extent similar redactional activity was at work in the pre-Hellenistic period. This final step depends on the readiness of these Hellenistic wisdom interpretations to offer some continuity and controlled analogy to earlier redactional moves in the formation of some of the OT books. This study of wisdom will, therefore, focus finally on the late redactional roles for wisdom rather than offer a general study of its phenomenology in early Israel.

In sum, the next two chapters will investigate the use of OT in the selected passages from Sirach and Baruch. Thereafter, the results of these studies will be summarized in order to test the thesis that wisdom has functioned in this material as a hermeneutical construct for a type of theological interpretation of non-wisdom texts. The last chapter will make some tentative probes into the redactional history of the OT in order to suggest an earlier and similar function of wisdom at work in the final shaping of certain biblical books.

Chapter II

Case Study One: Sir. 24:3–29

Preface to the Sirach Case Studies

Sirach, for many reasons, is ideally suited for a study of wisdom interpretation. The style of the book frequently parallels that of Proverbs and its express intent is to instruct students in the way of wisdom.[1] Unlike the other so-called "apocryphal" books, its authorship is known and its composition can be reasonably established in the period preceding the Maccabean Revolt in 168 B.C. It is thus one of the earliest representatives of Palestinian Judaism which laid the foundation for the later rabbinical parties of the Pharisees and the Sadducees. Consequently, most of the present OT lies before it and provides the primary object of its reflection and learned interpretation.

Two general limitations must, however, be acknowledged at the outset of these studies. First, uncertainties regarding the respective texts and their transmission histories affect the accuracy of any formal analysis. Unfortunately, the original texts of Sirach cannot always be reconstructed exactly. Likewise, the language and character of the OT texts to which the author makes reference can often be disputed. Besides the question of written texts, one must acknowledge as well the possibility that OT allusions may have been changed into more specific recollections of OT texts during a period of oral transmission. Such alterations may have occurred at a time when Sirach was passed along as a memorized lesson within scribal schools.

Middendorp's critique of this latter phenomenon isolates the more probable instances of such secondary expansion in a helpful manner.[2] Although the present investigation has been too restricted to propose

---

[1] See p. 16.

[2] Middendorp, op. cit., pp. 35 ff.

definitive solutions to many of these textual difficulties, these factors are usually minimal ones in the light of our stated purpose. Fortunately, scholars agree that the role of exotic word plays on syllables or consonants has almost no place in the OT usage exhibited in the case studies.[3]

A second limitation arises from the lack of extracanonical oral or literary resources that may have been available to these authors but no longer to us.[4] Extant post-exilic Jewish literature hints at the persistence of early conventions or traditions for interpreting the OT. For example, the references to the giants in Sirach and Baruch seem to reflect not only a consensus regarding the major issue in the text, but they also follow two different, though well established, paths of interpretation.[5] Furthermore, the tendency of the Aramaic Targums to shed light on some "novel" interpretations is a witness against their uniqueness and suggests familiar conventions for understanding certain texts within which the special treatment of a given author must be cast to be fully appreciated.[6] Finally, the presence of imported Hellenistic ideas and expressions cannot be ignored as an influence on post-exilic biblical interpretation.[7]

Adequate control over this range of limitations is made possible by the publication of several recent monographs on these subjects.[8] In addition, the success of this study is not dependent on a reconstruction of all the features in the ancient world relevant to each line of the Sirach prose.

The following studies are quite limited in focus and not intended to contribute significantly to a resolution of the larger historical problems of text and redaction. It must be emphasized that the case studies of Sir. 24 and 16:24–17:14, which follow, are designed to examine only some of the more compelling evidence of wisdom interpretation in Sirach. The aim is to achieve a minimal assessment through a selective analysis of certain promising texts. Moreover, there is no assumption that every use of the OT in Sirach constitutes a wisdom interpretation, nor is it assumed that Sirach qualifies at every point as wisdom literature.

---

[3] The general lack of this type of interpretation stands in contrast to the *pesher* readings in the Habakkuk commentary from Qumran. See W.H. Brownlee, "Biblical Interpretation Among the Sectaries of the Dead Sea Scrolls," *BA*, 14 (1951): 54–76.

[4] See p. 15, n. 60.

[5] See the discussion of Bar. 3:26–28 in ch. IV.

[6] For example, see the following analyses concerning the אד of Gen. 2:6 in Sir. 24:3, the giants in Bar. 3:26 and in Sir. 17:3.

[7] For a recent investigation of this matter, see Middendorp, op. cit., pp. 7–34.

[8] The important new contributions in Sirach studies are surveyed in Marböck's "Sirachliteratur seit 1966. Ein Überblick," *TRev*, 71 (1975): 178–83.

Preface to Sir. 24:3–29

The discourse under examination is a Wisdom Song reminiscent of Prov. 8. Its place at the middle of the book of Sirach is indicative of its priority in defining the total context of the book. Its unique contribution as a guide to the interpretation of the entire book is further signaled by the rare appearance of the author in a first person address at its conclusion (vv. 30ff.). The self-praise of Wisdom and her identification with the book of the Torah in v. 23 has the practical effect of leading in turn to the author's self-praise regarding his own prolific sagacity. Even as Wisdom makes an earnest appeal to her hearers (vv. 19–22), so the author invites all those who diligently seek wisdom to learn it of him (v. 34). The whole book is thus predicated on the author's special claim to wisdom, a claim grounded particularly in the accessibility of Wisdom through the presence of the written Torah in Israel.

Sir. 24:3–29 Analysis

Sir. 24:3 ἐγὼ ἀπὸ στόματος ὑψίστου ἐξῆλθον
καὶ ὡς ὁμίχλη κατεκάλυψα γῆν
I came forth from the mouth of the Most High,
and as a dark cloud I covered the earth.

In these opening lines, Wisdom begins her cosmic resume with an account of her origins, "from the mouth of God." Marböck finds in these words an allusion to Second Isaiah in which the Word of God likewise goes forth "from my (God's) mouth" and is effective in creation and in determining Israel's history (Is. 45:23; 48:3; 55:11).[9] If Sirach indeed considers the prophetic Word from Isaiah as indicative of Wisdom, then an even broader sapiential understanding of Isaiah's message may emerge.[10]

[9] Marböck, op. cit., p. 59.

[10] In Isaiah this phraseology was in the context of asserting God's control over history. He is presently carrying out his "plan" which he unfolds from the "beginning." Cf. Is. 43: 1–19, 46:8–11, 48:3, 5, 16, 55:11. There may be a conscious parallel between the *Word* and *plan* of God, which is "hidden" (e.g., Is. 48:6) only to be revealed in part by the prophet Isaiah, and *Wisdom*, which is beyond man's grasp (Sir. 24:28) though found in both the Torah (Sir. 24:23) and the teaching of the sage. If both Word and Wisdom equally "come from the mouth of God," then they share revelatory status. In this respect the Word or plan of God, which is efficacious in redemptive history for the prophet Isaiah, is paralleled by Wisdom who participates in God's "works" in redemptive history [cf. Sir. 1:9, 11:4, 16:27, 36:15 (33:20)]. Likewise, Isaiah's interest in ordering history according to "former" and "latter things" is paralleled in Sirach by the claim that Israel

Marböck's suggestion, however, rests at most on a singular usage of Isaiah in Sir. 24, a loose allusion which at best offers little control (cf. Lam. 3:38). Its probability must depend *a fortiori* on the accumulation of other more obvious examples in Sir. 24 that suggest a program of such wisdom interpretation. For that reason it should be noted only at this point in the analysis that this first phrase affirms Wisdom's special divine origins, after the manner of the Wisdom Song in Prov. 8 (cf. Sir. 24:9). The Latin sharpens this correspondence by appending to the verse, *primogenita ante omnem creaturam* (cf. Prov. 8:23).

Fortunately, the second clause of this verse offers a better intrinsic case for literary dependence on the OT. The second, like the first phrase, stands in continuity with Prov. 8 by moving from a statement of origins to a description of Wisdom's role in creation. Nevertheless, Sirach's description exceeds that of Proverbs by specifying a creative activity for Wisdom both within the process of creation itself and in the language of the Genesis traditions. The expression "cover[ing] the earth" recalls both Gen. 1:2 and 2:6 in which primordial entities ("darkness," "Spirit of God,"[11] and the אד) extend over the "surface" (פני) of the earth or its watery chaos. Moreover, the Latin text of Sir. 24:3 regards this phrase as an allusion at least to Gen. 1:2 and underscores that assumption by prefacing the clause with a recollection of Gen. 1:3, *ego feci in caelis, ut oriretur lumen indeficiens* (cf. Sir. 17:30).

In terms of grammatical analysis of this phrase, the most difficult expression to control is the subject which is also the critical point of identification with Wisdom. The two versions which are dependent directly on the Hebrew are instructive. *G* reads ὁμίχλη with a semantic

---

is "the first of your works" (Sir. 39:33, 43:33). In general, Middendorp (op. cit., p. 69) is led to conclude about Sirach's use of Isaiah: "Der Einzelne statt des Volksganzen wird angesprochen. Jesaia ist für Ben Sira eine Fundgrube, der er die ihm zusagenden Wendungen entnimmt. Ähnlich kommen die übrigen Propheten zur Anwendung, wie wir sehen werden."

We may ask what controls Ben Sira's selectivity of passages from the prophets. At least here, he seems to choose a recognizable phrase and to apply it to a similar thematic setting: creation, movement from the transcendent to the sphere of man, a divine expression (of Word or Wisdom). The point of connection is one in Isaiah which invites further definition (the divine Word) and is connotatively quite compatible with "Wisdom." The correspondence is held in place by employing an unusual expression reminiscent of the interpreted text, namely, "from the mouth of God [the Most High]." By this means Wisdom located in the heart of the sacred text, and the sage reads Isaiah in a new light on account of it.

[11] If Sirach is identifying Wisdom and the רוח אלהים, he probably intends reference to it as the רוח הקדש and not simply with the Targums as "the breath of the Lord."

range of "cloud-like darkness," "mist," "fog," and "gloom,"[12] whereas *S* offers ܥܪܦܠܐ, a term ordinarily employed to mean "dark cloud," "darkness," or "gloom."[13] The only other occurrence of ὁμίχλη within Sirach is found in a difficult phrase of Sir. 43:22a in which *G* appears to assume a slightly different Hebrew *Vorlage* than that of MsB.[14] Nevertheless, ὁμίλχη does seem to translate Hebrew ענן at that place.

However, despite Sir. 43:22a, there are two strong reasons to suggest that the Hebrew behind 24:3 was not ענן, but ערפל. First, of the ten occurrences of ὁμίχλη in the LXX (6 ×) and its deviating recensions (4 ×, in Aq. and Symm.), the Greek word usually translates Hebrew ערפל (6 ×).[15] The other Hebrew translation equivalents for it are חשך (2 ×),[16] עיפה (1 ×),[17] and perhaps כפור (1 ×),[18] but never ענן! Second, of the five times that ענן does appear in the extant Hebrew texts of Sirach, each occasion is translated in *G* by νέφελη–excepting 43:22a–and in *S* by ܥܢܢܐ. Except for the textually problematic 44:22, it is never rendered in *G* by ὁμίχλη nor in *S* by ܥܪܦܠܐ as it is here in Sir. 24:3. Therefore, the Hebrew of Sir. 24:3 was most probably ערפל which, unlike ענן, can readily account for both the *G* and *S* translations of the verse.[19]

Although no commentators argue for an allusion only to Gen. 2:6, a few suggest sole dependence on Gen. 1:2. For such a position the recognition of ערפל requires that the connection between "Spirit" and "cloud-like darkness" be explained adequately by an appeal only to Gen. 1:2. Fritzsche can deduce only that since the "Spirit" is "veiled" in the primordial condition of תהו ובהו at the beginning of creation, "darkness" is a suitable metaphor for it.[20] Segal cites Is. 60:2, which he regards as alluding

[12] H. G. Liddell and R. Scott, *A Greek-English Lexicon*, 9th ed., rev. by H. S. Jones (Oxford: Clarendon Press, 1940), p. 1222.

[13] C. Brockelmann, *Lexicon Syriacum* (Berlin: Verlag von Reuther & Reichard, 1895), p. 262. Also, L. Koehler and W. Baumgartner, *Lexicon in Veteris Testament Libreos* (Leiden: E. J. Brill, 1953), p. 738.

[14] R. Smend, *Die Weisheit des Jesus Sirach, erklärt* (Berlin: Verlag von George Reimer, 1906), p. 409. Smend thinks that the Greek translator simply misunderstands the previous word and consequently gives ענן a very inexact translation. Unfortunately, there is no extant Syriac translation of this text.

[15] Job 38:9, Joel 2:2, Zech. 1:15, Dt. 4:11 (Aq.), Ex. 20:21 (Symm.), Ps. 96 (97):2.

[16] Is. 29:18, Job 3:5 (Aq.).

[17] Amos 4:13.

[18] Ps. 147:5 (16).

[19] So Otto Rickenbacher, *Weisheitsperikopen bei Ben Sira* (Göttingen: Vandenhoeck & Ruprecht, 1973), pp. 133–34.

[20] Otto F. Fritzsche, *Die Weisheit Jesus-Sirach's erklärt*, 5th ed., rev., Kurzgefaßtes Exegetisches Handbuch zu den Apokryphen des Alten Testamentes, Vol. 5 (Leipzig: Verlag von S. Hirzel, 1859), p. 125.

to Gen. 1:2, though it relates there only to the glory of God and not specifically his Spirit. He makes no attempt to explain how in Is. 60:2 the adjective "darkness" is characteristic of the Spirit.[21] None of these explanations resolves adequately the question of why an understanding which centers on an identity with the Spirit and uses only Gen. 1:2 should evoke both the metaphors of "cloud" and "darkness" to express it.

Most commentators postulate a dependence by Sirach on *both* Gen. 1:2 and 2:6, but they do so intuitively and do not provide any detailed analysis of this conclusion, nor do they explain how ערפל could link elements in both verses into a single comprehensive expression. Yet, there are some tangible indications that these verses were interpreted by Sirach together rather than singly. A combination of unique features from each verse is required to sustain the paraphrase of Sirach 24:3. On the one hand, Gen. 1:2 has מרחפת which, taken by the reader either as "brooding" (cf. Dt. 32:11) or as "coming upon" (LXX of Gen. 1:2, ἐπεφέρετο), conveys the idea of "covering" even more directly than does a deduction from the imagery of the אד "watering the entire surface of the earth" in Gen. 2:6. Also, an identification of Wisdom only with the אד in Gen. 2:6 would appear less likely or satisfying theologically than an identification which included the Spirit of 1:2.[22] On the other hand, Gen. 2:6 does expressly mention "the earth," whereas 1:2 recalls only "the waters." Though one can argue, as does Segal,[23] that the earth lies below the waters, a purely deductive explanation for the difference in intention should be only a last resort. Moreover, the reading of 1:2 *with* 2:6 does supply a valid exegetical rationale for Sirach's use of the phrase.

But the strongest evidence for a synthetic hearing[24] of these two verses behind Sir. 24:3 rests on the choice of ערפל which proves a satisfactory link between the subjects of the two verses. This can be shown to be true in each case. In Gen. 1:2 the grammatical parallelism between the last two phrases provides the ground for an association in Sirach's intention be-

---

[21] Segal, op. cit., p. 147.

[22] There is, unlike the case for אד, evidence later than Sirach of an identification of the Spirit with Wisdom, for example, Wis. 1:4–7, 11:17 and *Bereshith Rabbah* 85 in which Solomon's wisdom is the Holy Spirit guiding him (see G. G. Box and W. O. W. Oesterley, "The Book of Sirach," *The Apocrypha and Pseudepigrapha of the OT in English*, ed. by R. H. Charles, 2 vols. (Oxford: Oxford Press, 1913), 1:397. Also, see n. 18.

[23] Segal, loc. cit.

[24] By this term, I mean the hearing of two or more diverse texts as a collective witness to the same subject. Seeligmann describes this tendency in interpretation as typical of "canon conscious" exegesis. See I. L. Seeligmann, "Voraussetzungen der Midrashexegese," *SVT*, 1 (1953): 152.

tween "the *darkness* upon the surface of the deep" and "the *Spirit* upon the surface of the waters." This term "darkness" (חשך) is a word closely allied in meaning with ערפל. Occasionally, the two words occur together in the OT along with ענן and sometimes אכלה in a pleonastic description of theophany. In Is. 60:2 ערפל and ענן appear in synonymous parallelism with the meaning of "darkness." Thus, the meaning of ערפל overlaps with that of חשך sufficiently so that, for Sirach, ערפל can fully include the concept of "darkness" which occurs in Gen. 1:2.

Conversely, in Gen. 2:6 אד as "cloud," "rain cloud," or "dark cloud" also falls into the semantic range of ערפל as "cloudy darkness" or "dark cloud." Although the LXX supplies πήγη ("streams" or "sources") for אד, there is another tradition, perhaps Palestinian in origin, which takes אד as a "cloud," specifically "a water-carrier" or contextually "a dark rain cloud."[25] The Targum of Onkelos and the Palestinian Targum both translate it ענן.[26] Further, the Palestinian Targum attributes to the ענן a numinous quality. It is "a cloud of glory" which "descended from the throne of glory," even as Wisdom is that heavenly entity which "came forth from the mouth of the Most High." Consequently, ערפל can allude suitably both to חשך as "darkness" in Gen. 1:2 and to ענן as "cloud," perhaps even "dark cloud" contextually, in Gen. 2:6. Therefore, we find that the choice of ערפל in Sirach 24:3 is semantically generic enough to entail an allusion to each of the subject elements in both Gen. 1:2 and 2:6. Naturally, this perspective helps clarify how in Gen. 1:2 the peripheral metaphor "darkness" is linked so directly to "the spirit of God." "Darkness," rather than the associated element "spirit," must be the point of focus in Gen. 1:2 in order to maintain a connection through ערפל with the "cloud" or "dark cloud" of Gen. 2:6.

Apart from this line of investigation one must also consider if there is anything about these two Genesis verses structurally that might provide an incentive for such a conflated interpretation of them. In fact, a number of closely related features could engender such a reading. First, each of these two verses in Gen. 1 and 2 stands within the opening lines of its respective creation narrative and each verse represents the *first* mention of activity within the circumstances of creation. Second, this first description of primordial activity includes references to an *agent*-like subject other

---

[25] See E. F. Sutcliffe, "The Clouds as Water-Carriers in Hebrew Thought," *VT*, 3 (1953): 99:103. Also, see C. Westermann, *Genesis*, Biblischer Kommentar: Altes Testament, Vol. 2 (Neukirchen-Vluyn: Neukirchner Verlag, 1970), pp. 273–74.

[26] The Fragmentary Targum contains no direct reference to this verse.

than simply to God himself. Moreover, the רוח/חשך (1:2) or אד (2:6) in either verse can be viewed as a participant with God in creation and is ambiguous enough to invite some additional speculation regarding its precise identity.[27] Third, in each verse the agent or agents act "upon the whole surface (פני)" of the primordial world or land, an expression which occurs elsewhere in these narratives only in Gen. 1:20 regarding the flight of birds, and in 1:29 concerning the location of plants. Logically, only in 1:2 and 2:6 could one imagine an activity of cosmic dominance in association with this expression. Fourth, as respective subjects of the verses, the terms "darkness" (1:2) and "cloud" or "dark cloud" (2:6) are sufficiently related ideas to allow for a common interpretation. This then makes possible the choice by Sirach of a single more generic metaphor (ערפל) in order to allude to both of them.

Hence, the two creation accounts in Genesis 1 and 2 are viewed as complementary and are harmonized together at this single point. Although Sir. 24:3a attests to Wisdom's temporal priority over creation, 24:3b declares her priority even within the process of creation itself. For this later depiction the writer of Sirach looked to the Genesis creation accounts and identified wisdom with those equivocal cosmic agents of the first activity distinct from that of God himself in the creation of the world. Structural and thematic similarities between these two verses induced a common hearing of them as a kind of commentary on each other which sought to express an aspect of creation in one overarching exposition. After all, for Sirach Gen. 1:1ff. and 2:4bff. were not records of the theologies of "P" and "J," but the one sacred tradition concerning creation. The writer, therefore, contrives a single holistic interpretation for two of the corresponding verses. The ambiguity of the agents has allowed him to identify them as implicit symbols for Wisdom in creation.

In this way, the writer is able to read the Genesis account of creation, which makes no reference to wisdom, as a statement about Wisdom's cosmic biography. Although the Wisdom Song of Prov. 8 portrays Wisdom as preëminent to creation or perhaps as a participant in some general sense (cf. v. 30), only Sir. 24 identifies a specific role for her from the opening chapters of the fixed Torah traditions. This slanted reading of Genesis in

[27] רוח is identified with "the Spirit of Messiah" in *Bereshith Rabbah* 2:4. Jub. 2:2f. may make a similar reference to the identity of רוח, perhaps with the אד as "cloud" also in mind, when it describes the host the spirits created on the first day. These include "angels of the spirit of clouds and darkness" among others. This passage might, likewise, account for the absence of reference to the primordial activity of רוח or the אד earlier in the detailed resume concerning "the complete history of creation" (Jub. 2:1).

order to gather information about Wisdom for a Song reminiscent of Prov. 8 provides a clear example of a wisdom interpretation of the earlier sacred narratives.

Sir. 24:4a ἐγὼ ἐν ὑψηλοῖς κατεσκήνωσα
I encamped (*S* pitched my tent) in the high places.

The Hebrew *Vorlage*, unfortunately, is difficult to determine with precision. Both *G* and *L (habitavi)* allow for the possibility of a simple verb meaning "to dwell," "to encamp," or "to lodge," e.g., שכן, חנה, ישב, or לון. However, the Syriac suggests the possibility of a verbal phrase common to the Old Testament, viz., נטה אהל (or תקע), "to pitch a tent."[28] Nor is there agreement on this subject among the experts. Smend regards the Syriac as "more exact,"[29] while Segal takes it as rather a "free" rendering.[30] Further complicating this matter is the possibility of textual variants even in the Hebrew which underlies these respective versions.

Before the text critical problem can be examined properly, the range of possibilities for the Hebrew *Vorlage* must be evaluated more explicitly. For that purpose, the following analysis will consider, first, the possibility of a simple Hebrew verb underlying the Greek text and, second, the possibility, that the Hebrew was a verbal phrase. Segal has suggested שכנתי perhaps because κατασκηνοῦν is substituted for שכן in 54 out of 60 cases in the LXX. Nevertheless, it can be shown for this instance that the LXX may be misleading as a paradigm for translation equivalents in Sirach. The evidence is as follows:

a. Including this one occurrence in 24:4, κατασκηνοῦν is used only four times in Sirach. In the only instance of an extant Hebrew texts it translates חנה with κατασκηνοῦν.

b. For the six appearances of שכן in extant Hebrew texts of Sirach, *G* never renders it κατασκηνοῦν. This is particularly important since, as mentioned before, the LXX consistently prefers κατασκηνοῦν for שכן in 90 percent of the occurrences.

c. Finally, שכן, which according to the limits of the extant Hebrew Sirach texts is never translated in *G* with κατασκηνοῦν, is usually rendered

---

[28] The Syriac is the common rendering of the Peshitta for the given Hebrew phrase. Clearly, the expression "pitch the tabernacle" (< משכן) with the verb ܢܨܒ. for Hebrew נטה or תקע does not occur. Therefore, if *S* renders the corresponding verbal phrase from Hebrew, then ܡܫܟܢ must stand in the translator's mind for אהל and not משכן. The repetition of this term would probably be the same throughout, as "tent" (אהל) rather than as "tabernacle" (משכן).

[29] Smend, op. cit., p. 216.

[30] Segal, op. cit., p. 148.

by *G* as καταλύειν (four out of six occasions). By contrast, the LXX rarely substitutes καταλύειν for שכן–only three out of 60 times, all in Jer. 29–32–but uses this Greek verb regularly for לון (16/39X).

Consequently, the frequent use of κατασκηνοῦν by the LXX for שכן cannot be used as simple supportive evidence that the underlying Hebrew of *G* in 24:4a originally had שכן as a form of the main verb. In fact, the available evidence suggests just the opposite conclusion. Since שכן is usually translated in *G* with καταλύειν and since there is as yet no extant case in which *G* gives κατασκηνοῦν for it, then one can estimate that שכן probably does not occur here in the Hebrew text underlying *G*. Moreover, since κατασκηνοῦν is not used for לון or ישב, but does occur once for חנה, חנה is the more probable candidate. Its contextual usage in Sir. 4:15 is also comparable to the occasion here in 24:4a.

Although there is some support for the occurrence of a simple verb rather than a verbal phrase on the basis of the length of the line or a syllable count, no firm conclusions can be drawn.[31] Any final analysis concerning OT allusions must consequently be done in full consciousness of these textual ambiguities. Therefore, the following assessments are presented under two separate sets of probable textual options: first, on the theory that the original text was either נטה אהל (or תקע) as suggested by *S* or חנה as implied by *G*, and second, on the theory that the original was neither of those possibilities of the first case, but some other common verb meaning "to dwell," "to lodge," and so forth, e.g., שכן, לון, or ישב.

Of the two, the first set is the more probable in light of the present information. If the original text intended the idiom "to pitch my tent," then Wisdom is depicted as sojourning and finding a home only after God

[31] There are a few arguments in support of an original simple verb of "dwelling," rather than a verbal phrase like that of *S*: (a) *G* in 14:25 and 24:8a supplies a fully articulated phrase in translation. If there were a verbal phrase in the Hebrew of Sir. 24:4b, then it is unclear why *G* would simplify it here. (b) The Hebrew as proposed by Segal without the phrase fits better in the lines as poetry. 24:3–4 are the opening stanzas of the poem. 24:3a and 24:4a, as well as 24:3b and 24:4b, are roughly of the same syllable length. The addition of "my tent" would break this pattern. Furthermore, each of the individual words in 24:3b and 24:4b are of roughly the same syllable length in their corresponding places in the line. 24:3a and 24:4a both begin with the same word and end euphoniously with a similar verb, first person singular Qal perfect. Since much of the poem consists of regular sets of distichoi with lines of roughly the same length, this seems to be a logical pattern here as well. (c) Circumstantially, at least, the verbal phrase in Syriac may be an attempt to give a contextually more specific translation of a single technical Hebrew verb, rather than the more general ܥܡܪ. Despite this strong evidence the central argument, based on length of stichoi, is weakened both by its appeal only to vv. 3–4 and by the irregularity in the lengths of lines that follow.

by command "fixed (her) tent" (v. 8) in the promised land, in Zion (v. 10). Combined with the motif of the "pillar of cloud" in the next verse, this language seems to be a direct play on the wilderness wanderings of the Hebrew people. Hence, the wilderness traditions are alluded to and given a distinct wisdom interpretation. What was true of Israel's earthly flight from bondage to a Promised Land is now applied to describe Wisdom's cosmic flight from a heavenly sphere to a special people, city, and country (cf. Sir. 24:10–12).

An even more enticing possibility is that the original was חנה, which is indeed the technical expression in Numbers and elsewhere for the camping along the stages of the wilderness journey.[32] In this instance, the Syriac could be fully explained simply as a dynamic equivalent of the verb. Although language of the wilderness traditions usually lacks the verbal phrase "to pitch a tent" because of its preference for the technical term חנה, the two expressions are virtually synonymous in meaning.[33] The *S* translation may have resulted simply because all the various Hebrew words for lodging or dwelling tend to be rendered in Syriac by the same colorless word ܫܪܐ. The translator noticed the technical use of the Hebrew term here as a *Stichwort* connection with the wilderness traditions, and rather than allow its special character to be lost in the general use of the Syriac verb "to dwell," he used the more precise expression ܢܨܒ ܡܫܟܢܐ, an expression which is the usual Peshitta equivalent of נטה אהל (or תקע), "to pitch a tent." Like חנה in Hebrew, ܢܨܒ ܡܫܟܢܐ would conceptually recall the transient lodging of Israel in the biblical traditions of the wilderness experience. This choice in language would explicitly link, by means of a technical term, the interpretation of wisdom's camping about the cosmos with the OT wilderness traditions. Since this particular textual restoration and analysis seems to conform judiciously to the best evidence, it is, in my opinion, the most compelling.

Because of the textual ambiguities, a complete analysis must allow for the second set of possibilities. This second hypothesis presumes that the underlying Hebrew was ישב, לון, or more probably שכן, as Segal and others have suggested. With the absence of a technical expression common to one particular OT tradition or of an unequivocal expression that links the action to the tent and journey motif, the evidence for a play on the

---

32 This verb becomes the regular term for all of Israel's temporary lodging along the way in the wilderness. Cf. esp. Num. 33:1.

33 For example, the two expressions occur with the same meaning in the same story in Gen. 26:17 and 26:25.

wilderness traditions is less obvious.[34] Only the references to the "pillar of cloud" and the settlement which follows sets this verb in a context of the Exodus wanderings.

With either set of lexical possibilities, the entire line, "I encamped in the high places," stresses Wisdom's preëminent status over the rest of creation and humanity as does her previous claim to derive from the mouth of God (v. 3 a). Similarly, God is often described in the Prophets and Psalms as "dwelling" (שכן) "on high" or "in the heights."[35] Those who find favor with him are consequently "made to stand" or "exalted" on high.[36] In 1 Kings 8:12 the dwelling place of God, as that of Wisdom in Sir. 24:3b, is "in thick darkness" (בערפל). Clearly, this familiar theophanic language about God is borrowed from the narrative literature and the Psalms and applied to Wisdom. The effect is to express the assumption of Wisdom's heavenly origin, originally found in Proverbs and Qoheleth, in language foreign to the biblical wisdom books and typical of theophany, for example, of God at Sinai (cf. Ex. 20:16–19).

However, despite the similarity in the depiction of Wisdom with that of God in the narrative and prophetic traditions, there is still a significant difference. While God dwells in the heavens, Wisdom only temporarily "encamps on the heights." This subtle distinction between God and Wisdom is strengthened by the occurrence of the "pillar of cloud" in the next stichos and by what follows in Sir. 24:7–8. Hence, one finds here, as elsewhere in the Song, that the language used in Wisdom's self-description vacillates between OT statements originally about God, on the one hand, and statements originally about Israel, on the other. In the latter case, even as Israel came out from (יצא מן) Egypt and encamped (חנה) in the wilderness,[37] so Wisdom came forth from (ἐξέρχεσθαι ἀπὸ) the mouth of God and encamped (κατασκηνοῦν) in the high places. While the transcendental character of Wisdom has been sustained by the adaptation for her of God language found outside the traditional wisdom literature, events in her history are borrowed from the narrative traditions of Israel's pilgrimage to a Promised Land. Because both of these applications use material found originally in narrative and psalmic contexts to inform a description of

---

[34] Outside of the wilderness wandering traditions the more general language of dwelling may be used to express the idea of tenting in the wilderness (e.g., Gen. 21:21, וישב במדבר).

[35] E.g., Ps. 113:4, 5; 132:14; Is. 33:5, 16; 57:15.

[36] E.g., 2 Sam. 22:34 (= Ps. 18:33); Ps. 107:41.

[37] E.g., Num. 33:1f.

Wisdom like that of the Wisdom Songs in Proverbs, both constitute examples of a secondary wisdom interpretation of biblical traditions.

Sir. 24:4b καὶ ὁ θρόνος μου ἐν στύλῳ νεφέλης.
And my throne was in a pillar of cloud.

Here one finds an unexpected combination of motifs without precedent in the Hebrew Bible. Each motif will first be examined in its wider OT context to understand how it might have been appropriated for Wisdom. If evidence of an intentional play on different OT traditions is found, then the effect of joining them together in this unusual manner will be explored.

The OT never describes Wisdom as having a throne. Instead, thrones appertain either to kings or to God. There are, however, aspects within the OT portrayal of the divine throne that do seem ideally suited to the claim of Wisdom here in Sir. 24. Like the concern in 24:4a with Wisdom's encampment, the cosmic location of God's throne in the OT involves the old problem of where the Creator of the universe can dwell–in the heavens or in the man-made temple, or both? The particular metaphor of God's enthronement does not occur in the Pentateuch but rather in the Psalms and in the Prophets, particularly in the theophanic visions of the prophets.

In some passages the divine enthronement is dissociated from any building or sanctuary. In Is. 66:1 God declares, "the heaven is my throne, and the earth is my footstool." He is sometimes described as simply enthroned "in the heavens," e.g., Ps. 103:19. In another set of passages, either implicitly or explicitly, his throne is seen in the temple. In Ezek. 43:6,7 the prophet hears God address him in the temple, "this is the place of my throne ... where I will dwell in the midst of the people of Israel forever." While a throne is a frequent symbol in prophetic visions, its appearance in Is. 6:1f. and Ezek. 10:1 strategically links the heavenly throne to the earthy sanctuary. This close association between the heavenly throne and the earthy sanctuary is presupposed by the statement in Jer. 17:12, "A glorious throne set on high from the beginning is the place of our sanctuary."

Wis. 9:4 illustrates a similar move to link Wisdom with the divine throne. There it is said that she "sits by thee [God] on thy throne." Even as the Wisdom Song in Prov. 8 includes concepts which were probably borrowed from the speeches of Egyptian gods and goddesses, so the writer of the Song in Sir. 24 borrows the imagery of the throne of Israel's God and identifies it with Wisdom.[38] This tendency to assign to Wisdom

[38] Kayatz, op. cit., pp. 76ff.; 134–39.

a share in the OT depiction of God's presence within Israel's sacred traditions proves to be a persistent interpretive device in Sir. 24.

Throughout the OT the imagery of a divine throne is associated frequently with theophanic symbolism. Prophetic vision accounts regularly employ the words, "darkness," "clouds," and "smoke." Ps. 97:2 describes this phenomena in relation to the throne: "Clouds [ענן] and cloud-like darkness [וערפל] are round about him, righteousness and justice are the foundation of his throne in the heavens." When the ark of the covenant first enters the holy of holies to dwell in the new Solomonic temple (1 Kings 8:6ff.), the building is filled with a cloud so dense that the priests, being overcome, cannot minister.

Similarly, Sir. 24:3–4 utilizes theophanic symbolism of divine "dwelling," "darkness," (pillar of) "cloud" and "a throne." The "pillar of cloud" is the characteristic symbol of divine guidance and presence in the wilderness traditions (e.g., Ex. 13:21, 14:19; Neh. 9:12,19).[39] Ex. 13:21 speaks of God as a visible presence, "in a pillar of cloud" leading Israel in the wilderness. Like the clouds, darkness, and smoke that accompanied the appearance of God in his later temple, the pillar of cloud periodically stationed itself before the portable tent of meeting, and God spoke either to the leaders or to the people (e.g., Ex. 33:9,10; Ps. 99:7).

While there is no reference specifically to a throne in the OT wilderness traditions, God is portrayed elsewhere as "seated" (ישב) between the cherubim in the accompanying ark.[40] The writer of Sirach was undoubtedly familiar with these later evaluations of the ark as the place of enthronement, e.g., Ezek. 10:1bff. From the standpoint of a history of religions it is not difficult to see how these early elements of the wilderness traditions allowed for such a developed interpretation of Wisdom's role in them. For example, Philo, although he shows no clear signs of direct dependence on Sirach in this matter, nonetheless views the cloud, which stood between Israel and the Egyptians in Ex. 14:20, as the symbol of both divine salvation and *wisdom* for the Hebrew people.[41]

In Sir. 24:4b the combination of these two images and the assignment of them to Wisdom can achieve its intended effect only when the reader is familiar with the biblical theophanic symbolism and particularly the past sacred wilderness traditions. Certain familiar language about God in the

---

[39] Cf. Marböck, op.cit., p.37. Despite the Syriac "pillars of cloud," *G* and *L* have the singular "pillar of cloud" suggesting בעמוד ענן which is more probable. Cf. Ex. 13:21.

[40] I Sam. 4:4.

[41] Philo, *Quis Rerum Divinarum Heres*, § 42 (LCL, Vol. 4, p. 385).

OT is read as applying not only to God but also to Wisdom.[42] As a result, Wisdom finds her identification in the rich and ambiguous spiritual reality behind the traditional biblical symbols of divine self-manifestation. The pillar of cloud, in contrast to more general references to theophanic clouds and darkness, causes the reader to think specifically about the wilderness traditions. Moreover, the historical sequence depicted in the Torah of Israel's wandering and settlement defines the larger pattern in which the author selects other biblical images for Wisdom. Even as in Num. 10:33, 34, the "cloud of the Lord" accompanies homeless Israel who "seeks a resting place," so Wisdom on her throne "in a pillar of cloud" moves along with Israel and like Israel "seeks a resting place" (v.7) in the land of Zion (v.10).

Sir. 24:5–6 γῦρον οὐρανοῦ ἐκύκλωσα μόνη
καὶ ἐν βάθει ἀβύσσων περιπάτησα
ἐν κύμασιν θαλάσσης καὶ ἐν πάσῃ τῇ γῇ
καὶ ἐν παντὶ λαῷ καὶ ἔθνει ἐκτησάμην

I encompassed the circle of heaven alone,
and I walked in the depths of the abyss.
In the waves of the sea and in all the earth
and among every people and nation I took possession.[43]

---

[42] It is possible that the choice of imagery in Sir. 24 is influenced by Song of Songs 3:6–11. The difficulty in dating the Song of Songs naturally complicates this hypothesis. However, early in the history of interpretation, the Song of Songs passage attracted exposition in terms of the ark of the covenant moving through the wilderness to Zion. See Gillis Gerleman, *Ruth–Das Hohelied*, Biblischer Kommentar: Altes Testament, Vol. 18 (Neukirchen-Vluyn: Neukirchner Verlag, 1965), pp. 135–36.
If one identifies Solomon with Wisdom, some interesting correspondences to the Sirach Song emerge. Solomon (the bridegroom?) comes up "from the wilderness" in a procession that appears like a "column of smoke" (כתימרות עשן, cf. Joel 3:3). Wearing his royal crown (v.11), he rides a majestic litter (v.6) or palanquin (v.9) which is equipped with silver posts, a gold back, and a purple seat. Observers from Jerusalem watch enthusiastically. The daughters of Zion rush forward to greet him on what seems to be his royal wedding day.
In Sirach 24, instead of Solomon, the alleged author of the wisdom books, it is Wisdom who comes "circling" (v.5a) and "walking" (v.5b) through the cosmos in search of a resting place and an inheritance, as did Israel and the tabernacle in the wilderness. Just as Solomon's royal litter appears as a "column of smoke," her throne is in a "pillar of cloud." Both are destined for the elect city of Zion. While Solomon rides on a portable throne, Wisdom is, likewise, carried on her throne in the transient pillar of cloud. With Solomon, the smoke is fragrant with "myrhh and frankincense," two of the elements which compose the sanctuary's perfumed holy incense with which Wisdom is intimately related in Sir. 24:15.

[43] This reading is based on the majority of the best texts of *G*. See Smend, op. cit., p. 217. Most commentators regard *G* as a misreading, but for arguments which defend an

Unlike the verses preceding and following, Sir. 24:5–6 no longer contains expressions reminiscent of the narrative Torah traditions. Rather, the language is unhistorical, referring solely to Wisdom's universal activity under and above the world and its people. In comparison with the Torah, the literary product of this abrupt shift in theme and vocabulary appears closer to that of a non-biblical source, namely, a form of Isis Aretalogy or its prototype.[44] The range of literary agreement between vv. 5–6 and the Isis Aretalogies include the parataxis of I-style predications together with the motifs of heavenly rule and solitary movement about the cosmos.[45] Because of these similarities, Conzelmann concludes that both verses and some elements in the preceding ones are borrowed entirely from an Isis hymn, and therefore contain in themselves "nichts spezifisch Jüdisches."[46]

original קניניתי, "I gained possession," see Fritzsche, op. cit., p. 126, and especially N. Peters, *Das Buch Jesus Sirach oder Ecclesiasticus übersetzt und erklärt*, Exegetisches Handbuch zum Alten Testament, Vol. 25 (Münster: Druck der Aschendorffschen Buchdruckerei, 1913), pp. 197–98. If it is taken as "possessing" or "winning possession" (cf. Prov. 8:22 in Aq., Symm., Theo. of Field's *Hexapla*, and in the Vulgate), then it may link with the latter theme of "inheritance/possession" (κληρονομία, cf. 24:7, 8, 12, 20, 23) in the rest of the Song and commentary. Ps. 82:8 speaks similarly of God. Conversely, if it is taken with *S* to mean "to rule," Prov. 8:14–16 may well be the stimulus. *L* helps little to resolve the matter.

If one follows the general rule of text critical decisions that the more difficult reading, namely, "to gain possession"—a reading which has strong manuscript support—is to be preferred, the Syriac "to rule" could be judged an attempt to make sense of a strange verbal form. In any case, the evidence for substantial dependence on such Isis statements as, "I am Isis, ruler of every land," rests on shakey textual grounds. Cf. Marböck, op. cit., p. 53. Moreover, the similarities of either alternative reading with phraseology in Prov. 8, upon which Sir. 24 depends repeatedly, makes a hypothesis of influence from an Isis Song both unnecessary and debatable.

[44] For the principal bibliography and an excellent summary of the discussion, see Marböck, op. cit., pp. 47–54. For a study of the Aretalogy *Gattung*, see A. J. Festugière, "A propos des Arétalogies d'Isis," *HTR*, 42 (1949): 290–334.

[45] Adolf Deissmann was the first to suggest that the paratactic I-style assertions in Sir. 24 find an exact parallel in the Nysa and Ios inscriptions of Isis Aretalogies. See his *Licht vom Osten* (Tübingen: J. C. B. Mohr, 1923), 4th rev. ed., p. 109, n. 3. For a comparison of other features in Sir. 24 with features in Isis Aretalogies, see Marböck, op. cit., pp. 49–54, and Martin Hengel, *Judentum und Hellenismus* (Tübingen: J. C. B. Mohr, 1973), pp. 165 ff.

[46] Hans Conzelmann, "Die Mutter der Weisheit," *Zeit und Geschichte*, ed. by Erich Dinkler [Tübingen: J. C. B. Mohr (Paul Siebeck), 1964, p. 228: "V. 3–6(7) sind nichts anderes als ein praktisch wörtlich aufgenommenes, nur an ein bis zwei Stellen leicht retouchiertes Lied auf Isis." In a footnote (n. 27) he explains his analysis of the verses: "In ὁμίχλη kann man eine Erinnerung an Gen. 1,2 finden; immerhin steht dort das Wort nicht. ἄβυσσος steht in Gen. 1, aber innerhalb eines anderen (überdies ebenfalls unjüdischen) Weltbildes. ὕψιστος wird vom Verfasser geschrieben sein, vgl. v. 2.23, ist aber gerade typisch als Aus-

The purpose of this study is not to resolve the question of how an Isis Aretalogy may or may not influence the structure of Wisdom's similar self-assertion in Sir. 24. Any final resolution of that question must consider all the evidence within the Song. It is sufficient to observe that the case for *direct* dependence relies primarily on these verses and labors under the assumption of their non-biblical origin. Moreover, this analysis refutes the later assumption by showing that the composition of these verses belongs to an anthological style of biblical interpretation.[47]

In the OT, Wisdom is never described explicitly as "alone" (μόνος = לבדו), as one acting in cosmic isolation. Conzelmann seizes upon this non-biblical depiction of Wisdom and compares it with the same motif in the self-description of Isis. [48] Nevertheless, throughout Sir. 24 the writer frequently takes over explicit biblical statements about God and applies them to Wisdom.[49] Since this is a routine convention in his use of Scripture, it deserves prior consideration over any other hypothesis. Indeed, an examination of the biblical evidence shows that God appears explicitly

---

druck der synkretistischen Situation, überdies Stichwort der Aretalogien [Kryrene 7; Isidor III (SEG 550)] I. 'Wolkensäule' wird eine Retouche in Erinnerung an Ex sein. Aber an die Geschichte Israels wird mit keinem Wort erinnert. Zudem ist es hier eine kosmische Säule. Das Motiv stammt also nicht aus der Bibel." For v. 6, he observes, "Damit ist der sicher zu rekonstruierende Isis-Text zu Ende" (ibid., p. 231), but he thinks v. 7a is probably a further motif from the Aretalogy because Isis ends her journey and *by implication* finds rest. By this logic he attempts to explain the language of "rest" and "inheritance" in v. 7. Marböck, by contrast, stops at this point and proposes, "das Suchen nach 'Ruhe' und 'Erbteil' gibt eine erste *interpretatio israelitica*" (op. cit., p. 62).
Helmer Ringgren is a vigorous dissenter from the theory that the material in vv. 5–6 is simply imported into the Song from an extraneous Isis-like hymn. In *Word and Wisdom* (Lund: H. Ohlssons Boktr., 1947), p. 146, he contends, "I do not think, however, that this theory is very convincing, since the differences seem to be greater than the resemblances, and the passages in question do not give the impression of being '*Fremdkörper*' in the context in which they stand." Since the publication of Conzelmann's article, some important recent investigations show similar reserve in this matter. For example, Middendorp does not press the point (op. cit., p. 20), and Marböck treats it cautiously (op. cit., pp. 34–96), although he is in substantial agreement.

[47] For a discussion and bibliography on "style anthologique" see Renée Bloch, "Midrash," in *Dictionnaire de La Bible: Supplément*, ed. by Henri Cazelles (Paris: Librairie Letouzey et Ané, 1957), Vol. V, 1263–82, esp. 1269ff. A. A. Robert in his entry under "Littéraires (Genres)" in the same volume defines the technique as one which seeks "réemployer, littéralement ou équivalemment, les mots ou formules des Écritures antérieures" (p. 411). The present analysis will show that a particular theme determines the choice of texts from which elements are taken and anthologically arranged.

[48] Conzelmann, op. cit., p. 230, n. 27.

[49] For example, see the discussion of Sir. 24:4 and 24:9b.

"alone" (לבדו) only in Is. 44:24 and Job 9:8. In Is. 44:24 God "stretches out the heavens alone." However, the language of Job 9:8 is remarkably similar to that of Sir. 24:5–6. In Job 9:8 God is he "who alone [לבדו, LXX μόνος] stretched out the heavens and *treaded* [ודורך, LXX περιπατῶν] *the* במתי *of the sea.*" The last construct phrase is a *hapax legomenon* in the *MT* and presented great difficulty for the early translators. While most translations interpreted it in terms of firmness or solidarity,[50] the Vulgate offered *super fluctus*, "over the waves," like the *G* and *L (in fluctibus)* of the phrase in Sir. 24:6a. Because of the divergency in the early translations of במתי, it cannot be proved that this phrase was taken over exactly from Job in the Hebrew of Sir. 24:5–6. Nevertheless, a minimal assessment is that three unusual features in the depiction of God in Job 9:8 have been applied similarly to Wisdom in Sir. 24:5–6. In both, God is alone; he "walks" or "treads" about the cosmos (both the LXX of Job 9:8 and the *G* of Sir. 24:5 have περιπατεῖν); and this activity occurs at a particular place, "the x of the sea."

In the light of this possible use of Job 9:8, another unusual reference in Job to God "walking" or "treading" about the cosmos deserves attention. In Job 38:16 God exposes the fallacy of Job's presumption in questioning the Creator, and, in turn, interogates Job, "Have you entered the springs of the sea or walked in the recesses of the deep?" Much as is the case with Job 9:8, the parallels in language are very close. A comparison of both the LXX and the *MT* of Job 38:16 with the *G* of Sir. 24:5–6 suffices to illustrate this point:

Sir. 24:5b	*(G)*	καὶ ἐν βάθει ἀβύσσων περιπάτησα
Job 38:16b	(LXX)	ἐν δὲ ἴχνεσιν ἀβύσσου περιπάτησας
	(MT)	ובחקר תהום התהלכת

In addition, the first phrase of the Job verse parallels the first of Sir. 24:6:

Sir. 24:6a	*(G)*	ἐν κύμασιν θαλάσσης
Job 38:16a	(LXX)	ἐπὶ πηλὴν θαλάσσης
	(MT)	עד נבכי ים

Wisdom's concern with "all the earth" (*G* and *L*, but *S* "the foundations of the world") recalls, likewise, the adjacent observation in Job 38:18 that God comprehends "the expanse of the earth" (רחבי ארץ). Even the devi-

---

[50] For examples, LXX ὡς ἐπ' ἐδάφους, "as on firm ground;" Targum על רום תקוף, "on the height of solidarity;" Peshitta ܥܠ ܬܘܩܦܐ, "on firmness."

ations in some of these construct phrases fall within the range of mere translation variants.[51] Other allusions to Job 38:16 in Sir. 1:3, and especially 16:18–19, suggest this passage is a favorite of the writer.

Finally, the uncommon phrase, "circle of heaven" (γῦρον οὐρανοῦ = חוג שמים), must be considered. In the Hebrew Bible it occurs only in Is. 40:22, Prov. 8:27, and Job 22:14. Once again the passage in Job is distinguished by its description of God: "He walks [יתהלך] on the circle of heaven." In Is. 40:22 God does not ambulate, but "sits" on the circle of heaven, and in Prov. 8:27 the phrase is employed only as a cosmic point of reference.

The most astounding evidence for dependence appears as the total pattern of scriptural usage emerges. The characteristic verses all come from Job (9:8, 22:14; 38:16). Each is concerned with a form of ambulatory activity and together are the only ones in Job to speak of God walking or treading in this manner. Each contains construct phrases which are collected in Sir. 24:5–6, in order to plot out the cosmic boundaries of created reality over which God alone exercises his will. Only the use of all three verses completes the four points of cosmic reference. Thus, Ps. 135:6 acknowledges, "Whatever the Lord pleases he does, in heaven and on earth, in the seas and all deeps."

The pattern of biblical phrases is based on an anthological use of features from all the verses in the book of Job concerned with the theme of God traversing the cosmos. The same method of interpretation occurs

[51] For example, חקר, "object of search, limit," in the phrase בחקר תהום (a *hapax legomenon*) occurs in the LXX as ἴχνος, "track, footprint." The same word in the Hebrew phrase מחקרי ארץ (Ps. 95:4) is rendered πέρατα from πέρας, "the measure of depth or height." Thus, βάθος, "depth," seems to orbit within the same semantic field as these other terms. Likewise, *S* may support this possibility of dependence directly on the Hebrew phrase in Job by its translation ܢܩܝܪ. This rendering is perhaps an intentional transliteration of חקר with change only in the first consonant in order to produce a sensible Syriac word. The reason for resorting to transliteration may result from the translator's difficulty in determining a precise equivalent. Other early translations show that the meaning of the word is indeed problematic; for example, LXX (mentioned above) "track, trace," Targum פשפוש, "exploration," and Peshitta ܫܬܐܣܘܗܝ, "foundations." In addition, a partial transliteration may be stimulated by the proximity of the *nomen rectum* תהום which is always transliterated in *S*.
As another example of a possible confusion in translation, *S* of Sir. 24:6a agrees with the Job 38:16 phrase "sources [נבכי] of the sea" against *G* and *L* which have "waves of the sea." Yet both *G* and *L* of Sir. 24:6a may represent translations like the Latin Vulgate, which takes the phrase in Job 9:8 as "waves of the sea." The difficulties in translating and the possibilities of influence from cross referencing by the different translators greatly complicate the matter. A precise reconstruction of the earliest Hebrew at this level of nuance must remain open to tenuous speculation.

elsewhere in Sirach (for example, see the analysis of Sir. 17:1–4 and Bar. 3:26–28). The genius of the interpretation lies in the writer's collecting from these verses a complete set of references to the four horizons of the cosmos. These features, together with the rare attribution that God walks "alone" in Job 9:8, account for all the distinctive language in Sir. 24: 5–6a. The exceptional language in v. 6b is probably reminiscent of either Prov. 8:22 or Prov. 8:14–16 (see n. 1).

The book of Sirach never suggests that the writer recognizes Job as a "wisdom" book. Since Job is not clearly associated by Sirach with wisdom and is mentioned historically along with Ezekiel in Sirach's Praise to the Fathers (Sir. 49:9), there is the probability that it lacks the more precise wisdom claim of Proverbs and Qoheleth as Solomonic books. In any case, the passages used from Job are in their own context not descriptive of Wisdom. Rather they are thematically related statements about God that are interpreted anthologically in Sirach for Wisdom. Although in Prov. 8:27 Wisdom is merely preëminently present when God "draws a circle on the face of the deep," in Sir. 24:5–6 she "encompass[es] the circle of heaven alone" and strides like the Creator throughout the universe. The function of Sir. 24:5–6 in the context of wilderness wanderings becomes clear in the verses that follow.

Sir. 24:7 μετὰ τούτων πάντων ἀνάπαυσιν ἐζήτησα
καὶ ἐν κληρονομίᾳ τίνος αὐλισθήσομαι
Among all these I sought a resting place,
And in whose inheritance I would lodge.

After the interlude of Sir. 24:5–6, which borrowed language from the poetic traditions in Job, this verse returns to the interpretation of Wisdom in terms of the wilderness narratives. Even as v. 4b recalled the "pillar of cloud," this verse draws upon the deuteronomic critique of the wanderings as a "search" for "rest" and "inheritance." Naturally, the structural question must first be asked concerning the relation of v. 7 to vv. 5–6, which interrupted the thematic pattern of a play on the wilderness traditions.

In this regard the transition in v. 7, μετὰ τούτων πάντων, is extremely significant. It abruptly sets the context of the preceding non-historical prose (vv. 5–6) within the larger framework of Wisdom's wandering in the wilderness. A similar literary device is used in Sir. 24:23. There ταῦτα πάντα sets the entire Wisdom Song in an unequivocal perspective by the direct identification of Wisdom with the book of the Torah. By a calculated use of demonstrative pronouns, these transitions mark an important change in the flow of prose and serve as pivot points upon which the whole of the previous passage is turned into one literary moment. The previous passage can then be set within a precise context of interpretation, one which overcomes any significant ambiguity otherwise detrimental to the guiding purpose of the author.

By means of this literary device every movement of Wisdom in vv. 5–6 illustrates the nature of her heavenly wandering parallel to Israel's earthly trek. Thus the author finds in the Job portrait of God walking about the cosmos the transcendental counterparts to Israel's desert journey. With the stage set by such an explicit transition, there remains but the unfolding of the wilderness theme.

Wisdom's search is in v. 7 a quest, like that of Israel, for rest and inheritance which is resolved by means of a decree from the Creator in vv. 8–9. In the section that follows she finds her place "in a sacred tent" (v. 10), "in a beloved city" (v. 11), and "among a praiseworthy people" (v. 12). In Zion, Wisdom ministers in the temple and proliferates like various hearty plants (vv. 13–17). Based on her identification and status in Israel's history Wisdom summons her hearers to partake of her knowledge. The larger structure of Wisdom's activity throughout the Song of Sir. 24 may be outlined as follows:

a. Wisdom's origin, v. 3.
b. Wisdom's search for rest and inheritance, vv. 4–7.
c. The Creator's command for settlement, vv. 8–9.
d. Wisdom's settlement and subsequent growth, vv. 10–17.
e. Her appeal to the readers based on the above credentials, vv. 18–22.

The central ideas in v. 7 of "rest" and "inheritance" are thematically interwoven throughout the rest of the poem. In v. 7 Wisdom seeks "rest," (ἀνάπαυσιν); in v. 8 the Creator "sets to rest" (κατέπαυσεν) her tent; and in v. 11 he "settles" (κατέπαυσεν) her in the beloved city. Again, in v. 7 she wonders in whose inheritance/possession (κληρονομία) she will settle. In v. 8 the Creator issues a command to "take up inheritance" (κατακληρονομήθητι) in Israel. Finally, in v. 12 she finds her κληρονομία in the portion of the Lord among a praiseworthy people. The word κληρονομία further links with v. 20 and is the critical thematic bond between the Song of Wisdom as a whole and v. 23. In sum, from v. 7 the reader confronts a well-articulated text with a careful selection of vocabulary which develops the same set of ideas.

The combination of the paired terms "rest" (נוח) and "inheritance" (נחלה) in v. 7 does not occur frequently in the OT except in the book of

Deuteronomy, e.g., Dt. 3:18–20; 12:1–11; 25:19.[52] Likewise, the same pattern is found in Jos. 11:13–15 in which the men of Reuben, Gad, and Manasseh are admonished into battle and reminded of the total requirements of the conquest. It is even more significant to find in all of these passages a surprising concentration of verbal and nominative expressions identical to those in vv. 7–12. As an illustration, the following Greek terms of the Sirach translation show up again in the LXX of these particular biblical passages: e.g., ἐντέλλεσθαι (vv. 8, 23–Dt. 3:18; 12:11, 14; Jos. 1:13); καταπαύειν (vv. 8, 11–Dt. 3:20; 12:9, 10; 25:19; Jos. 1:13, 15); κατακληρονομεῖν (v. 8–Dt. 3:20; 12:10; 25:19; κληρονομεῖν (v. 8 in MsA for κατακληρονομεῖν – Dt. 12:2, 29; 25:19; Jos. 1:15); κληρονομία (vv. 7, 12–Dt. 3:20; 12:9; Jos. 1:15 (cf. κλῆρος – Dt. 3:18; 12:1, 12; 25:19); ἐπικαλεῖν = שכן (cf. vv. 4, 8 κατασκηνοῦν – Dt. 12:5, 11). Without the Hebrew of Sir. 24 it is difficult to circumscribe the nuances in the borrowing of language, but this comparison should suffice to prove a high degree of literal correspondence.

The significance of this evidence is that it demonstrates a close dependence on biblical vocabulary from texts concerned with Israel's instruction and preparation for the conquest of the land. The paired terms "rest" and "inheritance" are indeed, as Marböck has already suggested, distinctive of Deuteronomy.[53] Only his conclusion that this is the first *interpretatio israelitica* must be questioned.[54] The effect of this shared vocabulary is suggestive of a general wisdom interpretation of the earlier wilderness traditions for they are now just as indicative of Wisdom on a cosmic plane as of Israel on the earth. It is important to note too that, in addition to numerous minor parallels, even the crucial elective commands by which God admonishes Israel to take the land for rest and inheritance (Dt. 3:18; Jos. 1:13, cf. Dt. 12:11, 14) are designated for Wisdom (Sir. 24:8).

Significantly, the verbal phrase "*to seek* a resting place" or "inheritance" is also a rare expression in the OT.[55] The Hebrew equivalents of the

[52] See Ex. 33:14 in which God at Sinai promises to give the people rest. For a discussion of the use of these terms in Sirach, see Rickenbacher, op. cit., pp. 138–41.

[53] Marböck, op. cit., p. 62.

[54] Ibid.

[55] Usually one seeks after other things in the OT: e.g., wisdom (Qoh. 7:25), peace (Ps. 34:15), knowledge (Prov. 15:14, 18:15), commandments (Prov. 2:4), Torah (Mal. 2:7), peace and a vision (Ezek. 7:25–26). Although the biblical wisdom literature is unusually concerned with "seeking after" various things or ideals, "resting place" and "inheritance" are never found there as objects of such a pursuit. Outside the wisdom literature it is made explicit that Israel's claim to a resting place is contingent on obedience

verb ζητεῖν in this context could be either בקש, or דרש or תור.[56] Judges 18:1 describes the Danites in the pre-monarchial period as a tribe that still "sought for itself an inheritance to settle upon" (מבקש לו נחלה לשבת = LXX ἐζήτει ἑαυτῇ κληρονομίαν τοῦ κατοικεῖν) because they had not yet received a land allotment among the tribes. For this reason they sent out men "*to spy out* the land" (לרגל vv. 2, 14, 17; a synonym for תור, cf. Jud. 1:23). Num. 10:33, in an even closer parallel to Sir. 24:7, describes Israel's three-day journey from Mount Horeb, with the ark of the covenant leading them, "to seek out a resting place" (לתור להם מנוחה = LXX κατασκέψασθαι αὐτοῖς ἀνάπαυσιν). According to the Scripture that follows, the "cloud of the Lord was over them by day whenever they set out from the camp." This image of the Hebrew people in search of a resting place, and accompanied by the pillar of cloud, is found again in Dt. 1:33, when God himself leads the children of Israel by means of fire and cloud "to seek out a place to pitch their tents" (לתור לכם מקום לחנתכם).[57] This last Hebrew phrase could be rendered into Greek by ζητεῖν ... κατασκῆναι.[58]

It is, therefore, evident that this particular expression, "to seek rest" or "inheritance," is used in the OT exclusively in reference to the tribes of Israel in pursuit of their allotments within the promised land. In at least two occasions (Num. 10:33; Dt. 1:33), there is a close association be-

to the covenant stipulations. Thus in Dt. 28:58–68 God threatens Israel with no resting place among the nations unless she obeys the commandments (cf. 1 Kgs. 8:56; Lam. 1:4). The prophet Micah later warns that in the midst of her transgression there will be no place for Israel to rest (Mic. 2:10; cf. Is. 32:18).

[56] תור has been overlooked by commentators, but it is a valid possibility, particularly since it is used in wisdom literature in precisely this way, e.g., Qoh. 1:13 לדרוש ולתור בחכמה and Qoh. 7:25 לדעת ולתור ובקש חכמה where it appears as a virtual synonym of בקש and דרש. Cf. Qoh. 2:3, Job 39:8, Prov. 12:26. Perhaps תור is used in Sir. 11:9a (MsB). Against this proposal is the fact that the LXX never translates תור in the OT with ζητεῖν, but prefers κατασκέπτεσθαι. Nevertheless, the translator has probably left us with good contextual rendering of the word without close adherence to the Septuagint's tendencies. See the previous discussion of κατασκηνοῦν in 24:4a. Segal's suggestion (op. cit., p. 145) of בקשתי has merit, but clearly is not the only option.

[57] LXX suggests "to lead them" for the final infinitive. Although the matter is hard to adjudicate, one can certainly understand how לחנתכם might shift to לנחתים by the simple transposition of two letters, particularly under influence from the Ex. 13:21 parallel and the following predication "to show you the way to go." A misreading the other way seems unlikely. Which text the writer of Sirach had before him is of course debatable. Assuming he had a Hebrew OT with reading like the *MT*, the writer of the verse probably shows dependence on the language of Dt. 12:5 and the similar statement in Num. 10:33.

[58] Cf. Sir. 4:15 in which κατασκηνοῦν is used for the root חנה. See also Sir. 4:13b, 14:24a and especially the discussion of 24:4.

tween this particular phraseology and the recollection of the pillar of cloud by day and fire by night which led Israel through the Sinai wilderness. This same correspondence in language and situation is paralleled by Sir. 24:7 in association with 24:4b.

Of the biblical passages with a high concentration of vocabulary on the rest and inheritance theme like that of Sir. 24:7–8,11 (Dt. 3:18–20; 12:1–11; 25:19; Jos. 1:13–15), only Dt. 12:1–11 also contains a command of God that his people *seek* the place he has destined for them (v. 5). For that reason, this passage provides an ideal point from which to probe after Sirach's wisdom reading of these traditions. Besides the above mentioned language parallels, Dt. 12:1–11 contains a number of other motifs similar to those in Sir. 24. Obviously the emphasis on a place which God will choose (e.g., Dt. 12:5) coincides well with Wisdom's appointment to Zion (Sir. 24:10b). The land is one of little constitutional and social order for the people. According to Deuteronomy the people do "whatever seems right in their own eyes" (Dt. 12:8). But once in the land the statutes and ordinances will be put in force (12:1), and there will be a central sanctuary (vv. 5–7). Likewise in Sirach, Wisdom is localized at the central sanctuary by divine mandate. One can easily see how the role of Wisdom as Torah (Sir. 24:23), which is here assigned to Israel and Jacob (Sir. 24:8) and flourishes in Jerusalem (vv. 13–17), parallels the constitutional ordinances of Deuteronomy, which are likewise to be enforced upon realization of the promised territory.

Finally, in light of the above analysis the meaning of the transitional expression "among all these things" in Sir. 24:7 can be more carefully considered. The material in 24:5–6 is reminiscent of Job's depiction of God moving about on the edge of the cosmos and offers no biblical language reminiscent of the wilderness traditions. Therefore, in order to maintain thematic continuity, the author subordinates the imagery of vv. 5–6 by the use of a transitional expression. Consequently, Wisdom's "circling" (ἐκύκλωσα, 5a)[59] and "walking" (περιπάτησα, *S* ܗܠܟܬ, v. 5b) now epitomize a *searching* for a resting place just as Israel had done in the wilderness. Indeed the verbs of movement are made to share a secondary correspondence with the depictions of "circling" (e.g., סבב = LXX κυκλοῦν: Num. 34:4,5; Dt. 2:1,3) and "walking" (e.g., הלך = LXX

[59] Sir. 45:9 has ויקיפהו in MsB for ἐκύκλωσεν although the context is quite different than here in 24:5 for which סבב seems more likely. A finite verbal form of קוף does not occur in the OT. Regardless, קוף and סבב share enough common semantic range to anticipate resonance.

πορεύσθαι Jos. 14:10; 19:8)[60] in the traditions of Israel's desert migration.

In sum, the writer of Sirach, while he has not cited particular OT passages, has, in fact, drawn freely upon the motifs of the OT narrative traditions. There is, moreover, an unusual predilection for Deuteronomic expressions specifically indicative of the wilderness traditions and the Mosaic allotment of land to the tribes of Israel. By means of key words and distinctive allusions, the writer binds the present text to the original OT traditions upon which it depends. The effect redactionally is to interpret past narrative traditions by re-stating them, although in an entirely different context. Once again, historical narrative from the Torah, originally not concerned with Wisdom, provides the principal content of a Wisdom Song like one finds in Proverbs.

Sir. 24:8 τότε ἐνετείλατό μοι ὁ κτίστης ἁπάντων
καὶ ὁ κτίσας με κατέπαυσεν τὴν σκηνήν μου
καὶ εἶπεν Ἐν Ιακωβ κατασκήνωσον
καὶ ἐν Ισραηλ κατακλρονομήθητι

Then the Creator of all things commanded me,
and he that created me set my tent to rest.
He said [to me], "Pitch [your tent] in Jacob;
Take up [your] inheritance in Israel."

The desire of Wisdom for rest and inheritance, expressed in the previous verse, here finds realization. Verse 8 begins with the temporal transition τότε after which follows a third person description of God's command to "*rest* [her] tent" and "take up [her] *inheritance.*" Again by τότε one is reminded that, unlike the situation in the biblical wisdom books, Wisdom has a complete personal history with temporal sequence.[61] The author recalls the motif of Moses' dividing the land among the tribes prior to the conquest in the plains of Moab.[62] Wisdom's share, however, in the distribution of inheritance is not a parcel of land like the tribes, but one with "the Lord's portion" (cf. v. 8 and esp. v. 12b). In accordance with her allotment, she ministers like the presence of God among a "praiseworthy people" (v. 12) in a "holy tent" (v. 10) prior to her subsequent

[60] A variety of verbs are used, e.g., רעה, Num. 14:33; נוע, Num. 32:13; also, commonly יצא, נסע, עבר, and others with the connotation of "walking," "wandering," "setting out," "proceeding."

[61] Cf. Marböck, op. cit., p. 63.

[62] Compare the Deuteronomy passages observed in the analysis of v. 7. Also, see Num. 36:2, 6, 13. Clearly the assignments of inheritance are legal commands which entail grants of land to the respective parties, as we have observed before.

settling in a "beloved city," Zion (vv. 10b–11).[63] Once again, in this section the writer depends on familiar traditions and themes from the OT, which he takes up synthetically. The complexity in his use of motifs is due in part to the author's holistic view of the sacred traditions. He is not merely citing texts, but constructing an intricate mosaic of themes. For this reason, individual elements cannot always be tracked down to a single quotation. Rather, in order to analyze the use of OT one must seek out distinctive patterns of terminology which expose whole sets of traditions or related passages at the focus of the interpretation.

At the outset, an important clue to an OT allusion comes with the honorific title for God, ὁ κτίστης ἁπάντων. According to an extant Hebrew text of Sir. 51:12, in all probability it read, יוצר הכל, "the Creator of all."[64] The phrase occurs only twice in the OT, in identical passages of Jer. 10:16 and 51:19. Each passage opens with the portrayal of God as the one who made the earth, "who established the world by his wisdom and by his understanding stretched out the heavens" (10:12; 51:15; cf. Sir. 24:9). In this context God is contrasted with the foolish idolators,

> Not like these is he who is the portion of Jacob,
> for he is the creator of all things
> and Israel is the tribe of his inheritance;
> the Lord of hosts is his name.
>
> לא כאלה חלק יעקב כי יוצר הכל הוא
> וישראל שבט נחלתו יהוה צבאות שמו[65]

It is significant to observe that the only OT reference to the epithet יוצר הכל, occurs in a context concerned with God's portion in Jacob and the designation of Israel as "the tribe of his inheritance." This combination of themes is noteworthy in as much as it echoes the same set of concerns

[63] By contrast, cf. Enoch 42:1,2: "Wisdom found no place where she might dwell; then a dwelling place was assigned her in the heavens. Wisdom came to make her dwelling among humanity and found no dwelling place; then Wisdom returned to her place, and took her seat among the angels." Also, 84:3, "... Wisdom departs not from the place of your throne, nor turns away from your presence ..." Cf. 94:5; Eth. Enoch 94:5; Syr. Bar. Apoc. 48:33–36; IV Ezra 5:9. She will return only in Messianic times, I Enoch 5:8; 49:1, 3; 91:10; II Bar. 44:14; IV Ezra 8:52.

[64] Cf. *S* ܡܪܐ ܟܠ, "Lord of all," and *L creator omnium*. The alternative phrase ברא הכל occurs neither in the extant Hebrew of Sirach nor in the entire OT, cf. Is. 40:28; 43:15; Qoh. 12:1. The LXX for the Jeremiah passage offered ὁ πλάσας τὰ πάντα! However, in 6 out of 11 times a finite verbal form of יצר appears in the extant Hebrew texts of Sirach, it is translated by κτίζειν, "to create" (excluding participial forms meaning "potter"). Likewise, in the LXX of Is. 22:11 יצרה is translated τὸν κτίσαντα αὐτὴν. For a discussion of this theme in Sirach, see Rickenbacher, op. cit., pp. 141–58.

[65] LXX omits this line.

as Sir. 24:8, but now with respect to Wisdom. Each of the Jeremiah passages records Jacob and Israel in parallel lines, with the principal related theme of "inheritance/portion/possession"[66] of the Lord. In terms of the OT itself, these citations may be examples of deuteronomistic influence on Jeremiah, since similar phraseology is found in Dt. 32:9, "For the Lord's portion is his people, Jacob his allotted heritage." Other expressions occur in Ps. 78:5,71 and 135:4. Although both psalms demonstrate interest in God's place in Zion, only Ps. 78 explores the transference of the *tent* to the settlement in Mount Zion, a theme which will be considered in the analysis of v. 10. Dt. 32:9 has a like setting, in the time when "the Most High" divided up the inheritance among the tribes. All of these passages are tied in some way to the land distribution, the Zion traditions, or the Creator epithet themes central to the issues related to Wisdom in Sir. 24.

The minimum conclusion which can be drawn from this analysis is that the writer has taken up a biblical motif around which his own ideas easily orbit in resonance with a variety of OT texts. Nevertheless, it is possible that the writer reflected specifically upon the twin Jeremiah passages. These graphic declarations which were previously applicable only to God, are now interpreted in terms of Wisdom. The preëminence of Wisdom and her special association with God makes this adaptation of God language appropriate. Quite naturally the NT writers could do the same for Jesus, the Word and Wisdom of God "through whom also he created the world."[67]

Sir. 24:9 πρὸ τοῦ αἰῶνος ἀπ' ἀρχῆς ἔκτισέν με,
καὶ ἕως αἰῶνος οὐ μὴ ἐκλίπω

He created me from the beginning, before the world,
(*G* & *L*) And unto eternity I shall not be cut off [cease or end]:
(S) And for all eternity my memory will not cease.

Within the third person descriptive segment (vv. 8–9) this verse stands out from the natural flow of the prose. The writer has abandoned momentarily the overarching theme of the tent, its settlement, and Wisdom's quest for an inheritance. The first line plainly recalls the traditional Wisdom

[66] Sir. 24:8, *G* κατακληρονομήθητι; *L haeres constituere*; *S* ܘܐܬܝܪܬܝ. As Smend indicates (op. cit., p. 217), these renderings allow for a possible האחזי. Cf. the Peshitta of Job 23:11. Yet for the same verb MsB of Sir. 36:16b has יתנחלו. Cf. *G* of Jer. 10:16; 51 (28):19: κληρονομία αὐτοῦ.

[67] Heb. 1:2. Note, for example, the use of Dt. 32:43b (cf. LXX, also the Odes of Solomon) in Heb. 1:6 in which a clear statement about God is applied directly to Jesus.

Song in Prov. 8, especially vv. 22 ff., by using the same familiar language.[68] The writer's concern here with the antiquity of Wisdom supports the prevailing intention of the Sirach Wisdom Song by stressing again (cf. v. 3 a) the preëminence and eternal value of that Wisdom which resides in Israel, ultimately in the Torah.[69] In addition, one is reminded that here is a Wisdom Song similar to that in Prov. 8 and that the similarities between the two songs are as remarkable as the differences.

There are also signs of continuity between this verse and those that precede and follow. The parallelism in v. 8 regarding the Creator prepared the reader for a restatement of Wisdom's creation and its significance. The assurance in the second line that Wisdom will not be "cut off" or "cease"[70] throughout eternity has inescapable implications for the security of Israel and her religious life in the sacred city. By means of these implications the second line marks a decisive return to the central motifs of the Wisdom's unique and enduring place in Israel's history. As Fritzsche has observed, this portrayal coincides beautifully with the theme of a home in Zion which follows.[71]

Thus far no evidence in v. 9 of sapientializing the OT has been found. The principal purpose for its reminiscences to Hebrew Scripture was to align the Wisdom Song of Sirach with that of Proverbs. However, the idea that Wisdom will endure "through all eternity" is something extraneous to the description of Wisdom in the biblical Wisdom literature.

---

[68] πρὸ τοῦ αἰῶνος is the same as *G* of Prov. 8:23. Sir. 42:21 indicates that the Hebrew was probably מעולם. The second prepositional phrase ἀπ' ἀρχῆς (cf. 16:26) would suggest מראש . Both phrases occur in the Proverbs verse. For a similar repeated construction used to stress antiquity, see Mic. 5:1. Additionally, ἔκτισέν με is probably a translation of (יהוה) קנני found in the previous line, Prov. 8:22. Nowhere else in the OT does this same full combination of elements occur.

[69] In *Der Thoraausleger Aristobulos, TUGAL*, 86 (1964): 44–48, Nikolaus Walter provides evidence that by the second century B.C.E. Hellenistic-Jewish apologists sought to affirm the antiquity of the Torah to a time before the poets Hesiod, Homer, and Linos. They purported that all of the Greek poets and later philosophers derived their wisdom originally from the Torah. Even if one allows for the full impact of equating Wisdom and the book of the Torah in v. 23 on the entire song, there is still no explicit support for such an apologetic position. Yet, cf. Marböck, op. cit., pp. 64–65. Indeed, the contrast between Walter's later citations and Sirach's silence on this same matter makes such an identification in ideology quite unlikely.

[70] Smend's suggestion (op. cit., p. 218) of ישבת זכרי (cf. 38:23) seems viable. Note also v. 9 in which Wisdom's "memorial is sweeter than honey." Likewise, the writer of 24:23 ff. hopes his instruction will be left for "eternal generations" (24:33). Similarly, Sir. 39:9 contends that the "memory" of the successful scribe will never fade away. Cf. 44:13.

[71] Fritzsche, op. cit., p. 127.

If this idea does not derive from the imagination of the author or from unknown sources, the attribution may well represent once again the free adaptation for Wisdom of a divine characteristic found throughout Scripture (cf. Ps. 90:2; 103:17).[72]

Sir. 24:10–12 [10]ἐν σκηνῇ ἁγίᾳ ἐνώπιον αὐτοῦ ἐλειτούργησα
καὶ οὕτως ἐν Σιων ἐστηρίχθην
[11]ἐν πόλει ἠγαπημένῃ ὁμοίως με κατέπαυσεν,
καὶ ἐν Ιερουσαλημ ἡ ἐξουσία μου
[12]καὶ ἐρρίζωσα ἐν λαῷ δεδοξασμένῳ,
ἐν μερίδι κυρίου κληρονομία μου.

[10]In the holy tent I ministered before him,
and thus in Zion I was established.
[11]In a city beloved as me I rested,
and in Jerusalem was my authority,
[12]I took root among an honored people
and in the portion of the Lord was my inheritance.

As suggested before, these three verses are linked together not only by their continuing participation in the theme of Wisdom's settlement and inheritance, but also in their repeated use of the prepositional phrases. The first line of each distichos contains a prepositional phrase with ב followed by a substantive of specification and an accompanying complementary attribution. Thus, Wisdom's new location is made very explicit: in a holy tent, in a beloved city, and among a praiseworthy people. This combination of nouns and adjectives does not recall OT phraseology, but is a product of the writer's own poetic imagination. These same adjectives, which are common ones to Ben Sira, appear freely elsewhere. For example, he bestows them as laudatory attributions upon heroes in the Praise of the Fathers (44:1ff.).[73] Since the selection of the adjectives in 24:10–12 is obviously a part of the common vocabulary of Sirach, it is illogical either to contrive a specific allusion to an OT text or to make textual decisions on the basis of some alleged biblical correlation.[74]

Verse 10 is interesting because it asserts that Wisdom migrated to Zion to perform a liturgical ministry in the sacred tent. This statement advances the imagery of Wisdom beyond her earlier relationship to the

[72] Marböck, op. cit., p. 64.

[73] E.g., "holy" in Sir.45:2 (Greek); 45:6; cf. 49:12 (ναὸν ἅγιον); "beloved" in 45:1; 46:13; "praiseworthy" (cf. *S* ܡܫܒܚ, for Hebrew כבד?) in 44:7; 48·6.

[74] Neither אהל קדש nor משכן קדש (Box and Oesterley, op. cit., p. 398) occur in the OT. One may question the suggestion that the phrase in v. 11 should perhaps read (ἐν πόλει) ἡγιασμένῃ (only in 248 *L* Aeth Arm 11) instead of ἠγαπημένῃ since עיר קדש "is supported by OT usage (Is. xlviii.2; lii.l; Neh. xi.1, 18; Dan. ix.24)." Such a position would

theophanic cloud and the tent. Wisdom thus engaged fully in the priestly administration, presumably in the pre-Davidic wilderness period and perhaps at Shiloh (cf. Ps. 78:60). She comes to reside in Zion/Jerusalem and to exercise her authority from there (v. 11b). In an interpretation of OT that is a familiar one in the Sirach Song, Wisdom identifies her inheritance with that of God, namely, "in the Lord's portion" (ἐν μερίδι κυρίου v. 12b). Significantly, her portion is not the Lord himself like that of both the Levites and of Aaron the High Priest,[75] but it is one with God's portion, the elect people of Israel (cf. 17:17). Instead of being equated with the priests themselves, Wisdom is identified closely with the essence of the priestly *ministry* which, as a result, allows a wisdom interpretation of the related sacred objects and symbols of divine presence in the cult (e.g., v. 15; cf. Sir. 4:11–19).

Does the author in fact draw on the OT for this depiction of Wisdom? Taken as a single complex of ideas, the combination of themes such as the transition to Zion (v. 10b), the settling to rest (v. 11a), the inheritance (v. 11b), taking root with God's people (v. 12b), and the general context of priestly ministry converge at no one point in the OT. Nevertheless, limited parts of it do occur frequently in the OT.[76] A proper assessment of Sirach's biblical reminiscences necessitates viewing the OT as did the author himself. Israel's sacred Scripture was envisioned with canonical divisions including at least the Torah and probably the Prophets (cf. the Twelve, 49:10).[77] Therefore, one must anticipate a use of Scripture that allows for a development of themes within the fixed traditions of the canonical context of books and certain book divisions. Only with such a perspective on the sacred traditions can one hope to hear them again as did Ben Sira.

The promise that Yahweh would plant his people on his holy mountain, the place of his divine sanctuary, occurs first within the context of the Hebrew canon in Ex. 15:17. Next, Dt. 12 takes up this theme which has already played a significant role in the composition of the Wisdom Song (cf. v. 8). This deuteronomic passage emphasizes the appointment of

---

result in a redundancy between the first and second prepositional phrases and dull the obvious eloquence of the work. Conversely, the first and third phrases require no such dependency and display a certain freshness in the expression of familiar things. In as much as Ps. 78:68 speaks of "Mount Zion, which [God] loves," the idea of calling it a "beloved city" is not surprising.

[75] Sir. 45:22.

[76] E.g., 1 Chron. 28:2, in which a "house of rest" is built in Jerusalem for the ark of the covenant. Cf. Joel 3:17, 21.

[77] See pp. 14–16.

a special place, obviously Zion, where God (Dt. 12:5) and his people (12:9,10) find rest and inheritance, and to which the people can bring their sacrifices to their God (12:5–7, 11–14).

In 2 Sam. 6 and 7 the promise in Ex. 15:17 finds concrete realization in the story of David's bringing the ark of the covenant up to Mount Zion with music, shouting, and dancing. According to the narrative David prepared a special portable "tent" (6:17) for transporting the ark. Nathan, in his famous oracle, reminded the new king that God moved about in a tent dwelling during the wilderness period prior to the final settlement in Jerusalem (2 Sam. 7:6). David was, therefore, not allowed to build a temple, but the ark remained, as did Wisdom in Sir. 24:10, within a *tent* in Zion. Moreover, even as Wisdom "took root" in Zion (Sir. 24:12) Yahweh "planted" Israel in the land (ונטעתיו, 2 Sam. 7:10).

Several different streams of inner-Biblical reflection on the conception of planting or taking root can be detected in the OT. Each of these different texts must be consided in relation to the others because, for Sirach, the resonance between various themes in Scripture is not dependent on any modern theory regarding when the parts of the Bible were written, but only on the functional capacity of related themes to be heard together in the whole context of a sacred Scripture. One finds in the Prophets and in the Psalter a frequent hope or remembrance of God's "planting" his people or making them "take root" (< שרש) in the Promised Land.[78] These passages, however, convey little of the concern in the Torah with the settlement of God, his tent, cultic sacrifies, and so forth. Of course, many general references to Zion and Jerusalem, as a place which God chooses for his habitation, are found in the Psalms and occasionally in the Prophets.[79]

Concerning the reference to Zion, Ps. 132 and 78 deserve special consideration, for they both speak of God's decision to dwell in Zion and both clearly depend on 2 Sam. 6 & 7 (= 1 Chron. 17). In addition, each has some special interest in God's movement to Zion that parallels Wisdom's migration in Sir. 24. In order to develop this point, each psalm will be considered independently.

Ps. 132:11–18 reads like a hymnic commentary on 2 Sam. 7: to hear one is to presume the other.[80] Ps. 132 also uses expressions not original

---

[78] 2 Kings 19:30, 31 (= Is. 37:31, 32); Jer. 32:41; 42:11; Amos 9:15 et al. Cf. esp. Ezek. 17:22–24. Also, Ps. 44:2.

[79] Ps. 74:2; 76:2; Joel 3:17, 22 et al.

[80] Its present interaction with the Davidic ideology, which finds its locus in 2 Sam. 6 & 7, is obvious enough. Compare also other uses of Deuteronomy, e.g., 32:40–43 with

to 2 Sam. 6 & 7, but reminiscent of Dt. 12 and related traditions which were discussed in connection with Sir. 24:7. For examples 2 Sam. 6 & 7 never portrays God as "choosing" or "finding" a "habitation" in Zion as does Ps. 132:5, 8, 13, 14 and Dt. 12:5,11. Like the language applied to Wisdom in Sir. 24, God desires a place to "dwell" (ישב, vv. 13, 14) and "rest" (נוח, v. 14) and finds it in Zion. The central motif of transfering the tent in Sir. 24:10 is, however, missing from the psalm. Nevertheless, an awareness of the way in which Ps. 132 can be heard together with 2 Sam. 6 & 7 as well as with Dt. 12 may be necessary for an emphatic understanding of Sirach's interpretation of related biblical texts.

Ps. 78:60–72 further exemplifies a terse composite picture of God's movement to Zion. According to v. 60, "He forsook his dwelling (משכן) at Shiloh, the *tent* (אהל) where he dwelt among men." This event coincides with the capture of the ark by the Philistines. Eventually, God awakes from his slumber (v. 66) and chooses "Mount Zion" as the place to build his sanctuary (מקדשו, v. 69). In turn, David is "chosen" to be a shepherd of his people (vv. 70f.), "Israel his inheritance" (נחלתו = LXX τῆν κληρονομίαν αὐτοῦ, v. 71b, cf. v. 62b). Again, there are similarities to Sir. 24. Like 2 Sam. 7 there is concern with the sacred tent, but the focus is not on the question of whether David should build a temple. Instead, Ps. 78 concentrates on the transference of God's presence in his tent sanctuary to his elect city Zion, much as Sir. 24 stresses the placement of Wisdom. Even as Israel is called God's inheritance, so Wisdom finds her rest and inheritance in Israel at Zion. God resides in Zion "which he loves," (v. 68) an expression the same as that of Zion, "a beloved city," in Sir. 24:11. Apparently, for the writer of Sir. 24 this prophetic emphasis upon the one place chosen by Yahweh in Dt. 12:5,11 certainly finds its fulfillment in the material of 2 Sam. 7 (= 1 Chron. 17) and in these hymnic interpretations.

Clearly, Ps. 78 and 132 illustrate an inner biblical activity of synthesizing traditions into new patterns of expression. Regardless of the historical questions, they appear to make explicit what was implicit in such canonically earlier passages as Dt. 12 and 2 Sam. 7. They speak more directly than the previous passages of God's perspective in the move to Zion. Primarily God, rather than Israel, desires a place to dwell and rest which he finds in the elect city. As Ps. 78 stresses, he moves to Zion in a tent (cf. 2 Sam. 7:6; 1 Chron. 17:5,6). Although it is impossible to say that the author of Sir. 24 has these specific psalms in mind, he applies this

---

Ps. 78:65–66. On this, see Claus Westermann, *The Praise of God in the Psalms* (Richmond: John Knox Press, 1965), pp. 92, 141.

same synthesis of OT traditions concerning divine activity to Wisdom. Once again, familiar narrative and hymnic traditions about God have been interpreted obliquely as part of Wisdom's autobiography so that in her Song, Wisdom has a share in God's own sentiments and historical involvement with Israel.

The image of Wisdom "rooted" (Sir. 24:12) in the Lord's portion is a unique one. In traditional wisdom literature the righteous and foolish are "rooted" in the earth and known by their fruits (cf. 24:19).[81] Here, however, another factor must also be considered. It is likely that the author's choice of the verb ἐρρίζωσα, which was not found in Ps. 132 or 78, was influenced by the related expression in 2 Sam. 7:10. God assures David that he will appoint a place for Israel and there he will "plant them" (נטעתיו).[82] The merging portraits of God and Wisdom break at this point. It is God who plants and Wisdom who, like Israel, takes root as a result. Yet, Wisdom is still kept distinct from Israel because her portion is the Lord's, viz., Israel "his inheritance" (v. 12b). Likewise, in Sir. 24:10 Wisdom ministers within the sacred tent in the provenance of the priests rather than in the commonplace tribal life of Israel. Moreover, her taking root is associated with the luxuriant growth of hearty plants (vv. 13–17) which in Sirach are detailed again only in reference to the splendor of Aaron the High Priest (Sir. 45:6–22). This same priestly metaphor is central elsewhere to Sirach's depiction of Wisdom.

Thus, the progressive coalescence of Wisdom's activity with that of God and the ministry of the priests is further crystalized. Scriptural references to the deuteronomic promises of rest and inheritance in a place chosen by God and to the claim in 2 Sam. 7 of a special relocation of the sacred tent to Zion have been read in concert with each other. Ps. 132 and 78 anticipate such a synthesis. All these elements of the Sirach Wisdom Song can be accounted for in this way. Once again, the author looks upon these sacred narrative and psalmic traditions of Scripture from the vantage point of Wisdom's history in the life of ancient Israel. Even so, it is not only a simple matter of all statements about God being taken over and assigned to Wisdom. Another factor has emerged. The narrative history of Israel

[81] Cf. Prov. 12:2, 3; Job 5:3. Finally, in her summons she offers the fruits of her garden to the hearers (24:19).

[82] Of the two occurrences of the verb ῥιζοῦν in Sir. 3:28 and 24:12, the former, in the only extant Hebrew text (MsA), supplies a nominal sentence composed of substantives of the root נטע. This same root is found in 2 Sam. 7:10. *S* has simply the metaphorical, "I grow high" (cf. v. 13f.).

may likewise apply to Wisdom because of Wisdom's identification specifically with the sacred tent and priestly ministry.

Sir. 24:13–14 (15) 16–17

[13]ὡς κέδρος ἀνυψώθην ἐν τῷ Λιβάνῳ
καὶ ὡς κυπάρισσος ἐν ὄρεσιν Αερμων
[14]ὡς φοῖνιξ ἀνυψώθην ἐν Αιγγάδοις
καὶ ὡς φυτὰ ῥόδου ἐν Ιεριχω,
ὡς ἐλαία εὐπρεπὴς ἐν πεδίῳ,
καὶ ἀνυψώθην ὡς πλάτανος.
---
[16]ἐγὼ ὡς τερέβινθος ἐξέτεινα κλάδους μου,
καὶ οἱ κλάδοι μου κλάδοι δόξης καὶ χάριτος.
[17]ἐγὼ ὡς ἄμπελος ἐβλάστησα χάριν,
καὶ τὰ ἄνθη μου καρπὸς δόξης καὶ πλούτου.

[13]I was exalted like a cedar in Lebanon,
and like an olive tree on Mount Hermon.
[14]I was exalted like a palm tree in Engedi
and as the rose bushes in Jericho,
as a fair olive tree on the plain
and I was exalted as a plane tree by the waters.
---
[16]I spread my branches like a terebinth,
and my branches were branches of glory and grace.
[17]I am like a grape vine putting forth lovely shoots,
and my flowers are the fruit of glory and wealth.

After Wisdom takes root in Zion, she blossoms like various trees and flowers and is compared to exotic spices reserved for Yahweh's perfumed anointing oil and incense (see the following analysis of Sir. 24:15). This imagery, together with other expressions throughout Sir. 24, recall the Eden paradise of Gen. 2. Even as Sir. 24:3b offers a word play on the dark cloud, which in Gen. 2:6 provided the first nourishment to a parched earth, Wisdom in Jerusalem thrives luxuriously like the first garden (Gen. 2:9; cf. Ezek. 31:2b–9, esp. v.9). References to the Creator in the vv.8 and 9 of the Song, likewise, have the effect of focusing attention back on the beginnings. The material in 24:23ff. picks up this same theme by its comparison of Wisdom with the paradisaical rivers (vv.25–27, cf. Gen. 2:10–14). In this way creation and the primordial bliss of the first garden provide one of the principal links between the Wisdom Song in Sir. 24: 1–22 and its interpretation in 24:23ff. The city of Jerusalem has been painted as a wonderland of Wisdom, a restoration of the garden of Eden. The lavish growth of diverse plants is indicative of Wisdom's vitality, her abundance and her priceless splendor. Some scholars have compared wisdom here with the Edenic "tree of life."[83] To partake of her is to experience paradise.

The symbolism of a vigorous tree or plant that bears desirable fruit is a common one in the OT. A close parallel to some of the flora in Sir. 24: 13–17 occurs in Hos. 14:4ff. There God's love is described as the dew[84] that causes Israel to take root and blossom like the olive tree, even as a garden, with a fragrance like Lebanon's wine. Similarly, the righteous man in the OT is compared frequently to a sturdy, well-watered tree which bears good fruit (e.g., Is. 58:11; Jer. 17:5ff.; Ps. 1:3; 92:12). Ezek. 31: 2b–9 is striking because Egypt is compared to various flourishing trees watered by abundant streams "round the place of its planting" (v.4) with a beauty "that all the *trees of Eden* envied ... in the *garden of God*" (v.9).

Then again, one should not ignore the prosaic sketch in Song of Songs 4–6 of the enticing lover.[85] There a young woman appears in a garden (4:12,15; 5:1) rich with the same kinds of vegetation like that in Sir. 24 (5:15, 6:10, 7:8,13). The garden is filled with costly perfumes and spices (4:6,14, 15:1); in its center a fountain is fed by the plentiful streams of Lebanon (4:12b,15). Either at the close or periodically within the different garden scenarios of Song of Songs the lover offers a summons to partake of the produce of her garden (e.g., 4:16). Sir. 24 has these same

---

83 P.E. Bonnard, *La Sagesse en Personne announcée et venue: Jésus Christ* (Paris: Les Éditions du Cerf, 1966), p.74. Also Marböck, op.cit., p.74. In Prov. 11:30; 13:12; 15:4, to follow wisdom is to obtain a "tree of life." Cf. Prov. 3:16 and Kayatz, op.cit., pp.105f. It is not clear from these passages that their authors intend an implied reference to the "tree of life" in Gen. 2:9 or 3:22. The appearance of this motif of exalted vegetation, in the light of other Edenic parallels, may certainly suggest the possibility that such an association is implied. Wisdom is portrayed as a tree from which one can partake and grow in Sir. 1:16–20; 6:19. However, in Sir. 24 the exact phrase "tree of life" does not occur, nor does "Torah of life" (Sir. 17:11; 45:5) which would have provided more substantial evidence for direct dependence.

84 Recall that Wisdom is the cloudy darkness that covers the earth, Sir. 24:3.

85 Marböck, op.cit., pp.74–75, observes that the symbolism of trees and spices are *topoi* of love songs, following Wolff's remarks on Hos. 14:6f. Cf. Hans Walter Wolff, *Dodekapropheton: Hosea*, Biblischer Kommentar: Altes Testament (Neukirchen-Vluyn: Neukirchener Verlag, 1965), Vol.1, 2nd ed., rev., pp.302, 306. While the theme in Hos. 14 describes the effect of God's love upon this people, other uses of this imagery do not fit as well into the context of a love song. That the *topoi* may originally be from love songs, or in some cases retain those connotations as in Hos. 14, does not imply that this factor is the controlling one in the use of the symbolism elsewhere. In Jer. 17:7f., it describes those who trust, in Ps. 92:12, those who are righteous, and in Ezek. 31:2b–9, the glories of a great nation. It is significant that Sir. 24:16b and 17b construe these figures as a promise of glory, grace, and wealth, which are the presumed profits of applied Wisdom.

motifs of flora (vv. 13–14, 15–17), spices (v. 15), garden rivers (vv. 25–27) and a call to indulge in the lavish fruits of the garden (vv. 19–22).[86]

Nevertheless, the more important question concerns how this imagery of Eden-like splendor relates to the overriding theme of Wisdom's journey, like Israel, to Zion. Once again, the writer of the Song shows dependence upon the OT by exploiting the connection already there between paradisaical metaphors of exaltation and the entrance into the land segment of the salvation-history narrative. Thus, in describing the abundance of the Promised Land, Dt. 8:7–10 affirms the agricultural ideal of "a land of wheat and barley, of vines and fig trees and pomegranates, a land of olive trees and honey, a land ... in which you will lack for nothing" (see vv. 8–9, cf. Dt. 32:13–14 and Is. 5:1ff.). Likewise, Ezek. 40–48 joins the experience of the return to Zion with that of a new paradise, even as a rejuvenation of nature accompanies the return to Jerusalem in Second Isaiah (e.g., Is. 35 and 55, cf. Is. 25). This same combination of motifs is picked up by the writer of Sir. 24 and applied to Wisdom.

Interestingly, the metaphors of abundant vegetation persist throughout Sirach to portray in general those adept in wisdom, even as the same language is used in the Prophets to describe the righteous. In parallelism with Hos. 14:5, the aspiring student scribe is admonished in Sir. 39,

> Hearken unto me, ye pious, and your flesh shall grow,
> Like the cedar that is planted by streams of water.
> Your scent shall be sweet as Lebanon,
> And ye shall put forth blossoms as the Lily.[87]
> (39:13–14a)

The description in Sir. 39 illustrates a practical realization of the summons in Sir. 24:19–22. The invitation to hear and obey comes from the master sage and results in productive students. Wisdom is efficacious in the lives of those who receive her. The above mentioned metaphorical imagery of the righteous in the OT has been made to apply specifically to Wisdom and those who obtain her. Hence, those who possess Wisdom are characterized in Sirach by an expression originally peculiar to the prophetic books of Scripture as a characterization of the righteous and the faithful.

---

[86] Cf. Sir. 1:20, 6:9.

[87] This is the translation of Box and Oesterley, op. cit., p. 457, whose notes illustrate the textual difficulty unresolved by more recent findings. The *G* "blossoms as the lily" (*S* "and like the root of the king's lilies") parallels Hos. 14:5, "he shall blossoms as the lily;" even as *G* "Your scent shall be sweet as Lebanon" (*S* "and like pleasant odours shall your scent be sweet, like the scent of Lebanon with its cedars") compares favorably with Hos. 14:6b, "and his fragrance like Lebanon." Cf. Rickenbacher, op. cit., pp. 162–64.

It is also important to observe that in the use of this imagery in Sir. 24:13–17 Wisdom is associated with the priests and their ministry. The precious spices of Sir. 24:15 are the same used in making the holy anointing oil and the sacred incense. The flora comparisons are found repeated exactly, almost element for element, in the eulogy to Aaron the High Priest (Sir. 45:6–22) and, to a lesser degree, in that of Simeon II, Aaron's post-exilic successor to the priestly office (50:5–13). Significantly, Simeon is the tinal hero in a series and concludes the list with his formal blessing (50:20–21). The primary focus, though on the priests, is not on the ritual of the cult. According to the preface (44:1–15) the pious heroes in Sir. 44–50 are epitomized predominantly for their sagacity.[88] The last verse of the preface provides an apt condensation of its intent: "the assembly recounts their wisdom and the congregation proclaims their praise" (44:15).

Within the Sir. 44–50 listing of heroes, the author distinguishes carefully between the offices of the priests, who make atonement, and the prophets, who speak an oracular word.[89] In spite of this distinction, it is significant that the two model representatives of priests and prophets, namely Aaron and Moses, share one cardinal qualification in common. Both are given the "commandment," "statutes," and "judgments"[90] by which they "teach" (cf. למד, 45:5,17) the people of Israel.[91] This point of agreement does not preclude the honoring of heroes for other unique acts of courage, spiritual power, and virtue. However, it locates the common denominator of their wisdom in the comission to teach, and to administer the Torah, not in the cult *per se*. This point of view in regards to the priests is summarized nicely by the comment of Box and Oesterly on Sir. 24:10: "The worship of the Tabernacle was the carrying out of the Law, so that, as personified, Wisdom could be said to minister before God."[92] Along these same lines, it is noteworthy that each of the sections dedicated to the priests, Phineas and Simeon, concludes with the short

[88] Edmund Jacob, "L'historie d'Israël vue par Ben Sira," *Mélanges Bibliques Rédigés en L'honneur de André Robert* (Paris: Bloud and Gay, 1957), pp. 288–94. That "wisdom literature" at this late stage can contain references to priests and cult is proven by their occurrence in Sir. 24 which is an obvious attempt at a Wisdom Song.

[89] For prophets, Moses is followed by Joshua, "a minister of Moses in the prophetic office" (Sir. 46:1); so also Samuel "in the prophetic office" (46:13); et al. For priests, Aaron is appointed a priest to Yahweh (MsB, 45:15b) and makes atonement (45:16) for all the people. Also, Phinehas is given "the High Priesthood forever" (45:24) to make atonement (45:23b) for them, even as Simeon the Priest (50:1) procures the pardon of God (50:21).

[90] Cf. Sir. 45:5, 17:11, MsB תורה חיים.

[91] Cf. Samuel (46:14); Phinehas (45:26).

blessing: "May God grant you wisdom of heart" (MsB, חכמת לב (ב), 45:26; 50:23). Likewise, the necessity that wisdom in practice must accompany the sacrifies, if they are to be efficacious, is made explicit in Sir. 32:1–13 (35:1–11).

Therefore, the later identification of Wisdom with the Torah in Sir. 24:23 is already anticipated in the Song itself by the relation between Wisdom and the priestly ministry.[93] Behind it lies the presupposition that the Torah which God commanded Moses to hand over to the Levites (e.g., Dt. 17:18–20; 31:9ff.) carries with it the duty of teaching it to the people (Dt. 33:10). Although some commentators suggest that this commission to Levites in Dt. 33 is applied to Aaron only by Ben Sira's ingenuity, there is a similar pentateuchal mandate given to Aaron in Lev. 10:11. For one to imply that the writer is hearing only the deuteronomic passages is to underestimate the sensitivities of a writer who demonstrates an obvious familiarity with all five books of the Torah.

Consequently, Sir. 24:13–14 and 16–17 recall a standard biblical motif concerning the righteous now applied to the vitality of Wisdom in Zion. The use of this motif in the Sirach Wisdom Song, likewise, follows the OT pattern of nature's exaltation when the people of God enter the Promised Land, although Wisdom has been made the subject rather than simply Israel. Moreover, this choice of imagery further reflects the writer's assumptions concerning the relation between Wisdom and the ministry of the priests (cf. Sir. 24:10 and 24:15) and is set in the larger patterns of the wilderness wanderings and the deuteronomic portrait of the conquest. The composition, once again, illustrates a consistent wisdom interpretation of motifs peculiar to OT narrative and prophetic literature.

Sir. 24:15 ὡς κιννάμωμον καὶ ἀσπάλαθος ἀρωμάτων
καὶ ὡς σμύρνα ἐκλεκτὴ διέδωκα εὐωδίαν,
ὡς χαλβάνη καὶ ὄνυξ καὶ στακτὴ
καὶ ὡς λιβάνου ἀτμὶς ἐν σκηνῇ.

As cinnamin and asphalthus of perfumes
and as choice myrrh I put forth a pleasant scent.
As galbanum, onyx and stacte,
I was as the smoke of incense in the tent sanctuary.

---

[92] Box and Oesterley, op.cit., p.397. Similarly Ringgren, op.cit., p.110; Smend, op.cit., p.218.

[93] One may question whether Marböck (op.cit., pp.66–67) has not overstated the position of Fritzsche, op.cit., pp.126–27). Fritzsche does not hesitate to view the ministry of Wisdom (24:10) in terms of the "Gesetzescultus" and to observe that Wisdom exercises her authority (24:11) in Zion "als Gesetz" (p.127). Also cf. Marböck, op.cit., pp.42–43.

Sir. 24:15 provides an excellent example of how the writer subtly incorporates earlier biblical traditions into his prose. By drawing its vocabulary from Ex. 30:23, the first half of the verse associates Wisdom's presence in Israel with the earthly tabernacle and its ritual preparations, specifically the "holy anointing oil" (Ex. 30:31). Similarly, the second half of the verse, excerpting its phraseology from Ex. 30:34, pictures Wisdom "as the smoke of incense in the tent/tabernacle." In both instances, the writer extracts key elements from the respective texts and redacts them into a single combined description of the sacred incense and anointing oil. A comparison of the respective texts confirms the writer's ingenuity (see Diagrams A and B).[94]

The writer of Sir. 24:15 intricately fuses Ex. 30:23 and 30:34 in a manner that preserves the distinctives.

Diagram A
Greek Texts

G of Sir. 24:15	LXX (B) of Ex. 30:23
	καὶ σὺ λαβὲ ἡδύσματα τὸ ἄνθος *σμύρνης ἐκλεκτῆς* πεντακοσίους σίκλους
ὡς *κιννάμωμον* καὶ ἀσπάλαθος ἀρωμάτων	καὶ *κινναμώμου* εὐώδους τὸ ἥμισυ τούτου σν'
καὶ ὡς *σμύρνα ἐκλεκτὴ* διέδωκα *εὐωδίαν*,	καὶ καλάμου *εὐώδους* διακοσίους πεντήκοντα
ὡς *χαλβάνη* καὶ *ὄνυξ* καὶ *στακτὴ* καὶ ὡς *λιβάνου* ἀτμὶς *ἐν σκηνῇ*	Ex. 30:34 λαβὲ σεαυτῷ ἡδύσματα *στακτὴν* *ὄνυχα χαλβάνην* ἡδυσμοῦ καὶ *λίβανον* διαφανῆ
	Ex. 30:36 ... *ἐν τῇ σκηνῇ* τοῦ μαρτυρίου

---

[94] Gasser (op. cit., p. 206) concluded from an examination of the phrase σμύρνης ἐκλεκτη in the LXX of Ex. 30:23 and 30:34, in comparison with the extant Greek translation of Sir. 24:15, that the grandson of Ben Sira relied on phraseology from the LXX for his translation of the respective texts. Yet, Gasser does not attempt to explain why the writer opted for ἀσπάλαθος ἀρωμάτων and did not follow the LXX καλάμου εὐώδους of the original Hebrew קנה בשם. Even if Smend (p. 219) is correct in postulating that ἀσπάλαθος derives secondarily from an original ὡς κάλαμος (cf. Syroh. 253, 23, S[ca], 248 κιννάμωμον), the hypothesis still does not explain the choice of the adjective. In fact, the

Diagram B
Hebrew Texts

Segal's reconstruction of Sir. 24:15[95]

כקנמון וקנה בשם
וכמר דרור נתתי ריח
כחלבנה ושחלת ונטף
וכלבונת עשן במשכן [באהל] [96]

MT of Ex. 30:23

ואתה קח לך בשמים ראש
מר דרור חמש מאות
וקנמן בשם מחציתו חמשים
ומאתים וקנה בשם חמשים ומאתים

Ex. 30:34

ויאמר יהוה אל משה קח לך סמים
נטף ושחלת וחלבנה
סמים ולבנה זכה בד בבד יהיה

Ex. 30:36

ונתתה ממנה לפני העדת באהל מועד

The precision and detail of corresponding elements illustrates once again the sophistication in the writer's use of the Hebrew Scripture. In this case, the two Exodus passages are found within Moses' instructions concerning Aaron and the priestly orders (Ex. 28:1ff.). Both the anointing oil and the incense were integral accessories for worship at the divine sanctuary.

---

adjective would present more of an enigma than ever, if indeed the translator is being consciously dependent upon the LXX. Also, Gasser's analysis overlooks entirely the additional borrowing from Ex. 30:23 of קנמן (LXX κινναμώμου and Sir. 24:25a κινάμωμον). One may further inquire concerning the reason why a close following of the LXX reading of Ex. 30:34 did not motivate the translator to reverse the order of the three spices mentioned in Sir. 24:15a. That there are some noteworthy similarities between the grandson's Greek translation of these exotic spices and that of the LXX is not particularly surprising since one might expect unusual or technical expressions to develop stereotyped equivalents in Greek. Hence, this passage does not, in my opinion, represent a very convincing example of the grandson's dependence upon the LXX as an aid in translating Sirach.

95 Segal, op. cit., p. 145.

96 Segal's proposal of במשכן is perhaps not the best choice. Against it is the explicit use of אהל in the Exodus passage to name the sanctuary in which the incense is offered. The word σκηνή occurs only four times in Sirach, once with a Hebrew equivalent of אהל (14:25). In the LXX's use of σκηνή, a distinction is not maintained between the related Hebrew terms. See n. 28.

For example, the oil served to consecrate the tent of meeting, the ark of testimony, and all other tabernacle paraphenalia (30:26–28). It was also used to sanctify Aaron and his sons for their ministry (30:30). The sacred incense was to be regularly brought "before the testimony in the tent of meeting" (30:36).[97] Consequently, the smearing of the anointing oil and the burning of incense before the ark of the covenant were both traditional testimonies to the presence and holiness of God during sanctuary observances.

According to Sirach, even these exotic implements of the cult appertain to Wisdom. This final link between Wisdom and the cult conforms to a larger pattern central to the structure of the total Song. The "darkness" and the "pillar of cloud" in 24:3,4 were theophanic symbols associated with the sanctuary. Wisdom, like the priests, is settled within the tabernacle *in Zion*, v. 8. Wisdom *ministers* in "the sacred tent," v. 10, and flourishes there in exactly the same metaphorical terms as applied elsewhere to Aaron the High Priest in 45:6–22. Finally, she appears as the oil and incense which the priests administer. Wisdom is associated throughout her Song with symbols of divine presence which in the course of her pilgrimage fall plainly within the purview of the priestly administration.

By these means the cultic symbols of divine presence, as well as the essence of the priestly ministry itself, is given a rationale in Wisdom. Wisdom is not made an abstract principle, but has a concrete function in the early institutions of Israel. The scriptural accounts of wilderness wandering and conquest are equally applicable to her. Hence, throughout the early pentateuchal narratives she appears *incognito* as God-with-Israel. Following the Torah's account of the priesthood, she finds her earthly existence with Israel in a search for rest and inheritance and is finally appointed to Zion, the holy city (v. 10). Like the ark sanctuary, Wisdom's domicile is never a constructed house or temple but remains the sacred tent. Once again these associations provide hints within the Song itself of Wisdom's true identification with the Torah as the Book of the Covenant, which Moses indeed handed over specifically to the care of the Levitical priests, e.g., Dt. 17:18–20; 31:9ff. In Moses' testimonial blessing of Levi in Dt. 33:10, the priestly duties are described, "They shall teach Jacob thy ordinances and Israel thy law; they shall put incense before thee and whole burnt offerings upon thy altar." For Sirach, both the priestly teaching and the offering of incense are in service of the Torah through which the Wisdom of God resides with the people of God.

---

[97] Cf. Lev. 4:7; 10:1; 16:12–13; Num. 4:16; 7:14f., 16f.; Dt. 33:10.

Furthermore, the use of Ex. 30 in Sir. 24:15 presupposes that the sacred oil and incense are proper symbols of Wisdom's role in the priestly ministry. However, there is no attempt in Sirach to reduce the sacrificial system to a moral lesson without a redemptive *mysterium*. Rather, the immoral and unwise gain nothing by their sacrifies, while those who act morally, who "keep the Torah" [(Sir. 32:1 (35:1)], increase their salvific participation in the cult [cf. Sir. 31:21–32:13 (34:18–35:11)]. For example, Sir. 7 contains short collections of gnomic advice on a man's duty to his friend, wife, children, cattle and so forth. In the one pertaining to man's duty to God, there are the two commands: "reverence his priests" and offer sacrifices (vv. 29–31). Cultic practice is in Sirach an admonition and reflection of Wisdom, even as of the Torah.

In this regard, Sir. 24:15 demonstrates again that for Sirach Wisdom concerns are not intrinsically antithetical to cultic practice. The interpretation is strategic in its choice of symbols. Traditionally, the sacred oil and incense have invited speculation regarding the deeper religious significance of these somewhat nebulous evidences of divine presence in Israel.[98] Even as others have sought to clarify the numinous in these sacred symbols, this author of Sir. 24 ventures an identification of them with Wisdom. The writer finds in the oil and incense a veiled witness to Wisdom and by implication a direct link between Wisdom and the priestly ministry.

Sir. 24:23 ταῦτα πάντα βίβλος διαθήκης θεοῦ ὑψίστου
νόμον ὅν ἐνετείλατο ἡμῖν Μωυσῆς
κληρονομίαν συναγωγαῖς Ιακωβ

All these things are the book of the covenant of God Most High,
The Torah which Moses commanded us
[as a] possession/heritage in the assemblies of Jacob.

The method of this investigation is, first, to describe the literary relationship of the verse to the preceding Song of Wisdom in Sir. 24:3–22. Second, the content of Sir. 24:23 and its citation of Dt. 33:4 will be evaluated in the context of similar statements in Deuteronomy. Finally,

---

[98] Incense is a metaphor for prayer in Ps. 141:2. Cf. Rev. 5:8. Anointing oil is also rich with symbolic potential. *Shir Hashirim Rabbah* 4:10 explains, "As perfumed oil yields all manner of fragrance, so the Scripture yields all manner of interpretations." Likewise, rabbinic interpretation of Eccl. 9:8 could view the oil as referring to "the honor conferred by the study of the law." See the article by Immanual Löw on "Oil" in *The Jewish Encyclopedia*, ed. by I. Singer, et al. (New York: KTAV Publishing House, no date), Vol. 9, pp. 391--92. In the New Testament it is used in reference to the reception of the Holy Spirit: Acts 4:27; 10:38; 2 Cor. 1:22, et al.

this assessment of Ben Sira's interpretation of Deuteronomy will be further supported both by the language in his address to the readers in Sir. 51:26 and by a corresponding interpretation of Deuteronomy in Bar. 3:9ff.

The literary structure. With the opening words ταῦτα πάντα the writer introduces to his readers an encapsulated summation or clarification of the whole previous section. These words mark both the end of the Wisdom Song (Sir. 24:1–22) and the beginning of commentary upon it. A comparable use of the demonstrative pronoun as a literary transition occurs in 24:7. Also, this final portrayal of Wisdom is not merely the last in a sequence, but it is critically differentiated from the preceding. While Wisdom throughout the Song is related to historical features or metaphors by a comparative "as,"[99] she is identified here in a more direct manner that speaks precisely to what she "is." All of Wisdom's previous associations are thereby grounded in a single more fundamental insight: "all these things (are) the book of the covenant." Subsequently, the writer elaborates this claim in words taken *verbatim* from Dt. 33:4 without a citation formula.

It is as thought the Wisdom Song in Sir. 24:1–22 were a kind of riddle, and one could speculate on how long a reader would take to discover the proper key. Now, if not before, the Song is plainly a recital of the history of Wisdom who resides in Israel as the Torah. The story begins (vv. 3–4) with creation when Wisdom is in the heavens and professes her origins in a manner not unlike that of the Wisdom books (cf. Prov. 8:22ff.). Then, the narrative picks up (vv. 5–7) the theme of a wandering in search of rest and inheritance, which coincides with Israel's same search (cf. Dt. 12) in the time when Moses received the Torah in the cloud at Sinai and delivered it to the safekeeping of the priests. Again, like Israel, she receives a divine command (v. 8) to posses the Land and, like the Israelite priests, she settles at last in Zion with the sacred tent (vv. 10, 15).

The center of attention is consistently on Wisdom who is or becomes the Torah in the possession of Israel. Therefore, the Song offers a selective application to Wisdom of some Torah traditions which can be associated with the divine presence in Israel. The writer's economy of purpose for the Song requires naturally only his selective treatment of historical traditions in the sequence of the Torah. For example, recollection of the Sinai event is not made in the Song, even though the citation of Dt. 33:4 in Sir. 24:23 recapitulates the essence of the entire Mosaic blessing (Dt. 33) as a eulogy

---

[99] The Greek has ὡς on Sir. 24:3, 13 (2 ×), 14 (4 ×), 16, 17. Ὡς is probably כ in Hebrew, as Segal (op. cit., pp. 145–56) has suggested.

of the Torah which God gave to Moses and to the people at the Sinai event (cf. Dt. 33:2).[100]

The closely worded opening phrase of 24:23 makes certain that Wisdom is not equated with some vague or general sense of Torah, but specifies "the book of the covenant," a synonym for "the book of Torah" elsewhere in Sirach and in the Hebrew Scriptures.[101] Moreover, like the νόμος ὑψίστου in 39:1, it is a canonical expression in Sirach.[102] The radical nature of this statement must not be overlooked. The writer finds in the Torah, the five books of Moses, a witness to Wisdom which provides the content for Wisdom's Song.

Whether 24:23ff. constitutes a later redactional addition to the earlier Song is hard to decide.[103] At least, these verses represent a literary, redaction-like shift in the prose and provide a clarifying framework for the previous Song. Moreover, 24:23 is worded thoughtfully with a play on the earlier prose. The title "Most High God" recalls the "Most High" in 24:2,3. The "command" to find a place in "Jacob" is the same theme and vocabulary as that of 24:8. Most important, by means of κληρονομία the citation of Dt. 33:4 provides a verbal link with key words on the same

---

[100] While economy of purpose allows for selectivity, certain omissions like this reference to Sinai are intentionally consistent for Sirach (cf. Sir. 17:11–14). If Wisdom were initially linked to Israel by the Sinai event, then the observations on Wisdom at Creation and particularly in Eden might be compromised (cf. Sir. 17:6–7). See E. Jacob, op. cit., p. 293.

[101] Marböck (op. cit., pp. 177–78) sets out the matter clearly. Cf. 2 Kgs. 2:8, 11 and 23:2, 21. In "Gesetz und Gnade." *ZAW*, 79 (1967): 30, E. Kutsch demonstrates the same for the deuteronomistic history. Also, see Sir. 17:12; 28:7. 1 Macc. 1:56–57 has both phrases in parallel.

[102] Segal, op. cit., p. 149; cf. K. Hruby, "Gesetz und Gnade in der rabbinischen Überlieferung," *Judaica* 25 (1969): 33. See pp. 14 (n. 59), 109.

[103] Cf. W. L. Knox, "The Divine Wisdom," *JThS* 38 (1937): 233, 236–37. Knox argues unconvincingly that 24:23ff. requires a Greek mentality distinct from the semitic flavor of the Song, for otherwise Hebrew *feminine* "Wisdom" and "Torah" would be identified with a *masculine* noun "river" (vv. 25ff.). He regards 24:23ff. as a secondary interpolation originating not before 132 B.C.E. U. Wilckens in *Weisheit und Torheit* (Tübingen: J.C.B. Mohr, 1959), 167–68, suggests that 24:23 represents what in a later redactor's mind "*für ihn* die zentrale Aussage des ganzen Liedes ist." In his *Judentum und Hellenismus* (Tübingen: J.C.B. Mohr, 1969), 289, n. 339, M. Hengel considers Knox's contentions of a later interpolation to be improbable. Marböck (op. cit., pp. 45–46, 77–78) notes the discontinuity and implies a redactional step which, in tune with the theme of the Song, concludes a series of personified concretizations with a final radical "reinterpretation." For further discussion of the textual and interpretative issues, see Otto Rickenbacher, op. cit., pp. 125–27.

theme throughout the entire earlier composition (see 24:7, 12, 20). Such learned and meticulous artistry, apparent even on the surface, is an indication that the writer's use of Dt. 33:4 and Deuteronomy in general, may be just as intricate and involving.

Deuteronomy and Sir. 24:23. The manner in which the writer incorporates Dt. 33:4 into the prose of verse 23 is significant. It is not a formal quotation, but is simply edited into the ongoing composition. Hence, the Scripture reference, like the allusions in the Song before, does not stand out with the independence of a special biblical authority. Instead, both textual resources and interpretation mingle together. This mixture parallels that left by inner-biblical redactors who organized and commented on earlier traditions in such a way as to identify the older traditions with their new interpretations, cast in a new and presumably better literary whole. Consequently, Dt. 33:4 has, by its placement in Sir. 24:23, been given a new redactional setting which successfully reveals the writer's own particular interpretation of it. For the writer, Dt. 33:4 is not only a statement about the Torah, but it is a commentary on the proximity of Wisdom in the history of Israel.

In the light of the writer's citation of Dt. 33:4 and the free employment of deuteronomic language elsewhere in the Wisdom Song, Deuteronomy plays an unusually prominent role in the composition of Sir. 24. It is not incidental that Dt. 4 is often noted by commentators for its unique claim of an association between Wisdom and Torah which, more than any other passage in Hebrew Scripture, comes closest to the assertion in Sir. 24:23. However, Dt. 4 does not propose the same full identification, as found in Sir. 24, between the book of the Torah and Wisdom. For example, unlike Sir. 24, Dt. 4 makes no mention of the Torah as a *book*, much less "the book of the covenant" as the Torah of Moses with its canonical connotations. Despite these differences, the writer's previous dependence on Deuteronomy,[104] his direct citation of Dt. 33:4, and his concern for the relation of law to wisdom as in Dt. 4, do suggest the possibility that a more profound interpretation of Deuteronomy as a whole may underlie the equation of Wisdom and Torah in Sir. 24:23.

One way to approach this matter is to examine the passages in Deuteronomy that share the most conspicuous vocabulary with canonical wisdom books, especially Proverbs. For example, words from the roots חכם, בין, and יעץ occur 14 times in Deuteronomy:

---

104 Compare the language of "rest and inheritance" in Sir. 24:7–8 with the same in Dt. 12. See Marböck, op. cit., pp. 62–63.

a. Four are in ch. 2 and 16.[105]
b. Four are found in ch. 4.[106]
c. Five occur in the Song of Moses (ch. 32).[107]
d. One instance (חכמה) is found in 34:9.

The "a" occasions are all in connection with the appointment of "wise" judges to assist Moses. Similarly in 34:9, Joshua is endowed with the רוח חכמה which seems to reinforce this requirement for leaders in the Israelite community.[108] Likewise in Sir. 39, the hope of the scribe is that through his studying of both the Scriptures and all worldly wisdom he might charismatically be filled with the πνεύματι συνέσεως (lit. "wisdom of understanding"). Therefore, outside of these explicit references to wise leaders in the community, only Dt. 4 and 32 (b & c) employ the same related vocabulary.

Dt. 4 and 32 not only contain the remaining passages that overtly mention wisdom, but these passages share in common the same motif and themes. Each is concerned with the judgment of Israel by the surrounding nations (α) in terms of her wisdom or lack of it (β) which is directly dependent on her obedience to the Torah (γ). The repetition of these three features can be demonstrated individually for each chapter.

On the one hand, one finds in Dt. 4:6 what is acknowledged as the closest parallel in the OT to Sirach's more explicit assertion in 24:23a. There exists a remarkable relationship between the "statutes and ordinances" (חקים ומשפטים v. 5), and the evaluation of "your wisdom and your understanding in the sight of the people" (חכמתכם ובינתכם לעיני העמים v. 6). The last phrase לעיני העמים emphasizes the consequence of Israel's obedience to "all these statutes."[109] It is that the nations may conclude, "Surely, this great nation (Israel) is a wise and understanding people." The two rhetorical questions in vv. 7 and 8 provide the ultimate ground for the relationship between the statues and wisdom in that no other nation has its God so "near" (קרוב) or a "Torah" (תורה) so righteous as Israel's. The judgment of the nations (α) can be viewed as the central motif by which

---

[105] 1:3 (2×), 15; 16:19.

[106] 4:6 (4×).

[107] 32:6, 28, 29 (2×).

[108] The phrase רוח חכמה does not occur elsewhere in Deuteronomy.

[109] For the use of אשר to introduce either purpose or result clauses in the OT, see R. J. Williams, *Hebrew Syntax: An Outline* (Toronto: University of Toronto Press, 1967), pars. 465–66. Also, C. Brockelmann, *Hebräische Syntax* (Neukirchen Kreis Moers: Verlag der Buchhandlung des Erziehungsvereins, 1956), 153 (§ 161 bαβ). Also, its use in Dt. 4:40 to introduce a purpose clause parallels somewhat the context here in 4:6.

the conclusion that Israel is wise and understanding (β) necessarily results from her obedience to the Torah (γ).

On the other hand, Israel is depicted in the Song of Moses (Dt. 32)[110] as corrupt, and is addressed as "a foolish people, without wisdom" (עם נבל ולא חכם v.6). Only in Dt. 32 is the designation of "foolish" (נבל) used for Israel. The same concept recurs in 32:15 in which a verbal form of this same root dramatizes the perfidy of a wayward generation, one that makes mockery of "the Rock of [their] Salvation." In v.21 Yahweh responds to Israel's vanities (בהבליהם) by threatening to deliver her over to a foolish or vile nation (בגוי נבל). God warns of an annihilation so complete that Israel will never again be remembered among mankind (v.26).[111]

God, however, does not actualize his angry gestures of destruction in Dt. 32 because his wrath might subsequently be misconstrued by the adversary nations. They would regard it as a private victory and not as the genuine retribution of Yahweh against his own people. The reason (vv. 28, 29) the nations would misapprehend the truth of the situation is that they, like Israel (vv.6, 15), lack "counsel" (עצות) and "understanding" (תבונה) and are neither "wise" (חכמו) nor "discerning" (יבינו) of their "end" (אחרית).[112] Still, the nations must judge (v.31). Finally, in the hortatory address immediately after the Song, Moses adjures the people on the basis of his Song "to observe to do all the words of this Torah" (דברי התורה הזה v.46b). Once again, we find the nations judging Israel (α), but now Israel too is foolish and without wisdom (β) which is the circumstance under which Moses demands as remedy a renewed obedience to the Torah (γ).

In the context of the present redaction of Deuteronomy, chs.4 and 32 bracket the legal corpus and complement one another by connecting Israel's hope of wisdom before the nations with her adherence to the Torah. Together they serve to reinforce the same ideas. Moreover, alongside these two chapters Dt.30 must also be mentioned. Like Dt. 4 and 32, Dt. 30 is once again engaged with the question of the place and significance of the Torah in Israel.

Dt.30:10 conditions promises of salvation and prosperity (30:3–9) by an obedience to "his commandments and statutes which are written in

---

[110] For a discussion of the Song of Moses and a complete bibliography of recent studies including those concerned with its Wisdom elements, see C. J. Labuschagne, "The Song of Moses: Its Framework and Structure," *De Fructu Oris Sui*, ed. I.H. Eybers, et al. (Leiden: E. J. Brill, 1971), pp.85–98, esp. 92.

[111] Cf. Sir. 44:10–15.

[112] For a discussion of this phrase as a possible wisdom feature, see Weinfeld, *Deuteronomy and the Deuteronomic School*, op. cit., pp.316–17.

this book of the Torah" (ספר התורה הזה). Israel is assured that "this commandment" is not hard or far off (v. 11); neither is it in heaven nor beyond the sea (vv. 12–13). Rather, "the word" (הדבר, v. 14) "is very near you so that you can do it." "The word" in v. 14 clearly refers back to "this commandment" which finds its definition in v. 10, in the "commandment and statutes," viz., "the book of the Torah."

The parallels with Dt. 4 are particularly important. Only in Dt. 4 and 30 do we find the same concern in that book for the *nearness* of God by means of the Torah (both Qal passive participles of קרב, 4:7; 30:14). In Dt. 4, as well as in Dt. 32, the Torah is the ground for the recognition of Israel as a wise nation. In ch. 4, likewise, obedience to the Torah leads the nations to acknowledge the unique nearness of Israel's God. However, unlike ch. 4, Dt. 30 does not mention wisdom. Conversely, while Dt. 4 has only the more general term "Torah," ch. 30 speaks explicitly of "the *book* of the Torah," similar to "the book of the covenant" in Sir. 24:23. In other words, if one reads Dt. 4 and 32 together alongside Dt. 30 the conception emerges of a *book of Torah* (ch. 30) which comes *near* to Israel (chs. 4 and 30) from beyond the heavens and is her *wisdom* (chs. 4 and 32). This imagery coincides perfectly with the presuppositions of Sir. 24:23 and probably reflects his hearing of Deuteronomy.

Deuteronomy in Sir. 51:26 and Bar. 3:29–31. The probability that the writer of Sir. 24:23ff. has understood Deuteronomy as here reconstructed, is confirmed by one of the other rare first-person accounts in Sirach. In Sir. 51:13–30 the writer-sage makes one of the final appeals to his potential students. An extant Hebrew copy (MsB from the Cairo Geniza) of 51:26 reads,

> וצואריכם בעלה הביאו ומשאה תשא נפשכם
> קרובה היא למבקשיה ונותן נפשו מוצא אתה
> Bring your necks under her yoke;
> let your soul bear her burden
> She is near to those who seek her,
> and whoever is determined [lit. gives his soul] finds her.

Once again a play on Deuteronomy can be observed. The subject is wisdom which is "near" as in Dt. 4:6,7, but this wisdom is also called a "yoke," a metaphor for obedience popularly associated with the book of the Torah (30:10).[113] The endeavor to attain wisdom in Dt. 33:10 is, as here, a commitment requiring total devotion of heart and soul. In harmony

[113] E.g., Jer. 5:5; Pirke Aboth III, 6. Cf. Hruby, op. cit., pp. 38–39. It is not used in the OT in association with Wisdom.

with the same theological ascription in Sir. 24, Ben Sira, who has studied the book of Torah as Wisdom made manifest in Israel, has now offered her to his aspiring readers, "Turn in unto me, ye unlearned, and lodge in my house of instruction" (51:23). In this context Sir. 51:26 means that the wisdom near to Ben Sira, both in his experience and in the Torah, can now be put *near* to his students in the form of "instruction" in this, *his* wisdom book. The idea that Torah is a special source of wisdom and that the writer has learned recourse to it suggests that the wisdom book of Sirach can have a special claim to wisdom. In Deuteronomy, those who pursued the commands of God found them near in the Torah. Likewise, Ben Sira's book brings instruction near to those seeking wisdom.

Finally, the Wisdom Song in Bar. 3:9ff. provides additional evidence of a similar parallel understanding. It imitates Sir. 24 in a number of features. Like the Wisdom Song in Sirach, the prosaic section in Baruch describes Wisdom's movement from a heavenly to an earthly sphere. She is shown repeatedly to be inaccessible to those persons in canonical history outside of Israel and consequently the cause of their destruction. Wisdom is identified at the conclusion of the prose, as in Sir. 24:23, with "the book of the commandments of God and the Torah which endures forever" (Bar. 4:1). But, unlike Sirach's Wisdom Song, in the body of Baruch's prose about the way of wisdom Dt. 30 is paraphrased! For a detailed examination that shows how Dt. 30 is interpreted in Bar. 3:29–31, see chapter IV.

Baruch's wisdom interpretation of Dt. 30 reveals the same assumption as that underlying Sir. 24, namely, that the Torah which God alone brings near (Dt. 30) is the same Torah which is wisdom near to Israel (Dt. 4). Because there is no direct reference to wisdom in Dt. 30, only our proposal regarding its resonance with Dt. 4 accounts for the assumed relationship of Torah with wisdom both in Bar. 3:29–31 and in Sir. 24. Even as Sir. 51:26 stresses "the yoke" of "instruction" which is "near" (קרובה) and which the diligent "find" (מוצא), so the Dt. 30 section in Bar. 3:9ff. is interpreted in terms of a searching for and "finding" (ἐξευρισκεῖν see 3:15, 32, 36) of *wisdom*. Therefore, our conclusion with respect to the writer's use of Deuteronomy in Sir. 24:23 and Sir. 51:26 has been further complemented by the analogous, if not directly dependent, interpretive activity in Bar. 3:9ff., especially 3:29–31.

In summary, the interpretation of Deuteronomy in Sir. 24:23 picks up the theme of the Torah as *wisdom* which appears the same in both Dt. 4 and 32 and incorporates from Dt. 30 the idea of the *book* of the Torah that is no longer in heaven but given to Israel. However, the writer of Sirach expresses the idea of *nearness* (Dt. 4 and 30) more concretely in the election vocabulary, found elsewhere within Deuteronomy (e.g., Dt. 3:18ff., 12:1ff.), of a divine "possession" or "inheritance" in Israel. In order to secure this connection he simply edits into his commentary the statement of Dt. 33:4. It is significant that 33:4 is the only verse in Deuteronomy that links the Mosaic law with the thematic catch-word, "possession/inheritance" (κληρονομία = מורשה), which was stressed before throughout the Wisdom Song (cf. Sir. 24:7, 12, 20).[114]

This combined interpretation of Dt. 4, 30, and 32 provides the biblical basis for Ben Sira's conclusion that "the book of the covenant" is Wisdom and results from simply one possible, selective reading of Deuteronomy. The method of using different, thoughes thematically related, OT texts to interpret each other obviously cannot be regarded in itself as a peculiarly sapiential device. Yet, the *book* of the Torah found in Dt. 30 has come to have a special meaning in Sir. 24:23, like the "Torah of the Most High" in Sir. 39:1. As in Sir. 39, it stands for one of the canonical divisions, the five books of Moses, and a primary source of Wisdom for the sage. So, here, the giving of the book of the Torah is synonymous with the settlement and unique presence of divine Wisdom in Israel. It is both a promise and a hermeneutical statement. The Torah can be read as a guide to wisdom and resides as a unique possession of Israel.

Sir. 24:25–29 [25]ὁ πιμπλῶν ὡς Φισων σοφίαν
καὶ ὡς Τίγρις ἐν ἡμέραις νέων,
[26]ὁ ἀναπληρῶν ὡς Εὐφράτης σύνεσιν
καὶ ὡς Ἰορδάνης ἐν ἡμέραις θερισμοῦ,
[27]ὁ ἐκφαίνων ὡς φῶς παιδείαν,
ὡς Γηων ἐν ἡμέραις τρυγήτου.
[28]οὐ συνετέλεσεν ὁ πρῶτος γνῶναι αὐτήν,
καὶ οὕτως ὁ ἔσχατος οὐκ ἐξιχνίασεν αὐτήν
[29]ἀπὸ γὰρ θαλάσσηςἐπληθύνθη διανόημα αὐτῆς
καὶ ἡ βουλὴ αὐτῆς ἀπὸ ἀβύσσου μεγάλης.

[114] The Hebrew for κληρονομία in the previous Song is probably נחלה which is the conventional expression for "inheritance" in the deuteronomic phrase "rest and inheritance." Cf. Sir. 24:7,8; see Dt. 3:18–20; 12:1–11; 25:19; Jos. 11:13–15 and Marböck, 62. Nevertheless, the Hebrew word in Sir. 24:23b is probably מורשה as in the *MT* of Dt. 33:4. So, Segal, op.cit., p. 146. The two Hebrew terms are quite similar in meaning, both terms are commonly translated in the LXX with κληρονομία: usually for the former and in one-third of the occurrences (12) for the latter. Clearly, the probability of a lexical distinction is overshadowed in Sir. 24 by the conceptual agreement between the two words and the importance of that agreement in the interpretation of the Wisdom Song. That κληρονομία is the translation equivalent in the LXX of the term in Dt. 33:4 confirms its contextual agreement in meaning with the use of נחלה in the preceding Song.

[25]Which [The Torah, cf. 24:23] is full of Wisdom like the Pison,
and like the Tygris at the time of first fruits,
[26]which overflows like the Euphrates with insight
and as the Jordan at harvest time
[27]which makes instruction flow like the Nile[115]
and as Gihon at the time of vintage.
[28]The first man did not know her perfectly,
nor will the last fully comprehend her.
[29]For her understanding is wider than the sea,
and her counsel is deeper than the great abyss.

The following comparisons of Wisdom with the rivers of Paradise, including the other well-known rivers of the ancient Near East, further undermine any theory that the Wisdom Song is merely a series of various personified concretizations of Wisdom which suddenly end in her identification with the written Torah.[116] Although Sir. 24:23 is the only direct identification, the other associations are similies which trace the presence of Wisdom as Torah from the beginning, through her participation with Israel in her election and inheritance of Zion. Now the writer advances the praise of Wisdom (= Torah) as the "water of life" in terms of the paradisaical rivers. This move is not a step backward into an earlier set of random personifications which were drawn from the course of Israel's history. Rather, in a style much like that of the Wisdom Song itself, it sustains and complements the previous praise of Wisdom as Torah in Israel, but now in terms of her presence in the Edenic garden of intellectual, material, and religious delights.

Several features in Ben Sira's use of Hebrew Scripture are noteworthy. First, the order in which he places the rivers sheds some light on the matter. Except in Gen. 2:10–14 the Pison and Gihon are not named elsewhere in the OT.[117] These rivers, idiosyncratic to the Edenic narrative of Gen. 2, serve as an *inclusio* in Sir. 24:25–29. By their positions at the first and the end of the list, they bracket the rest of the rivers to make them appear as additional streams of paradise. While the Pison, Gihon, Euphrates, and Tigris (for Hiddekel) are fully in keeping with Gen. 2:10–14, the Jordan and Nile are foreign to the Genesis account. At the outset these are, however, the two other prominent rivers in that part of the Semitic world and might seem to deserve a place among the great arterial resources which are

---

[115] *G* of v. 27a has probably misconstrued an original Hebrew, המשפיעה כיאר מוסר. So Segal, op. cit., pp. 146, 150.

[116] Cf. Marböck, op. cit., p. 76.

[117] The LXX of Jer. 2:18 is an exception, but is probably inaccurate.

tributaries from the one great river that flows through the center of Eden (Gen. 2:10).

Both the Prophets and the Psalms exhibit the imagery of Eden in their depictions of a future bliss, but the naming of rivers is absent from them.[118] For that reason, Ben Sira's description is probably reflective of another set of OT traditions, namely, those concerned with the dimensions of the Promised Land. For example, in Gen. 15:18 God promised Abraham a land "from the river of Egypt [Nile] to the great river, the river Euphrates." A reference is made to this same promise in Dt. 1:6–8, and instruction is offered throughout Deuteronomy to those who are about to cross over "the *Jordan*" to "the land which the Lord your God gives you [to us]."[119] As G. von Rad and others have notes, this land "beyond the Jordan" is seen in terms of Paradise[120] and its possession is for Israel contingent upon her obedience to the divine law:

> ... and you shall write on them [the pile of stones] all the words of the Torah, when you pass over to enter the land which the Lord your God gives you, a land flowing with milk and honey, as the Lord, the God of your fathers, has promised you. And when you have passed over the Jordan ... (Dt. 27:3, cf. 12:10).

The effect of this description is to portray the Nile, Euphrates and Jordan as the great river boundaries of the Promised Land,[121] which in Deuteronomy and the Prophets is pictured in paradisaical terms and insured for Israel only by obedience to the Torah.[122] By Ben Sira's naming the Pison, Gihon, and Tigris, there is a similar portrayal of an Eden-like Promised Land where the Torah, as the wisdom of God, abounds. Likewise, the wealth of wisdom is compared to the great rivers which periodically overflow and flood the land with life-sustaining water.

Once more, one finds a comprehensive evaluation of the past traditions with some continued preference for Deuteronomy and its influence on the later OT books. The play on Genesis sharpens the parallelism with Eden as a prototype of the Promised Land. By positioning the key words

---

[118] Cf. Joel 4:18; Zach. 14:8; Ezek. 47; Ps. 46:5, 36:9.

[119] E.g., Dt. 2:28, 4:21–22, 11:31, 12:10, 27:3.

[120] Cf. Dt. 11:8–15. G. von Rad, *Deuteronomy*, trans. by Dorothea Barton (Philadelphia: Westminster Press, 1966), p. 85.

[121] The more accurate boundaries of the land, for example, in Num. 34:1–12; Jos. 13:19; and Ezek. 47:13–23 represent greater geographical precision and a wider variety of reference points. For instance, the northern boundary cited otherwise at the Euphrates (Gen. 15:18, Dt. 1:6–8, 11:24) is there set at the entrance to Hamath. The distinction between the "brook" and the "river" of Egypt can be viewed in this same manner.

[122] Dt. 4:23, 11:26f., 12:10, 30:18, 32:46–47.

Pison and Gihon before and after the list, the writer cleverly brackets the rest. That this depiction of Wisdom flourishing in Israel, in harmony with the earlier picture of flora in Sir. 24:13–17, is not just a detached metaphorical use of Genesis is evident in the writer's subsequent observation. He assures the reader that neither the "first man" (in the garden) knew her perfectly, nor will "the last." The reason for this state of affairs is simply that Wisdom is too vast and inexhaustible: "more full than the sea," "greater than the deep." This assessment recalls the cosmic dimensions of her activity (24:5–6) which she professed before being appointed with Israel to her inheritance/possession. Even as the "first man," Adam, obtained Wisdom in the garden and could not master her, the same applies to "the last [man]" who meets her again in the form of the Torah in the Promised Land. Hence, the glorification of Palestine as a Second Eden, based on the unique presence of wisdom within it, finds its justification in a wisdom interpretation of the Genesis narratives.

Chapter III

Case Study Two: Sir. 16:24–17:14

Preface to Sir. 16:24–17:14

These verses stand in the larger discourse of Sir. 15:9(11)–18:14 concerning the execution of God's wrath on man's sin. In the verses immediately preceding 16:24 there is a series of questions about whether God who dwells "in the heights" (v. 17) really pays attention to the relatively insignificant deeds of each earthly individual. At the end of the series the writer provides a candid subscription that these inquiries are paradigmatic of what a foolish person thinks: "They that lack understanding think these things, and the man of folly thinks this" (v. 23). Consequently the instruction that follows in 16:24ff. is presented as a full and digressive response to the misguided imagination of the previous questions. It begins appropriately with a formal, didactic introduction typical of wisdom literature:[1]

> Hear me [*G* 'O son'] and receive my wisdom,
> And set your heart upon my words.
> I will pour out my spirit by weight,
> And by measure will I declare my knowledge.
> (vv. 24–25)

Sir. 16:24–17:14 Analysis

Sir. 16:26–28 [26]Ἐν κτίσει κυρίου τὰ ἔργα αὐτοῦ ἀπ' ἀρχῆς,
καὶ ἀπὸ ποιήσεως αὐτῶν διέστειλεν μερίδας αὐτῶν.
[27]ἐκόσμησεν εἰς αἰῶνα τὰ ἔργα αὐτῶν
καὶ τὰς ἀρχὰς αὐτῶν εἰς γενεὰς αὐτῶν
οὔτε ἐπείνασαν οὔτε ἐκοπίασαν
καὶ οὐκ ἐξέλιπον ἀπὸ τῶν ἔργων αὐτῶν

---

[1] Cf. Prov. 4:10f.; 8:6f. The Hebrew in MsA and the Syriac are against the *G* "O son" (τέκνον), which occurs after "Hear me." If *G* is indeed secondary, then the translator has apparently recognized this as a didactic introduction like those in Proverbs and added the usual reference to students as "sons." τέκνον frequently stands for בן elsewhere in Sir. 3:12; 6:32; 7:23; 34:33; 41:6,14; 44:12.

[28]ἕκαστος τὸν πλησίον αὐτοῦ οὐκ ἐξέθλιψεν,
καὶ ἕως αἰῶνος οὐκ ἀπειθήσουσιν τοῦ ῥήματος αὐτοῦ.

[26]When God created his works from the beginning,
After making them he assigned them [their] portion.
[27]He set in order his works forever,
And their authority unto their generations.
They neither hunger nor grow weary
And they cease not from their work.
[28]Not one thrusts aside its neighbour,
They never disobey his word.

In v.26, *G* and *L* "their portions" seems more probable than *S* "laws." Segal's proposal of חלק חלקיהם for the phrase, "he assigned them their portions," is certainly plausible but not conclusive.[2] While *S* is suggestive of the verb חלק,[3] a Hiphil of בדל is also conceivable.[4] The object of creation is God's "works" (v.26), and the process is one of sorting out the elements into their proscribed arenas of activity. The following v.27a amplifies this depiction according to *G*'s use of ἐκόσμησεν, "he set in order" or "he meted out," which probably translates תכן (cf. 42:21).[5] Is. 40:12 similarly pictures God measuring out and weighing the apportioned masses of creation. Consequently, the theme here is that of God orchestrating his "works" (cf. vv.26, 27, 28) into a single harmonious cosmos, a cosmos resonating in perfect obedience to "his word" (v.28b, cf. 43:9–10, Ps. 148:6).[6]

If Sirach's interest in the ordered universe is receptive to the Stoic concept of νόμος as the world principle, then the philosophical idea has been completely translated into OT terminology.[7] There is certainly no jarring sense of hellenistic novelty, but the greater insight into the passage

---

[2] Segal, op.cit., p.102. Smend (op.cit., p.154) suggests חלק חקותם.

[3] Of the 6 cases in which ܦܠܓ occurs alongside an extant Hebrew text, it translates חלק 4 times (16:16b; 44:2a; 44:23a; 45:22b), otherwise נאוה (10:18a) or פלג (30:23a). *G* is problematic since it recurs only once, 44:23, and seems to misread the Hebrew and duplicate in the wrong place the חלק that follows.

[4] Frequently in the LXX διαστέλλειν renders the Hiphil of בדל, particularly when it is used for distinguishing in a religious or forensic sense (cf. Lev. 10:10; 13:47; Num. 8:14; 16:19; Dt. 10:8; 19:27; 29:21; 1 Kgs. 8:53; Ezek. 22:26; 39:14; 42:20).

[5] See Segal, op.cit., p.106; Smend, op.cit., p.154, and their respective discussions.

[6] Cf. Is. 40:26; Enoch 2:1–2; Wis. 11:21.

[7] Middendorp's proposal (op.cit., p.30), that the noetic elements in Sir. 17:6–8 derive from the Stoic conceptualization of Reason, is not very convincing. V.5 is obviously a late addition (see n.18) which sought to impose a Stoic context to the material that follows. Without it as evidence for original Hellenistic intrusions, Middendorp's suggestion of Stoic influence in what follows is precarious and not firmly established. Cf. Marböck, op.cit., p.138.

bears on its conformity to and adaptation of the Genesis narratives. It is important to observe initially that v. 26 not only introduces the subject of the passage but starts a temporal sequence ("when ...") which is picked up later by v. 29 ("after these things pass"). In vv. 26–28 the works of creation are brought into being and attain clockwork precision. In vv. 29ff., "after these things," God creates human beings and endows them with knowledge to perceive his works (v. 8) and, as a result, to praise their Creator (v. 9, cf. 17:8, 10). These temporal designations within the passage are significant because they provide a framework in conformity with creation accounts in Genesis.

The clause "when God created" (Sir. 16:26a) corresponds to Gen. 1:1ff. and particularly its counterpart in 2:4bff. in which, as in Sir. 16:26–29, the creation of the elemental orders is fully completed before there are any appearances of life on the planet.[8] The apportioning of the elements recalls the repeated divisions between various created things in Gen. 1 (הבדיל בין, vv. 4, 6, 7, 18). These separations serve to underscore the complexity and perfection of the universe. Elsewhere, Ben Sira speaks of similar distinctions made among humanity, though, unlike here, they are strictly moral in nature [33(36):10–15]. In reminiscence to Gen. 1:16 and the celestial lights that "rule" (משל) over the world by day and by night, the cosmos in Sir. 16:27 exercises a delegated "rule" or "authority" (*G* ἄρχας, *S* ܘܫܘܠܛܢܗܘܢ, cf. 43:6 ממשלה). So far, these OT recollections show no explicit signs of wisdom interpretation, although it may be suggested, on the basis of the introduction (vv. 24–25), that the writer condenses the Genesis traditions into a didactic lesson.

Sir. 16:29–17:4 [29]καὶ μετὰ ταῦτα κύριος εἰς τὴν γῆν ἐπέβλεψεν
καὶ ἐνέπλησεν αὐτὴν τῶν ἀγαθῶν αὐτοῦ
[30]ψυχῇ παντὸς ζῴου ἐκάλυψεν τὸ πρόσωπον αὐτῆς,
καὶ εἰς αὐτὴν ἡ ἀποστραφὴ αὐτῶν.
17 [1]Κύριος ἔκτισεν ἐκ γῆς ἄνθρωπον
καὶ πάλιν ἀπέστρεψεν αὐτὸν εἰς αὐτήν.
[2]ἡμέρας ἀριθμοῦ καὶ καιρὸν ἔδωκεν αὐτοῖς
καὶ ἔδωκεν αὐτοῖς ἐξουσίαν τῶν ἐπ' αὐτῆς.
[3]καθ' ἑαυτὸν ἐνέδυσεν αὐτοὺς ἰσχὺν
καὶ κατ' εἰκόνα αὐτοῦ ἐποίησεν αὐτούς.

---

[8] The "works" need not refer only to the stars, for such is not the case elsewhere in Sirach (e.g., 1:9; 18:4). The question of where vegetation belongs in the scheme (cf. Gen. 1:11) is irrelevant to Sirach's present concern. See the discussion of v. 29 by Smend, op. cit., p. 154; and also that of C. Spicq, *L'Ecclesiastique*, La Sainte Bible, vol. 6 (Paris: Letouzey et Ané, 1946), p. 650.

[4]ἔθηκεν τὸν φόβον αὐτοῦ ἐπὶ πάσης σαρκὸς
καὶ κατακυριεύειν θηρίων καὶ πετεινῶν.

[29]And after these things the Lord looked upon the earth,
And filled it with his good things.
[30]With every living thing he filled the earth;
And into it is their return.

17 [1]God created man out of dust
And turned him back thereunto.
[2]He granted him a fixed number of days
And gave him authority over all things on the earth.
[3]He clothed them with strength like his own,
And made them according to his own image.
[4]He put the fear of them upon all flesh,
And caused them to have power over beasts and birds.

The phrase "after these things" marks a new stage in the creation commentary. Now God surveys the earth and fills it with living things (v. 30). This event may be intended to echo the divine decision, "Let the earth bring forth living creatures" in Gen. 1:24 (also cf. 1:20). However, Sir. 16:29b is textually corrupt. If Smend is correct in taking the verb to be "he blessed" (following *S*), then this terminal event in the creation of life may reflect Gen. 1:22 in which God blessed on the fifth day the fish and the birds who were the first living creatures.[9]

If *G* ἄγαθος, "good things" is the true object of the verb, then there is likely also an allusion to God's daily pronouncements that his creation is "good" (Gen. 1:4, 10, 12, 18, 21, 25). Unfortunately, the text cannot be recovered with absolute certainty.

Sir. 17:1a is directly dependent upon Gen. 2:7, "Yahweh formed man out of the dust of the earth." *S* ܡܢ ܥܦܪܐ, "from the dust," is more exact in contrast to *G* ἐκ γῆς, "from the earth" and recalls the Genesis עפר. The Hebrew undoubtedly had אדם "men," as suggested by the literal rendering of *S*.[10] The Hebrew of Sirach may match Gen. 2:7 word for word, but the textual evidence is too uncertain to establish such a conclusion.[11]

---

9 Smend, op. cit., pp. 154–55.

10 Although *S* may use a variety of words to translate אדם (e.g., 5:13; 11:27; 32:24; 49:19), the extant Hebrew texts suggest that whenever ܐܕܡ occurs it always translates this same word (e.g., 36:10b; 49:16b).

11 Both *S* and *G* find support in the phrase, "of dust from the earth" (עפר מן האדמה). The former seems to pick up the first part, and the latter the last part of the phrase. The subject and main verb could be identical with Gen. 2:7, but the translations prevent any exact reconstruction.

Sir. 17:1b clearly alludes to Gen. 3:19 and to the judgment on Adam that he must labor for his bread until he "return[s] to the ground from out of [which] you were taken."[12] This usage is noteworthy since in the Genesis narratives the statement belongs to God's judgment against Adam and Eve for their rebellion in the garden. Here, however, it is simply recognized as a universal axiom of created humanity. Its original relation to man's sin in the garden has been intentionally obscured.

That God "granted them a fixed number of days" (17:2a) may reflect the writer's understanding of the opaque statement in Gen. 6:3 that "[man] is flesh, but his days shall be a hundred and twenty years."[13] There God first appears to restrict the lifespan of mankind because of the same apostasy that precipitates the Flood. Once again, a statement that arises out of an etiological setting of requisite divine judgment upon the emergence of postcreation sin is now taken simply as generally indicative of created humanity.

Sir. 17:2b addresses the authority appointed to mankind "over all."[14] This expression parallels that of Gen. 1:28 in which, first in self-reflection, God wills that mankind subdue (רדה) all the various creatures he has made. Then, in Gen. 1:28 after God creates mankind in his own image, he puts his thoughts into action by commanding the first couple both to subdue (רדה) the earth and to have dominion (כבש) over all the creatures in it. While the Sirach text is perspicuous enough to support the case for dependence, it can not be reconstructed sufficiently to know if either of the two Genesis verbs was actually used in Hebrew (cf. Sir. 16:27a).

Sir. 17:3a is a difficult line to analyze. *S* prefaces it with "by his wisdom" and adds, "and covered them with fear." This latter phrase in *S* is probably secondary and has picked up the word "fear" that follows in the next line. The claim in both in *G* and *S* that God "clothed them with strength" may suggest that Sirach has allegorized Gen. 3:21 in which God "made for Adam and his wife garments of skins [עור] and clothed them." This event occurs after he expelled them from the garden.[15] On the one

[12] Cf. Qoh. 12:7.

[13] Cf. Ps. 90:10, Job 14:5. See discussion by Fritzsche, op. cit., p. 82, and that of V. Ryssel, "Baruch," *Die Apokryphen und Pseudepigraphen des Alten Testaments*, ed. by E. Kautzsch, 2 vols. [Tübingen: Verlag von J. C. B. Mohr (Paul Siebeck), 1900], 1:313.

[14] Cf. *G*, "over the things upon it;" *L eorum quae sunt super terram.*

[15] *Bereshith Rabbah* 20:12 interprets עור, "skin," with אור, "light," which closely resembles it in sound. Therefore, "garments of skin" are "garments of light," that is, like fine linen garments. No moralizing of this interpretation follows. Whether Ben Sira ventures a similar grammatical play between עור and עוז, "strength," is not certain, but possible.

hand, Targum Onkelos contemplates a bestowal of virtue in Gen. 3:21 and paraphrases, "vestments of honor [דיקר] upon the skin of their flesh," while the Palestinian Targum offers, "vestures of honor [דיקר] from the skin of the serpent." Similarly, *L* of Sir. 17:3a appends to the phrase in question, *et secundum se vestivit illum virtutem.* On the other hand, in the sacred Wisdom literature Prov. 31:17 observes that the wise woman "girds her loins with strength [עוז]" and later that "strength [עוז] and honour/beauty [הדר] are her clothing." Therefore, the phrase in Sirach may represent a symbolic re-interpretation of Gen. 3:21 in a manner idiomatic to proverbial wisdom. If so, then again a motif associated with the consequences of the Edenic rebellion is collapsed into a synopsis of characterizations for created humanity without attention to the larger narrative context of the Fall.

The claim in 17:3b that God "made them according to his own image" directly reflects Gen. 1:26a, 27a (cf. Gen. 9:6b).[16] Moreover, the following lines (17:4) appear to depend directly on Gen. 9:2.

> The fear of you and the dread of you shall be upon every beast of the earth, and upon every bird of the air, upon everything that creeps on the ground and all the fish of the sea into your hand that are delivered.

Gen. 9:2 stands after the Flood story in the recapitulation of the Creation commands. There one finds repeated, as here, that mankind is made in the image of God (cf. Gen. 9:6b). The command to subdue the animals is like that of Gen. 1:28, but only in Gen. 9 is fear mentioned as an instrumental means. Apparently, a holistic approach to scriptural interpretation facilitates the writer by allowing him to hear all the related passages as a common witness to the one tradition of creation.

In summary, Sir. 17:1–4 illustrates again the thoughtfulness and intricacy with which the writer weaves related biblical themes into a single fabric. The individuality of Adam and Eve has been forfeited in the desire to gather various statements of universal significance for mankind as they appear in the Genesis chapters. They have been carefully arranged in an unnumbered anthological list which emerges as a gnomic and scripturally

---

[16] This line is omitted in *S*, which offers instead an awkwardly expanded form of the first part of the verse, "In his wisdom he clothed them with strength and covered them with fear." Smend (op. cit., pp. 155–56) proposes to reconcile both *G* and *S* by an original, "und nach seinem Bilde bedeckte er sie mit Fruchtbarkeit" (p. 156). Middendorp (op. cit., p. 52) acknowledges that the original probably reflects Gen. 1:26, but on the basis of 17:6f. concludes that it is purely noetic in function and therefore corresponds strictly to the Stoic image of man.

based abstraction of created humanity.[17] Except for the larger context of a didactic lesson there are no outstanding parallels to the biblical wisdom literature. Although the writer compresses the content of the traditions into a descriptive, anthological style, he exercises extraordinary respect for the sacred text and permits no conspicuous intrusion from the standpoint of distinctive wisdom phraseology into the selections employed. In this regard, the suggestion in *S* that a phrase in 17:3 begin with "in his wisdom" is anomalous and probably secondary. Nevertheless, the interpolation in *S* does imply the Syriac translator has recognized the implicit wisdom context but lacked the reticence of the original writer of these verses. Only in the broadest definition could these verses *by themselves* be called "wisdom," a definition so broad as to obviate any critical advantage for normative insight into literary analysis. This circumstance changes in the verses that follow.

Sir. 17:6–10 [6]διαβούλιον καὶ γλῶσσαν καὶ ὀφθαλμούς,
ὦτα καὶ καρδίαν ἔδωκεν διανοεῖσθαι αὐτοῖς.
[7]ἐπιστήμην συνέσεως ἐνέπλησεν αὐτοὺς
καὶ ἀγαθὰ καὶ κακὰ ὑπέδειξεν αὐτοῖς.
[8]ἔθηκεν τὸν φόβον αὐτοῦ ἐπὶ τὰς καρδίας αὐτῶν
δεῖξαι αὐτοῖς τὸ μεγαλεῖον τῶν ἔργων αὐτοῦ,
[10]καὶ ὄνομα ἁγιασμοῦ αἰνέσουσιν,
[9]ἵνα διηγῶνται τὰ μεγαλεῖα τῶν ἔργων αὐτοῦ.

[6]He created for them *[S]* tongue, and eyes, and ears,
And he gave them a heart to understand.
[7]With insight and understanding he filled their heart
And taught them good and evil
[8]He put his fear upon their hearts
To show them the majesty of his works,
[10]And they will praise his holy name
[9]To declare the majesty of his works.

---

[17] The above analysis of 17:1–4 can be displayed graphically to show this effect:

v. 1a – Gen. 2:7
1b – 3:19
2a – (?) 6:3
2b – 1:26b, 28b
3a – (?) 3:21
3b – 1:26a, 27a (cf. 9:6b)
4 – 9:2

Since the original versification is difficult to recover, that of Box and Oesterley has been employed for this limited purpose. Note that v. 5 is a later Stoic insertion in *G*, as recognized by all modern commentators. It is also absent from *S*. Smend (op. cit., p. 156) preserves Grotius' classic remark exposing it.

Both the writer's selectivity in alluding to sacred tradition and the degree of elaboration which he gives a particular selection provide several clues to his dominating point of view. On the one hand, 17:6–10 stands in continuity with 17:1–4 which lists statements universally descriptive of created humanity, taken at random from the Genesis narratives. Accordingly, 17:6–10 simply appends to this series a complementary statement regarding mankind's knowledge of good and evil (v. 7b). On the other hand, the writer does not list it in the same terse disinterested manner as before but surrounds the statement in phrase upon phrase of free and copious embellishment in celebration of mankind's intellectual capacity. The language is not everywhere replete with biblical allusions and the loquacious style contrasts sharply with that of the previous series of short, compact paraphrastic references in 17:1–4.

In Genesis the phrase "good and evil" occurs in both 2:17 and 3:1ff. and is related to the forbidden fruit of the tree from which Adam and Eve were commanded not to eat. Their cognizance of good and evil is a consequence both of the serpent's deceit and of Adam and Eve's usurpation of illicit knowledge. Ben Sira completely reverses this negative connotation and presents this new awareness as God's "revelation" (*G* ὑπέδειξεν) or his "teaching" (*S* ܐܠܦ) to them. Perhaps the writer takes as his own presupposition the statement in Gen. 3:6 that the tree was desirable to Eve precisely because it would make her wise (להשכיל). Regardless, good and evil now go hand in hand with "discretion [שכל] and insight [בינה]" (v. 7a), the very cornerstones of wisdom.[18]

The writer's method of using Scripture is similar to that of 17:1–4. More particularly, it parallels those occasions in which statements from connotatively pejorative contexts associated with the Fall or the pre-Flood apostasy now function along with others as neutral, universal attributes of created humanity. Moreover, certain individual ascriptions about humanity which were originally found scattered throughout the course of the Genesis narratives have been abstracted out of their original settings in the traditional epic story-line. They now form a coherent list of statements which in its order violates the original sequence of occurrences in

[18] My translation of the phrase "discretion and insight" differs only slightly with that of Box and Oesterley. *S* ܣܘܟܠܐ along with *G* ἐπιστήμη suggests שכל for the underlying Hebrew (cf. Sir. 10:30). The *G* "skillfulness of insight" is within the translator's freedom to interpret a hendiadys expression of two nouns related by *waw*. The expression itself is idiomatic to biblical Hebrew. In 2 Chron. 2:11 Huram, the king of Tyre, sends a letter to Solomon and addresses him in relation to his Father David as, "a wise son, endued with discretion and understanding" (בן חכם יודע שכל ובינה). Also, see 1 Chron. 22:12 and Prov. 4:1, 5, 7.

the Genesis narratives. For our purposes it is significant that in Sir. 17: 6–10 the knowledge of good and evil is made a witness to the presence of wisdom in the garden of Eden. Further, this special knowledge is accommodated by the creation of the essential vehicles of its perception and demonstration: tongue, eyes, ears, heart (v. 6).

Although the technique of collecting and listing topically related statements is not in principle a sapiential methodology, it can certainly be employed as in 17:6–10 to suggest a wisdom interpretation. However, the centrality of this final wisdom interpretation for 17:1–10 as a whole is obvious only from an overview of the entire list. For example, the recognition of good and evil follows at the end of the list as its culmination and in ultimate service to the goal of praising the works of God (cf. vv. 8–10 Also, by contrast in the degree of elaboration the singular ascription in 17:6–10 stands out in comparison with the statements of 17:1–4 as the one of greatest significance for the entire section 17:1–10.

This assumption of wisdom at creation and implicitly in the garden of Eden conforms to similar imagery in Sir. 24 and inspires the claim in 40:27 that "The fear of God is a very Eden of blessing."[19] In addition, the idea of transgression in the garden remains throughout Sirach, as here, a suppressed feature which surfaces only by implication in the persistent dogma found elsewhere that "From a woman did sin originate and because of her all must die" (25:24).[20] Conversely, Adam's glory is estimated in the Praise to the Fathers (44ff.) as "above all living things" (על כל חי, 49:16). Edmund Jacob construes this assertion to imply that Adam is eulogized as the sage *par excellence*.[21]

If this assessment is correct, then Adam's extraordinary claim to wisdom is probably a logical outgrowth of an identification of the knowl-

---

[19] For the identification of the fear of God with wisdom in Sirach, see 1:16; 19:20; 21:11.

[20] Marböck (op. cit., p. 152) observes the same remarkable absence in Sirach of concern with the Fall as a source of evil or the later sinfulness of humanity.

[21] Edmund Jacob, op. cit., pp. 288–294. He concludes, p. 293, "Utilisant peut-être et combinant ces textes, Ben Sira voit à l'origine de la création ne pas la Sagesse personnifiée ni un Adam ravissant la sagesse par ruse, mais un Adam glorieux et parfait comme la sagesse elle-même. Cette grandeur d'Adam transparaît aussi dans ce qu'il dit de L'image de Dieu dont il est le premier à reprendre le thème, en insistant plus que ne le fait La Genèse sur la force et l'intelligence de l'homme qui inspire la terreur à toutes les autres creatures (17:1 s.)." For references in Jewish and Christian interpretation of Adam in royal, sacridotal, and prophetic terms see, W. Staerk, *Die Erlösererwartung in den östlichen Religionen* (Berlin: W. Kohlhammer, 1938), pp. 3f. and B. Murmelstein, "Adam, ein Beitrag zur Messiaslehre," *Weiner Festschrift für Kunde des Morgenlandes*, 35 (1928): 242–75.

edge of good and evil in the garden with God's teaching of wisdom to nascent humanity. It is this wisdom that provides mankind with the genius to apprehend God's works, which will naturally elicit pious praise for the creator (vv. 8–10). A frank recognition of Adam's reciprocity in the Edenic rebellion would inveigh against the sufficiency of his wisdom and might even challenge the efficacy of wisdom itself. Clearly, as in most good literary exegesis, some complicating details best serve the scholar's intention when left quietly and unobstrusively in the netherworld of the uninterpreted.

Sir. 17:11–14 [11]προέθηκεν αὐτοῖς ἐπιστήμην
καὶ νόμον ζωῆς ἐκληροδότησεν αὐτοῖς
[12]διαθήκην αἰῶνος ἔστησεν μετ' αὐτῶν
καὶ τὰ κρίματα αὐτοῦ ὑπέδειξεν αὐτοῖς
[13]μεγαλεῖον δόξης εἶδον οἱ ὀφθαλμοὶ αὐτῶν
καὶ δόξαν φωνῆς αὐτοῦ ἤκουσεν τὸ οὖς αὐτῶν.
[14]καὶ εἶπεν αὐτοῖς Προσέχετε ἀπὸ παντὸς ἀδίκου
καὶ ἐνετείλατο αὐτοῖς ἑξάστῳ περὶ τοῦ πλησίον.

[11]He set knowledge before them.
The law of life he gave them for heritage.
[12]He made an everlasting covenant with them,
And showed them his judgments.
[13]Their eyes beheld his glorious majesty,
And their ear[s] heard his glorious voice;
[14]And he said unto them, Beware of all unrighteousness
And he gave them commandment, to each man concerning his neighbour.

The theme shifts abruptly to the Torah. The identification of Torah and wisdom is plainly to be inferred from the first expression that God gave to mankind "the Torah of life" (νόμον ζωῆς), a phrase which occurs again only in Sir. 45:5, when at first Moses receives "the Torah of life and discernment" (MsB, תורה חיים ותבונה, cf. Bar. 4:1). Furthermore, the phraseology in these verses recalls the biblical narratives of the giving of the Law at Sinai. For example, the "covenant" *(S)*[22] is "set before them" (v. 11a, cf. Dt. 4:44), and it is called "the Torah of life" (v. 11b, cf. Dt. 30:15, 19). As at Sinai, the people "beheld his glorious majesty" (v. 13a, cf. Ex. 24:16–17) and heard "his glorious voice" (v. 13b, cf. Ex. 19:19; 20:19; Dt. 4:12; 5:4; 30:2, 10, 20). Even the charge to "beware of all unrighteousness" (v. 14a, *S* "unfaithfulness") summarizes in traditional terms the legal demands of Torah, if not specifically the Decalogue.[23] The following injunction concerning "one's neighbor" (v. 14b, cf. Lev. 19:18) concludes

[22] If *G* is correct, then the Torah is identified immediately with "insight" (ἐπιστήμη, v. 11a).
[23] So all the commentators.

the Sirach pericope with an epitomization, once again in biblical language, of the essential content of the Law.[24]

In Sir. 17:11–14 the Torah is not described as an abstract principle, like the Stoic νόμος or a manifestation of Natural Law. Rather, it is precisely from the biblical milieu that the Torah in 17:11–14 finds its literary characterization.[25] Moreover, in order to sustain the common nexus between wisdom as delivered to humanity in the garden, though chronologically at creation, and wisdom given as The Torah, though chronologically at Sinai, the writer merely juxtaposes the two themes together without a temporal transition. Even with the careful omission of any explicit reference to Moses or Sinai, the implicit configuration of scriptural history remains strained without resolution. The same tension over when Israel received wisdom may be said to be reiterated in the Song of Wisdom in Sir. 24 and may account for the silence there about Sinai in relation to Wisdom's autobiography.

Nevertheless, it is surely wrong to deduce from Sirach's use of the term "Torah" that it is fully dogmatized to be a pre-existent entity like that of later Judaism. The issue is not set forward so plainly as that. The writer seems clearly here, as well as in Sir. 24, to hold the literary dimension in a historical perspective such that the *book* of the Torah (e.g., Sir. 24:23) derives from the gift of the Torah to Moses at Sinai, yet the Torah *as Wisdom* finds its origin with God at creation. In other words, the sage studies "the Torah of the Most High" as a literary canonical source in Sir. 39, yet it is also a guide to Wisdom which is present long before the time of Moses and the literary composition of the canonical book of the Torah. Though the implication of the eternality of the Torah may seem only a nuance away, it remains open to further speculation. For Sirach it is the perception of the Torah as the wisdom of God, not the eternality of the Torah, that is the chief issue at stake.

In general the evidence for wisdom interpretations of OT narrative is more elusive in Sir. 16:26–17:4 than in the preceding case study of Sir. 24. Nevertheless, 17:6–10 and 17:11–14 present in overt sapiential terms both the knowledge of good and evil in the garden and the Mosaic

---

[24] Cf. Segal, op. cit., p. 106. Abot de Rabbi Natan B: 27:9–11 [Text "A" (16:33f.) attributes the saying to Simeon ben Eleazar] calls this the "commandment" (דבר) upon which "the whole world is suspended."

[25] Ryssel (op. cit., p. 314, n. "f") refutes such positions similarly. Significantly, he observes that even allowing for maximum decisions against biblical language within the textual differences of *G* and *S*, v. 14 alone provides conclusive proof that the law of life is seen in terms of the Mosaic Torah.

reception of the Torah in Israel. In the former, the interpreter brings a dramatically different perspective to the original texts. In the latter, the same theme of wisdom is continued but now with descriptive phrases indicative of the reception of the Torah at Sinai. These latter verses (vv. 11–14) are intentionally linked with the earlier 17:1–4. Even as God *taught* mankind good and evil (v. 7b), God likewise *teaches* them the law of life (*S* of v. 11b, *G* has "He gave them for a heritage"). Even as the Edenic bestowal of wisdom helped mankind to have ears and eyes to apprehend the majesty of God's works and the glory of his acts, so the Torah facilitates mankind to see God's glorious majesty and hear his glorious voice (v. 13).

Baumgartner, in his investigation of literary *Gattungen* in Sirach, considered 16:24ff. to be a prime example of the mixing of forms throughout the composition of the book.[26] After the didactic introduction of 16:24–25, 16:26–17:24 offers a creation hymn which by a shift in its focus is gradually transformed into a didactic discourse on the theme of forgiveness. Sir. 17:25ff. offers in prophetic style an appeal to repent and to return to God. However, it is not in the recognition of the different form critical units, but rather in the literary subjugation of various *Gattungen* that one finds the greater insight into the type of literature that is Sirach. Here the introductory and concluding remarks are the most telling. In 16:23 the preceding skeptical questions are described as thoughts of "the man of folly." Vv. 24–25 present what follows antithetically as a wisdom lesson, "receive my wisdom," in a categorical manner determinative for the reader. Much like a title to a psalm, these two verses offer a definitive framework to help overcome the intrinsic ambiguity within parts of the following hymnic prose and lend emphasis to the more obvious moments of a wisdom interpretation in 17:6–10.

---

[26] Baumgartner, op. cit., p. 194f.

Chapter IV

Case Study Three: Bar. 3:9–4:4

Preface to the Baruch Case Studies

Although Baruch, in its entirety, purports to be from the pen of Jeremiah's secretary, most scholars, since the nineteenth century, agree that none of the literature likely derives from Baruch. Obvious literary differences between the various parts of the single work betray a complex redactional history. The middle section, 3:9–4:4, is distinguished in both its form and content from the material on either side. Only here is "the way of wisdom" the unifying theme. Similarly, this section is introduced by a summons to hear which resembles the address in Dt. 6:4 (cf. Dt. 4:1, 6 32:1; Is. 1:2, 10); yet, its goal is explicitly that the readers may "learn understanding" (γνῶναι φρόνησιν).

This last concern in the purpose clause of a summons to hear is typical only of Proverbs and sets the whole of what follows in the context of a wisdom lesson (cf. Prov. 1:2; 4:1). In what follows the author illustrates that a failure to adhere to the way of wisdom accounts for the fall of various biblical paragons of human power. These are presented as a series of negative examples drawn from Scripture and prove that God alone knows the way and has only made it known to Israel. As a conclusion, the way of wisdom is identified with "the book of the commandments," i.e., "the Torah" (4:1), even as in Sir. 24:23.

Admittedly, the date of Bar. 3:9–4:4 is widely debated though most scholars estimate its origin within the first two centuries B.C.E. The Greek text *(G)* supplies the best textual evidence of a possible Hebrew original.[1]

[1] The question of the original language of Baruch is still widely debated. I find the arguments for a Hebrew original slightly more convincing than those of the other position. This working hypothesis for our study of Bar. 3:9–4:4 is shared by J. J. Kneucker, R. R. Harwell, E. König, R. H. Charles, W. O. E. Oesterley, C. C. Torrey, A. Bentzen, R. H. Pfeiffer, O. Eissfeldt, and others. A number of scholars contend that only 1:1–3:8 was originally composed in Hebrew, e.g., O. F. Fritzsche, E. Schürer, H. L. Strack, H. St. J. Thackeray, and R. Mayer. A few scholars, including C. F. Keil and E. J. Goodspeed, conclude that the entire book was written in Greek. For bibliographical annotation to the

The Syriac *(S)* may also be dependent upon a Hebrew precedent but probably simply reflects an earlier Greek translation. Other language versions, likewise, provide helpful secondary witnesses to the early Greek copies of the text. The following study will make no systematic attempt to clarify these perplexing textual problems. Rather attention will be given to problems of textual duplicity only in so far as they impinge directly on the goals of this investigation.

This analysis, like the preceding ones on Sirach, neither assumes that every adaptation of OT represents an example of wisdom interpretation nor that such interpretation is the only significant type of OT usage in this literature. Its purpose is only to examine a few instances in which wisdom interpretations of OT narrative or prophetic traditions are likely to occur. While it is historically probable that Bar. 3:9–4:4 originates from a period close to that of Sirach, only exegetical evidence can confirm a use of wisdom analogous to that found in the earlier studies.

Bar. 3:9–4:4 Analysis

Bar. 3:26–28 [26]ἐκεῖ ἐγεννήθησαν οἱ γίγαντες οἱ ὀνομαστοὶ οἱ ἀπ' ἀρχῆς,
γενόμενοι εὐμεγέθεις, ἐπιστάμενοι πόλεμον.
[27]οὐ τούτους ἐξελέξατο ὁ θεὸς
οὐδὲ ὁδὸν ἐπιστήμης ἔδωκεν αὐτοῖς
[28]καὶ ἀπώλοντο παρὰ τὸ μὴ ἔχειν φρόνησιν
ἀπώλοντο διὰ τὴν ἀβουλίαν αὐτῶν.

[26]There the giants were born, the renown of old,
great in stature and skilled in war.
[27]These God did not choose,
neither did he give to them the way of understanding;
[28]So they perished because they had no wisdom,
they perished through their own foolishness.

The wording of v. 26a follows closely that of Gen. 6:4b:

Gen. 6:4b (LXX)[2]	Bar. 3:26a *(G)*
ἐκεῖνοι ἦσαν οἱ γίγαντες	ἐκεῖ ἐγεννήθησαν οἱ γίγαντες
οἱ ἀπ' αἰῶνος οἱ ἄνθρωποι οἱ ὀνομαστοί	οἱ ὀνομαστοὶ οἱ ἀπ' ἀρχῆς

above and some further discussion, see J. J. Battistone, *An Examination of the Literary and Theological Background of the Wisdom Passage in the Book of Baruch* (Ph.D. dissertation: Duke University, 1968), pp. 7–8, n. 1. The recent publications of critical Greek texts of Baruch greatly facilitate the present investigation. See J. Ziegler, *Ieremia. Baruch. Threni. Epistula Ieremiae*, Septuaginta: Vetus Testamentum Graecum, vol. 15 (Göttingen: Vandenhoeck & Ruprecht, 1957), pp. 450–67 and E. Tov, *The Book of Baruch* (Missoula, Montana: Scholars Press, 1975), pp. 28–31.

[2] The LXX here follows fundamentally the same text as the *MT*.

Despite close dependence upon Gen. 6:4b, a few significant changes have been introduced. The author has inserted a passive form of the verb ילד in order to retain full continuity of thought with this familiar passage in Gen. 6. Moreover, the use of a passive, rather than an active (cf. v. 4a), renders the agent of the verb indefinite and absolves the interpreter from the necessity of commenting on the peculiar details of the giants' birth in Gen. 6:1–4a. In this way, the writer cleverly restricts attention exclusively to the subject of the giants themselves.

The Hebrew behind *G* οἱ γίγαντες is probably, as *S* (ܓܢܒܪ̈ܐ) suggests, גברים (cf. Gen. 6:4b), although Kneucker's proposal of נפלים from Gen. 6:4a is plausible.[3] Certainly by the time of Baruch both the Gibborim and the Nephilim in Gen. 6:1–4 were being interpreted similarly. In the LXX both terms are translated the same, οἱ γίγαντες, "the giants."[4] This same assessment of them occurs in the abundance of early Jewish interpretations of Gen. 6.[5] The Midrash on Gen. 6 affirms this same point of view when it states that the "mighty men" were called by seven names: "Nephilim, Enim, Rephaim, Gibborim, Zamzumim, Anakim, and Awim" (*Bereshith Rabbah* 26:7). Consequently, all these ancient tribal groups came to be numbered among the descendants of the legendary giants of Gen. 6.

This early Jewish interpretive tradition, which identified the giants of Gen. 6 with the conquest giants as their descendants, provides an important clue to the origins of the phraseology of Bar. 3:26b. In Baruch the giants are described in a manner foreign to the Genesis narrative as "extremely tall." Yet, for two reasons this phrase must not be considered to be merely an imaginative attribution. First, in contrast to *G* "giants," the original Hebrew of גברים or נפלים does not lexically entail any implied characterization of unusual height. Second, and more significantly for this study, the source of this expression is found in the description of the con-

[3] J. J. Kneucker, *Das Buch Baruch: Geschichte und Kritik, Übersetzung und Erklärung auf Grund des wiederhergestellten hebräischen Urtextes* (Leipzig: F. A. Brockhaus, 1879), pp. 301, 356.

[4] There is a general tendency in the LXX to translate all such terms by γίγαντες. For example, in 1 Chron. 20:6, 8 רפה is translated Ραφα (v. 8) in one place and γίγαντες (v. 6) in the other. Similarly, in 2 Sam. 21:20b–22, v. 20b speaks of the descendants of Ραφα, but the LXX of v. 22 (*MT* להרפה בגת) is expansionistic and speaks of the children τῶν γιγάντων ἐν Γεθ τῷ Ραφα οἶκος. For Num. 13:33 the *MT* has הנפילים בני ענק מן הנפלים while the LXX simply has οἱ γίγαντες even as it offers υἱοὺς γιγάντων for Dt. 1:28b בני ענקים.

[5] E.g., 1 Enoch 7; Jub. 5; Sir. 16:7; Wis. 14:6; 3 Macc. 2:4; Testament of Reuben 5:6–7.

quest giants as אנשי מדות, "men of stature." This attribution applies specifically to those called the descendants of the Nephilim, "the sons of Anak who come from the Nephilim" (Num. 13:33–34; cf. Dt. 1:28), and the supposed descendant of the Rephaim (1 Sam. 21:20; 1 Chron. 20:6). The original Hebrew of the phrase in Bar. 3:26b may be precisely that employed in Scripture to describe these conquest giants;[6] however, even if the Hebrew is not an exact parallel, such close conceptual correspondence within this kind of controllable context is as convincing as lexical fidelity. Hence, the biblical material after Gen. 6 supplies the requisite biographical information for filling out the meager imagery of the giants given initially in Gen. 6.

Earlier in the analysis of Sirach this mode of synthesizing elements from related texts was noted and described as anthological. This same logic can similarly account for the remaining assertion in v. 26b that the giants are "skilled in war." In the same biblical accounts of the conquest, the spies, who were sent out by Moses, report that the Nephilim are not only of great stature, but that they are "stronger" than the Hebrew people, and have well fortified cities (Num. 13:28, 31; 14:12; Dt. 1:28). Likewise, the Philistines employed these giants as warriors in the front lines of battle (e.g., 2 Sam. 21:20). Consequently, the giants confronted in the conquest are portrayed as extraordinary creatures of extreme height and military expertise, which are exactly the same qualifications that Bar. 3:26 ascribes to them. Furthermore, this recollection of their fighting ability serves the purposes of Baruch in that it helps explain the "renown" of these giants according to Gen. 6. In addition, it enhances his interpretation because their fame is, like that of the international wisemen in v. 23, grounded in public recognition of a superior skill which, nevertheless, proves ineffective against the revealed "way of wisdom." For Baruch the giants are not pale symbols, but men of might, who stand out in the perception of the period as convincing images of magnificent and self-sufficient creatures in sacred Scripture.

The claim in v. 27 that God did not "choose" these giants is peculiar to Baruch and ingeniously linked by Reusch to Dt. 4:37:

> Because he loved your fathers and chose (ויבחר) their descendants after them and brought you out of Egypt with his own presence, by his great power, driving out before you nations greater and mightier than yourselves, to bring you in, to give you their land for an inheritance, as at this day.[7]

---

[6] Kneucker, op. cit., p. 302.

[7] F. H. Reusch, *Erklärung des Buches Baruch* (Freiburg: Herder'sche Verlagshandlung, 1853), p. 157.

These nations which God has driven out of the land are the nations of the conquest. The giants function as a part of this same tradition and substantiate the threat of nations "stronger and mightier than us" (גדול ועצום ממנו Num. 14:12; 13:28,31; cf. Dt. 1:28 גדול ורם ממנו). The fact that the election formula is a part of the biblical tradition in which the conquest giants appear lends some further support to Reusch's thesis. All the key elements in the Baruch passage come, therefore, from two coherent sets of related biblical traditions about giants, namely, from Gen. 6 and from the conquest traditions. The synthesis of these elements results in a terse, anthological portrait of the giants in Scripture.

So far as this analysis is concerned, it is readily apparent that the writer of Bar. 3:26 collected information from different narrative traditions in order to provide a single, comprehensive depiction. However, in the context of Bar. 3:9ff. the depiction of the giants is not an end in itself, but directs the attention of the reader to a particular problem in the text of Gen. 6:1–4, a dilemma which, to a lesser degree, concerns the giants of the conquered nations. Curiously, this question is not the obvious one, namely, how the primeval giants who are destroyed by the Flood can survive to produce children to be destroyed again in a later conquest of the Land. Rather, the enigma explored by Baruch is the question of why these remarkable creatures should suffer judgment at all. Gen. 6:1–4, except for lauding them as "men of renown," is silent on the subject. In the biblical accounts, the conquest giants are not given a moral or religious judgment except by implication of their role in battle.

One dimension of contemporary Jewish thought proposed that before the Flood the giants degenerated to extravagant wickedness and moral transgression. This situation is depicted in 1 Enoch 7:3–6 as follows:

> ... They bore great giants, whose height was three thousand ells: Who consumed all the acquisitions of men. And when men could no longer sustain them, the giants turned against them and devoured mankind. And they began to sin against birds, and beasts, and reptiles, and fish, and to devour one another's flesh and drink the blood. Then the earth laid accusation against the lawless ones.[8]

1 Enoch 10:7b–8 adds,

> ... all the secret things that the Watchers have disclosed and have taught their sons. And the whole earth has been corrupted through the works that were taught by Azazel: to him ascribe all sin.[9]

---

[8] R. H. Charles, "Book of Enoch" in *The Apocrypha and Pseudepigrapha of the Old Testament,* ed. by R. H. Charles, 2 vols. (Oxford: Clarendon Press, 1913), 2:192.

[9] Ibid., p. 194.

Jub. 5:1bff. imagines similarly,

> ... they bare unto them sons and they were giants. And lawlessness increased on the earth and all flesh corrupted its way, alike men and cattle and beasts and birds and everything that walks on the earth–all of them corrupted their ways and their orders, and they began to devour each other, and lawlessness increased on the earth and every imagination of the thoughts of all men [was] thus evil continually. And God looked upon the earth, and behold it was corrupt, and all flesh had corrupted its orders, and all that were upon the earth had wrought all manner of evil before his eyes. And he said that he would destroy man and all flesh upon the face of the earth which he had created. But Noah found grace in the eyes of the Lord. And against the angels ... And against their sons went forth a commandment that they should be smitten with the sword, and be removed from under heaven.[10]

In both accounts, which show signs of a common tradition, the noble giants soon discard the armor of righteousness to commit unholy acts, presented in the language of the Torah as transgression of the Law: "sin" (1 Enoch 7:5; 10:8; Jub. 5:12), "lawlessness" [1 Enoch 7:6; Jub. 5:2 (2 ×)]; "corruption" [1 Enoch 10:8; Jub. 5:2 (2 ×); 5:3 (2 ×); cf. Gen. 6:11, 12]; "evil" (Jub. 5:2, 3; cf. Gen. 6:5). The addition of the terms "sin" and "lawlessness" over those found in Gen. 6 serves to heighten the picture of giants participating in a corporate violation of divine law. In Jub. 5:12 the creatures after the Flood are even given a new "righteous" nature that they might not sin against their orders.

In contrast to 1 Enoch and Jubilees, Bar. 3:27–28 offers an alternative interpretation. Instead of using the vocabulary of "evil" and "corruption" found in Gen. 6, the writer evaluates the fall of the giants in an entirely different, though perhaps complementary, light. The giants, he reasons, were destroyed because they were not "elected" (v. 27a) by divine providence to be given "the way of understanding/wisdom" (v. 27b). Significantly, this last key phrase is drawn from the vocabulary of Proverbs and Job, and is not found in the Torah (cf. Prov. 21:16). It is synonymous with the epitomization of the teaching of the sage in Prov. 4:11, and now describes the one way by which the giants might have escaped destruction. Bar. 3:28 restates the consequences in the most unequivocal terms, "They perished because they had no wisdom; they perished through their own foolishness." Similarly, Sir. 16:7, Wis. 14:6, and 3 Macc. 2:4 explain the delinquency of the giants as a result of foolish pride, or false confidence in their own height and strength. None of these depends for its interpretation upon a reconstruction of the ante-deluvian events in Gen. 6:1–3. In this respect they contrast sharply with inter-

---

10 R.H. Charles, "The Book of Jubilees" in *The Apocrypha and Pseudepigrapha of the Old Testament*, op. cit., 2:20.

pretations like those of Enoch and Jubilees. That all these comments on the giants and the problem of their survival in Sirach, Wisdom of Solomon and Bar. 3:9ff. happen to take the same tact of interpretation indicates the possibility of a common tradition of such interpretation intrinsic to early Jewish, Wisdom–like literature.[11]

In sum, the author of Bar. 3:26–28 has given a synthetic description of the giants based on the characterizations in Gen. 6:4 and in the traditions concerning the conquest of Canaan. The manner of the destruction of the giants, whether by the primeval Flood or by the invasion by the Hebrew people into Palestine, is left intentionally ambiguous. Moreover, it is noteworthy that, although the portrait of the "mighty men" of antiquity is drawn entirely from the sacred narrative traditions, the final judgment of them is couched in language distinctive of the wisdom literature, particularly that of Proverbs. Since the movement of Baruch's assessment of the narrative is chiefly from the historical context peculiar to the Torah and the Former Prophets towards a sapiential evaluation in the language of the biblical wisdom literature, it is valid to speak here of a wisdom interpretation of biblically non-wisdom traditions.

Bar. 3:29–31 [29]τίς ἀνέβη εἰς τὸν οὐρανὸν καὶ ἔλαβεν αὐτὴν
καὶ κατεβίβασεν αὐτὴν ἐκ τῶν νεφελῶν;
[30]τίς διέβη πέραν τῆς θαλάσσης καὶ εὗρεν αὐτὴν
καὶ οἴσει αὐτὴν χρυσίου ἐκλεκτοῦ;
[31]οὐκ ἔστιν ὁ γινώσκων τὴν ὁδὸν αὐτῆς
οὐδὲ ὁ ἐνθυμούμενος τὴν τρίβον αὐτῆς

[29]Who has gone up into heaven and taken her,
and brought her down from the clouds?
[30]Who has gone over the sea, and found her
and acquired her with choice gold?
[31]There is neither one who knows her way,
nor one who comprehends her path.

These verses show substantial verbal dependence on Dt. 30:12–13:

Bar. 3:29–30	Dt. 30:12–13
τίς ἀνέβη	τίς ἀναβήσεται ἡμῖν
εἰς τὸν οὐρανὸν	εἰς τὸν οὐρανὸν
καὶ ἔλαβον αὐτὴν	καὶ λήμψεται αὐτὴ ἡμῖν
(καὶ κατεβίβασεν αὐτὴν ἐκ τῶν νεφελῶν)	(καὶ ἀκούσαντες αὐτὸ ποιήσομεν)
	οὐδὲ πέραν τῆς θαλάσσης
	ἐστιν λέγων

[11] That 3 Macc. 2:4 may belong with these would only illustrate that a sapientialized interpretation need not be confined to a wisdom-like book. Our interest has only been in the opposite consideration, whether wisdom-like literature may not show signs of a similar hermeneutical predisposition at certain points.

τὶς διέβη	τίς διαπεράσει ἡμῖν
πέραν τῆς θαλάσσης	εἰς τὸ πέραν τῆς θαλάσσης
καὶ εὗρεν αὐτὴν	καὶ λήμψεται ἡμῖν αὐτήν
(καὶ οἴσει αὐτὴν χρυσίου ἐκλεκτοῦ)	(καὶ ἀκουστὴν ἡμῖν ποιήσῃ αὐτήν καὶ ποιήσομεν)

Dt. 30:12–13 forms part of Moses' last address to Israel before she enters the land. In it he admonishes the elect people of God to obey the commandments of God. If they are obedient, they will prosper and have abundant life (Dt. 30:8ff.). Moses emphasizes that God's laws are not hidden, harsh, or obscure, but written plainly and simply in a public document, "the book of the Torah" (v. 10). The existence of a fixed accessible Torah means that "the word [דבר] is very near you" (v. 14). The statements in vv. 11–13 eloquently establish this point by stressing the accessibility of the Torah, and at the same time, in v. 5, by underlining the severe penalties for disobedience.

The rhetorical questions asked in Dt. 30:12 and v. 13 are examples of inquiry utterly ruled out by the literal accessibility of the Torah. These are for Israel the untenable questions which, after the provision of the Torah through Moses, can only be seen as illegitimate excuses not "to hear and to do it" (vv. 12b, 13b). The importance of this latter phrase is evident both by its repetition in these two verses and with some elaboration of the first verb, by the occurrence again in v. 14, which states conclusively: "the word is very near you; it is in your mouth and in your heart, so that you can do it." The centrality of this particular thematic phrase and its absence in Baruch is important to this study.

The changes made in the allusion to Dt. 30:12–13 show a discernible pattern that gives valuable insight into the author's adaptation of it. In Deuteronomy these two questions are both presented as specious ones. The writer of Baruch alters this by a very simple deletion. He removes the particularity of the questions for Israel by dropping in each case the prepositional phrases, "for us" (לנו). Now the questions are no longer incongruous self-reflections of Israel regarding a purported hiddenness of the Torah, but instead are universalized to serve as an incisive rhetoric that points up the limits of all purely human efforts to grasp "the way of wisdom" (cf. v. 31). Within the presupposition of Wisdom's original status in the heavenly domain of God, they satirize any pretense of grasping her by mere earthly genius and agility. By quite similar logic Prov. 30:3–4 portrays "wisdom" as synonymous with "the knowledge of the Holy One" and interjects, "Who has ascended to heaven and come down?"

In addition, the two central, purpose clauses from Dt. 30:12b and v. 13b, "to hear and to do it," have been judiciously dropped from each deuteronomic verse in favor of other biblical phraseology. In v. 29, the verbal expression, "and take it for us" (ויקחה לנו) has been slightly changed and given a new context by what follows. Not only has the לנו been omitted in keeping with the aforementioned deletion of לנו in the first part of the question, but in the place of the deuteronomic purpose clause the verbal idea of "taking it" has been supplemented by the sequential activity of "bringing" Wisdom "down from the clouds." The addition of "clouds" in parallel with "heavens" now conveys a frequent biblical metaphor for divine transcendence. For example, this metaphorical pair is used to express God's uniqueness (Dt. 33:26), the mystery of his way (Job 35:5), and his exaltation above humanity (Ps. 36:5; 57:11; 108:4). Consequently, the final verb "brought down" stands in sequential contingency with "taken it [her]." By formulaic biblical parallelism these actions have been cast as a vain human attempt to overcome divine transcendence, even as implied in Job 35:5. Moreover, this action of taking and bringing down may be reminiscent of the aforementioned Prov. 30:4.[12]

The second question in v. 30 likewise omits thé deuteronomic purpose clause. The main verb in this substituted phrase, οἴσει, "to obtain" or "to acquire," probably translates קנה (Qoh. 2:7, 8; Gen. 12:5; 31:1; Dt. 8:17, 18; Jer. 17:11) rather than סחר (Prov. 3:14) or עשה (cf. LXX of Hos. 9:16).[13] קנה in this case would be idiomatic to the injunction in Proverbs that one should "obtain wisdom."[14] Moreover, the deuteronomic verb "take her" has been changed to "find her" (εὗρεν αὐτήν, prob. מצאה). The resulting combination of verbs represents, as in v. 29, a sequence of activity which here entails first "going up," then "finding," and finally "acquiring" with money. Like the verb קנה in relation to wisdom, מצא is also idiomatic to the canonical wisdom literature (Prov. 1:28; 2:5; 4:22; 8:9; 12:17); and the combination of לקח and מצא occurs similarly in Prov. 8:9, 10 (cf. Sir. 30:39; 51:28). At exactly this point Job 28:15–19 shares same theme as here: "It [Wisdom] cannot be obtained for gold" (v. 15 a).

By contrast, in the Torah and the Prophets one never speaks of "finding" or "obtaining" the Torah, but rather as in Deuteronomy, of "hearing" and "doing it" (cf. Dt. 27:26; 28:58; 29:29; 31:12; 32:46). In addition, Kneucker builds a convincing case for a series of motifs in

[12] R. B. Y. Scott, *Proverbs*, The Anchor Bible (Garden City: Doubleday & Co., 1965), p. 176, n. 4. Scott observes similar expressions in Gilgamesh, Tablet III, and in the *Dialogue of Pessimism*, 83–84. Also, Rom. 10:6–8 introduces the same motif of "bringing down" in an obvious play on Dt. 30:12–13.

[13] Kneucker, op. cit., p. 304.

[14] Prov. 4:5, 7; 8:22; 16:16; 17:16; 23:23; cf. 1:5; 18:15; 19:8.

Bar. 3:30bff. reminiscent of the same series in Job 28:15–28: v.30b parallels Job 28:15–19; v.31, Job 28:20–22 (= 28:12–14); vv.32ff., Job 28:23ff.; v.36, Job 28:28.[15] Thus v.30b is the first crucial step toward a shorthand paraphrase dependent upon the sequence of motifs in Job 28:15–28. The deleted deuteronomic phrases, had they been retained, would have further distracted the reader from the controlling imagery throughout Bar. 3:9ff. of "finding" (εὑρίσκειν v. 15) or "finding out" (ἐξευρίσκειν, vv. 32a, 36) wisdom in order that she may be known. Hence, both by omitting certain words and phrases from Dt. 30:12–13 and by adding others, the writer conforms the older deuteronomic material, concerned only with Torah, to a new context, concerned explicitly with wisdom.

The denouement of the lesson is that only God has "found out" wisdom, and he has subsequently "given her" to Israel (v.36). This conscious motif throughout Bar. 3:9–4:4 of first locating wisdom and then making her accessible is the same as that now reflected in vv. 29–30. The change in the verb "take" from Dt. 30:13 to "find" in v.30a overtly adjusted the vocabulary to suit the familiar theme of a quest for wisdom consistent with that of Job 28. Here too, Baruch stresses the *knowledge* of the way of wisdom, rather than obedience to commandments intrinsic to it. Likewise, Israel's exile is not cast sharply as a transgression of commandments, but as a "forsaking" (ἐγκαταλείπειν, prob. עזב) of the way, an expression used in Scripture both in reference to the Mosaic Torah and to wisdom (cf. Ps. 89:30; Prov. 28:4; 4:2, 6). It must be remembered that Dt. 30 does not mention wisdom but refers only to the commandments of the Torah. However, by selective citation, alteration in vocabulary, and additional complementary statements, Dt. 30 is intentionally conformed in Bar. 3:29–30 to the special themes and vocabulary of the biblical wisdom literature. Just as Dt. 4, Dt. 30:12–13 now reads as a statement regarding the accessibility of wisdom to Israel.

Bar. 3:32–37a [32]ἀλλὰ ὁ εἰδὼς τὰ πάντα γινώσκει αὐτήν,
ἐξεῦρεν αὐτὴν τῇ συνέσει αὐτοῦ·
ὁ κατασκευάσας τὴν γῆν εἰς τὸν αἰῶνα χρόνον,
ἐνέπλησεν αὐτὴν κτηνῶν τετραπόδων
[33]ὁ ἀποστέλλων τὸ φῶς, καὶ πορεύεται,
ἐκάλεσεν αὐτό, καὶ ὑπήκουσεν αὐτῷ τρόμῳ
[34]οἱ δὲ ἀστέρες ἔλαμψαν ἐν ταῖς φυλακαῖς αὐτῶν καὶ εὐφράνθησαν,
[35]ἐκάλεσεν αὐτούς, καὶ εἶπον Πάρεσμεν,
ἔλαμψαν μετ' εὐφροσύνης τῷ ποιήσαντι αὐτούς.

---

[15] Kneucker, op. cit., p. 303.

[36]οὗτος ὁ θεὸς ἡμῆν,
οὐ λογισθήσεται ἕτερος πρὸς αὐτόν.
[37]ἐξεῦρε πᾶσαν ὁδὸν ἐπιστήμης καὶ ἔδωκεν αὐτὴν
Ιακωβ τῷ παιδὶ αὐτοῦ καὶ ἰσραηλ τῷ ἠγαπημένῳ ὑπ' αὐτοῦ.

[32]But he who knows [sees?] all things knows her.
He found her out in his understanding.
He established the earth for evermore;
he filled it with four-footed beasts.
[33]He that sent forth the light, and it went;
he called it, and it obeyed him with fear.
[34]The stars shined in their watches and rejoiced
[35]He called them and they said, "Here we are."
They shined with gladness to the one who made them.
[36]This is our God,
with whom none can be compared.
[37]He found out all the way of understanding and gave it to
Jacob his servant and to Israel whom he loved.

At this point the investigation will center on the vv. 32–35 which form a hymnic interlude in the middle of the author's prose presentation in Bar. 3:9–4:4. First of all, the surrounding narrative must be held in view before a study of scriptural dependence can properly be undertaken. In vv. 16–28 the author has painted a series of portraits of human power. Each is either generally or specifically drawn from Scripture. Together they exhibit the range of human pretense for success and survival: world rulership (v. 16), wealth (vv. 17–18), superior understanding (vv. 22–23), renown physical strength and military expertise (vv. 26–27). Having these qualities and lacking wisdom, the worldly heroes perish to be heard of no more. In vv. 27–28 the writer of Baruch summarizes and theologically pinpoints the reason for their downfall, "These God did not choose, neither did he give to them the way of understanding. They perished because they had no wisdom; they perished through their own foolishness."

Once this conclusion is set forth, vv. 29ff. pursue the same matter from a different angle. Questions are now raised about who has ever passed beyond the earthly horizons to grasp the salvific way of wisdom. The answer is graphically given in vv. 31–32, "no one except he who knows all things!" Although the implication that this statement refers to God is unambiguous, it is left unexpressed in order to achieve a literary effect at the end of the hymnic elaboration of divine power (vv. 32–35). Throughout the hymn the author carefully portrays this one who knows the way as the Creator and sustainer of the universe. This creation activity is delineated by a short series of terse, dynamic predications: he "established," "filled," "sent," "called." Only in v. 34 does the style shift away from the action of he who knows all things, in order to document the felicity of the stars under his divine command.

Finally, at the end of the prose, the obvious conclusion is given in a stark, dramatic statement, "This is our God" (v. 36a). This statement contrasts sharply with the previous narration both by its tight, pungent style and its cool, deductive stance over the earlier material. In this way the author of Baruch purposely sacrifices poetic imagination for the sake of spelling out his over-riding intention. He elaborates in vv. 36ff., "... with whom none can be compared. He found out all the way of understanding ..." Indeed, the transcendant power of God defies any comparison with the human heroes of power (cf. vv. 16–28). The express purpose of the prose in vv. 32–35 is to show, as stated in the verses which precede and follow it, that God alone is capable of "finding out" (ἐξευρίσκειν, vv. 32a and 37a) the way of understanding. Only the earlier hymnic interruption of vv. 24–25, between the examples of the famous wisemen and the giants, openly anticipated this same idea. In the end the author concludes that created humanity can know the way only if God gives it by his elective will and that he has so chosen Israel (v. 37b).

In the light of this concern with wisdom, Baruch's use of scriptural resources for the language in vv. 32–35 is significant. Kneucker has shown that starting with v. 30b the sequence of thought through v. 36 roughly corresponds to the same in Job 28:15–28.[16] In v. 32a the *G* phrase ὁ εἰδὼς τὰ πάντα reflects direct influence from Job 28:24 (cf. LXX εἰδὼς τὰ ἐν τῇ γῇ πάντα). The following verb phrase, ἐξεῦρεν αὐτὴν (prob. חקרה) has the same expression in Job 28:27 (*MT* חקרה, LXX ἐξηγήσατο) even as does the next, ὅ κατασκευάσας (*MT* הכינה, LXX ἑτοιμάσας).[17]

By contrast the subsequent clause, "he filled it with four-footed beasts" does not recall Job 28 at all. It shares only the temporal context of Job 28:25–27: "when he gave to the wind its weight ... when he made a decree for the rain ..." In a scholarly elaboration of the biblical text, the author has drawn upon the imagery of the Genesis narrative. In Genesis God commands the fish to "fill" the sea, and humanity to "fill" the earth (cf. Gen. 1:22, 28). The author of Bar. 3:32 applies this same motif by logical extension to the four-footed beasts (prob. בהמה, LXX τετράποδα, Gen. 1:24–26). As a result, an important shift has been made from the Job material. In Job 28:24–27 the theme is that of God at the dawn of creation looking about all of the heaven and earths and discerning the

[16] Kneucker, op. cit., p. 305.

[17] Ibid.

enigmatic way of wisdom. It is this way of wisdom that he then "declares," "establishes," and "searches out." By contrast, in Bar. 3:32b God "establishes" not the way of wisdom but the earth! In order to enhance this departure from the original text of Job 28:27, the author adds a specific allusion to the beasts from the Genesis account of the creation.

While the next lines continue to report divine activity on a cosmic scale like that of Job 28:25–26, the actual expressions in vv. 33a und 35a are taken from Job 38:35:

Bar. 3:33a, 35a *(G)*	Job 38:35
ὁ ἀποστέλλων τὸ φῶς	*MT* התשלח ברקים
	LXX ἀποστελεῖς δὲ κεραυνοὺς
καὶ πορεύεται	*MT* וילכו
	LXX καὶ πορεύσονται
ἐκάλεσεν αὐτούς	*MT* ויאמרו לך הננו
καὶ εἶπαν Πάρεσμεν	LXX ἐροῦσιν δέ σοι Τί ἐστιν

The related passages in Job 28 and 38 are concerned with the same theme of wisdom in the cosmos, a wisdom which only God is capable of knowing. The additional statements in vv. 33b, 34, and 35b cement the whole presentation together and do not refer at all to specific scriptural passages.

Another significant change from Job is Baruch's use of the word φῶς (ܢܘܗܪܐ) in v. 33 which suggests אור rather than ברקים as in Job 38:35a.[18] This alteration in language once again brings the expressions into greater harmony with the Genesis traditions. The element "light" may now be taken as reminiscent of the creation אור (cf. Gen. 1:3–4). The following plural verb which in Job 38:35b had ברקים for its subject now corresponds to the response of the "stars" in Bar. 3:34–35.

In sum, the author in Bar. 3:32–35 has excerpted material from Job 28 and 38 as well as from the resources of his own imagination to characterize divine power. The Job passages share with Baruch the same contextual concern with a proof that God alone can find and know wisdom. The allusions to the appearance of four-footed creatures on the earth and the primordial "light" are important because Job does not show the same direct dependence upon the details of the narrative creation tradition in Genesis. Thus, the Job material which speaks of God's activity at the beginning of time has been interpreted in correspondence with the biblical creation narratives. To accomplish this, the writer adapts a part of the Genesis tradition to the imagery already present in Job. Hence, the Genesis narratives are used as a source of information to describe God the Creator,

---

[18] In the LXX φῶς never translates ברקים or ברק.

who alone reveals the way of wisdom to Israel. They have, by such an accommodation, been given a wisdom interpretation, for God's actions at creation are now viewed as evidence for his comprehension of universal wisdom.

Bar. 3:37(36)–4:1 [19] [37]ἐξεῦρε πᾶσαν ὁδὸν ἐπιστήμης καὶ ἔδωκεν αὐτὴν Ιακωβ
τῷ παιδὶ αὐτοῦ καὶ Ισραηλ τῷ ἠγαπημένῳ ὑπ' αὐτοῦ
4 [1]Αὕτη ἡ βίβλος τῶν προσταγμάτων τοῦ θεοῦ
καὶ ὁ νόμος ὁ ὑπάρχων εἰς τὸν αἰῶνα
πάντες οἱ κρατοῦντες αὐτῆς εἰς ζωήν,
οἱ δὲ καταλείποντες αὐτὴν ἀποθανοῦνται.

[37]He found out all the way of understanding / wisdom,
and he gave it to Jacob his servant and to Israel his beloved.
4 [1]This is the book of the commandments of God
and the law which endures forever.
Everyone who obtains her [is appointed] unto life,
but whoever forsakes her is destined to die.

Much as in Sir. 24:8b, God assigns a place for the way of wisdom "unto Jacob ... to Israel." Within Bar. 3:9ff. this activity answers the question posed in v. 15, "Who has found her place?" God himself has found and, in an act of divine election, "given" her to Israel rather than to other famous nations and peoples (cf. v. 27). The appositions τῷ παιδὶ αὐτοῦ, "his servant," and τῷ ἠγαπημένῳ ὑπ' αὐτοῦ, "his beloved," occur frequently in Scripture, as here, in association with a singular or combined reference to the tribal patriarchs, Jacob and Israel. Likewise, this pair of names is commonly part of the election motif for Israel.[20] While there is substantial thematic agreement with passages like Dt. 33:10, Ps. 78:5 and Ps. 147:19, no case for direct dependence upon any particular instance can be established (cf. Sir. 24:8–11; 1:13).

However, both in the selection of the names of the patriarchs and in the choice of appositions, the writer has followed a familiar biblical formulation. In a typological application the author assesses Israel's election in terms of wisdom and seals its authority in the language of Scripture. In this way he is freed from the obligation of detailed attention to the finite linguistic context of any single sacred passage and succeeds in evaluating a general biblical teaching.

---

[19] The intervening verse (v. 38), though well attested in Greek texts, is generally suspected by commentators to be a later Christian gloss. The Greek and Latin Fathers cite it frequently in support of the Logos doctrine of Christ. For our purposes, it is not essential to the analysis and has, therefore, been dropped.

[20] Kneucker, op. cit., pp. 309–10.

It must now be asked whether this generalized formulation shows signs of wisdom interpretation. This kind of formulation, in fact, never occurs in biblical wisdom literature like Proverbs, Qoheleth, or even Job. It is composed rather of language scattered throughout the Torah, Prophets, and Psalms. In its fullest expression, the OT election motif signifies Israel as the recipient of either the Torah or the Promised Land. By contrast Baruch offers ὁδόν ἐπιστήμης, "the way of understanding," as the reward of Israel's election. As previously noted, Baruch's central theme, "the way of wisdom," is distinctive of wisdom literature, particularly of Proverbs. Indeed, this phrase is the summation of wisdom teaching (Prov. 4:11).[21]

The articulation, therefore, of Israel's election in Bar. 3:37 is typical of that found in the so-called non-wisdom books, though it is interpreted here as a background for the gift of "the way of wisdom," a phrase indicative of the sage's teaching in sacred wisdom tradition. Since the basic formulation of Scripture derives originally from the narrative traditions and concerns the giving of Torah or the Land to Israel, its unique interpretation as the moment in which wisdom is given to Israel can be described as a wisdom reading of an earlier non-wisdom motif within the context of the sacred canon.

Finally, 4:1 deserves careful consideration for two reasons. First, it is similar in theme and syntax to the Greek of Sir. 24:23:

Sir. 24:23	Bar. 4:1
Ταῦτα πάντα βίβλος διαθήκης θεοῦ ὑψίστου	Αὕτη ἡ βίβλος τῶν προσταγμάτων τοῦ θεοῦ
νόμον ὅν ἐνετείλατο ἡμῖν Μωυσῆς	καὶ ὁ νόμος ὁ ὑπάρχων εἰς τὸν αἰῶνα
(κληρονομίαν συναγωγαῖς Ιακωβ)	(πάντες οἱ κρατοῦντες αὐτῆς εἰς ζωήν οἱ δὲ καταλέιποντες αὐτὴν ἀποθανοῦνται)

Second, like Sir. 24:23, Bar. 4:1 makes explicit what is implicit in the preceding prose. The demonstrative pronoun αὕτη refers to the central theme of the prose regarded as a whole, namely, "the way of wisdom."[22]

[21] The exact phraseology varies somewhat with the *nomen rectum*, although the meaning remains essentially the same. For example, in Bar. 3:9–4:4 the *G* occurrences may have for the *nomen rectum* either σοφία (v. 23) or ἐπιστήμη (vv. 20, 27, 37; cf. v. 31), while the *MT* instances in Proverbs have חכמה (4:11, LXX σοφία); בינה (9:6, LXX φρόνησιν); or שכל (21:16, LXX δικαιοσύνης). The noun ἐπιστήμης does not occur in the LXX of Proverbs. Elsewhere it can translate forms of בינה or תבונה, דעת, חכמה, or שכל.

[22] The suggestion of R. R. Harwell, *The Principal Versions of Baruch* (New Haven: Yale University Press, 1915), p. 16, that αὕτη should be αὐτη overlooks the common feature of an indefinite near demonstrative pronoun as a summarizing particle both here and in Sir. 24:23. Kneucker, op. cit., p. 313, regards the *G* ἡ βίβλος τῶν προσταγμάτων of

Up to this point, language or narratives indicative of the Torah have been interpreted successfully in the idiom of wisdom. Bar. 4:1 only confirms this interpretation and the expressed implication that the Torah provides the only sufficient source of lifegiving wisdom (4:1b).

An older connection between the goals of Torah and the wisdom literature is fully exploited by the author. Traditionally, wisdom literature offered "life" (e.g., Prov. 3:18; 4:13, 22, 23; 13:14; 16:22), even "the way of life" (e.g., 2:19; 5:6; 6:23; 10:17; 15:24), in a manner fully compatible with the same promise, based on obedience to the Torah (e.g., compare Dt. 30:15 with Prov. 3:1ff.). This symbiosis of Torah and wisdom, apparent already in Proverbs, has in the time of Sirach and Baruch led to a relatively more aggressive reunion of the different parts of the canon. One part of the literature offers a theological vitality to clarify another. It is significant that this mode of interpretation involves at least the recognition of the Torah as a distinct canonical collection which now invites a wisdom interpretation.

Bar. 4:1 as a bad translation of ספר התורה. If his hypothesis is correct, then it may have been conditioned by the desire of the translator to avoid ὁ νόμος in order that the appositive phrase could begin with it, so as to mimic the statement of Sir. 24:23. However, against his hypothesis is the occurrence in Bar. 3:9 of ἐντολαὶ ζωῆς which is a *hapax legomena* instead of the more familiar νόμος ζωῆς (= תורת חיים, cf. Sir. 45:5). The novelty there as well as here in Bar. 4:1 may well be due to the creativity of the author, rather than a fluke of the translator.

Chapter V

An Assessment of the Case Studies

The case studies undertaken have confirmed the existence of recurring wisdom interpretations of fixed OT traditions in the post-exilic period. Fortunately, because of the advanced stage of OT canonization at the time of Ben Sira and the writer of Bar. 3:9–4:4, it is possible for the modern scholar to achieve relatively objective literary control in describing such a phenomenon. By recalling the original OT context of these references to fixed narrative and prophetic traditions, the nature of interpretation can frequently be measured as a function of the literary changes in the post-exilic re-application of the biblical material. Whether this re-application involved alteration in wording or the re-contextualizing of familiar OT traditions, the case studies provide ample evidence of a desire to prove exegetically that the Torah and the prophetic writings inform and anticipate the concerns of the biblical wisdom traditions.

A Review of the Technical Evidence

In order to illustrate the type of evidence found in the case studies, a more systematic presentation of specific features within the analysis is required. Naturally, this condensation will not cover all of the more complex instances within the studies, but, without offering a substitute to the studies themselves, will provide a representative sample of their content. In the light of the method employed in conducting the previous research, a brief survey of the various means by which these early Jewish writers made reference to biblical texts and traditions will precede the listing of conspicuous types of redactional alterations in their actual use of OT.

Means of Referring to Specific OT Texts or Traditions

1. Full citation of a single biblical text (at least several words in length) without alteration in wording.

Sir. 24:23 cites Dt. 33:4 in a form which appears to be a *verbatim* rendering of the Hebrew text. Significantly, no citation formula distinguishes the citation from the rest of the prose.

2. Partial citation of a single biblical text with alterations in wording, including additions and omissions.

Sir. 24:15a excerpts the ingredients of perfumed anointing oil from the recipe of Ex. 30:23, and Sir. 24:15b cites those required for the making of incense from Ex. 30:34. Only the numerical proportions for mixing these components have been deleted. Then again, Bar. 3:29–30 quotes directly from parts of Dt. 30:12–13, with careful omission of prepositional phrases, with alterations in verbs and insertion of additional OT material reminiscent of Job 28.

3. The use of key words or phrases as *Stichwort* connections to specific texts or traditions.

The "pillar of cloud" in Sir. 24:4b recalls the wilderness traditions in the Torah; "rest" and "inheritance," as paired terms of the divine "command" to occupy the Land, are distinctive of the respective deuteronomic traditions (cf. Dt. 12); the observation in Bar. 3:32b that God "fills" the earth with "four-footed beasts" links the interpretation unequivocally with the creation narrative of Gen. 1.

4. Allusions to specific texts or traditions.

While Sir. 16:26a, "when God created his works," is reminiscent of Gen. 1:1 and 2:4b, the Sir. 16:26b language of assigning places to the various parts of creation recalls the God's dividing (הבדיל בין) the primordial elements in Gen. 1. The elaborate description of various flora in Sir. 24:13–14, 16–17 alludes to the biblical tradition of Edenic exaltation connected with the motif of entrance into the Promised Land (cf. Dt. 32:13–14 and Ezek. 40–48). The general sequence of motifs in Sir. 24:3–22 clearly reflects the traditional pattern found in the Torah of exodus, wandering, desire for rest and inheritance, divine appointment, and assignment of the sacred tent to Zion.

5. Paraphrase of specific texts or traditions.

Job 28:15–28 is selectively paraphrased in Bar. 3:30a; Job 28:15–19 parallels v. 30b; Job 28:20–22 (28:12–14) v. 31; Job 28:23ff.

vv. 32ff.; and Job 28:28 v. 36. Other less extensive examples occur throughout the case studies.

6. Imaginative choice of metaphors that allow for a variety of free associations with biblical imagery.

Sir. 24:13–14, 16–17 uses the metaphor of Wisdom flourishing in Zion like various plants or trees. Though these expressions are not direct citations, they conform stylistically and by their choice of flora to the same kinds of metaphors for the righteous in the Prophets. In addition, the extensive nature of this metaphor gives the impression of a garden which, in the light of the later naming of Edenic rivers in 24:25–29 and the reference to "the first man," alludes to the garden of Eden. However, in the context of Wisdom's Song it is also part of an appeal by Wisdom to come and partake of the fruit of the garden, and it recalls the similar imagery for Wisdom in Proverbs and for the lover in Song of Songs. The garden imagery has still another function in that it is reminiscent of the historical pattern of Wisdom, even as Israel, in pursuit of a home in the Promised Land. There the vegetation flourishes as the result of Wisdom's "taking root" (v. 12) in "the portion of the Lord," namely, in Israel her "inheritance." Wisdom, therefore, as Israel, is "planted" in the land (2 Sam. 7:10; Amos 9:15), and these flora metaphors confirm and fill out this idea by logical extension. In the final analysis, the writer's imagination is the decisive factor in recognizing and in exploiting the multi-sidedness of a biblical metaphor.

More significant insight into the use of OT appears after consideration of the ways in which the writers change the original functions of specific texts and traditions. By concentrating on the way citations and allusions are taken from their original context and edited into another, the writer's most fundamental assumptions about Scripture can be explored. Although this investigation is primarily concerned with the nature of wisdom interpretation, the following list of redactional alterations of biblical contexts is not limited to such examples. As will become apparent, a wisdom interpretation is not bound to a specific set of techniques, but uses a common fund of technical expertise in a specialized manner. Once again, the list is not exhaustive and the examples are selected, in many instances from the previous list of means for referring to the OT. This correspondence, despite some minor repetition, provides the best impression of how the interpretation of OT is taking place.

Redactional Means of Interpreting
Specific OT Texts or Traditions
with Alterations of Their
Original Contexts

1. The fusing together of different texts or traditions by partial citation, paraphrase, key words or allusions.

a. By means of partial citation or paraphrase. Sir. 24:3b fuses Gen. 1:2 and Gen. 2:4 into a single statement. It is accomplished by some literary dependence on each verse and by the choice of an object noun generic enough to include the respective subjects. Likewise, Sir. 16:24ff. uses expressions for an account of creation in temporal sequence, based on a combined interpretation of Gen. 1 and 2. To this material is added thematically related prose from the Psalms and the prophetic literature. Bar. 3:32–35 entails a selectivity of phrases from Job 28:24, 27 and Job 38:35 (cf. vv. 32a, 33a, 35a). The subtle alteration in wording suggests an intentional conflation of OT texts. "Lightnings" become "light" in Bar. 3:33a, which recalls creation in Gen. 1:3ff. even as does the added statement in Bar. 3:22b that God "filled" the earth with "four-footed beasts" (cf. Gen. 1:24–26). This combination of phraseology extracted from Genesis and Job serves the writer's singular description of God as the cosmic Creator, who alone knows the way of wisdom. Similarly, examples of "anthological style" (cf. discussion below) illustrate a programmatic attempt to gather thematically related information throughout parts of Scripture. This propensity for literal citation or paraphrase illustrates the writer's preference for the sacred text over free imagination or the blurring of text with later tradition.

b. By means of key words. Sir. 24:4b offers, "my throne was in the pillar of cloud," a combination of familiar motifs not found together originally in Scripture. The term "throne" occurs only in books outside the Torah as a theophanic symbol within the temple, associated with clouds of smoke and prophetic visions. Conversely, "the pillar of cloud" belongs to the wilderness traditions in the Torah and to the later wilderness summaries (e.g., Neh. 9:9–21 and Ps. 98:6–7). By placing these terms in a close relationship to one another, the writer links the two traditions together in a common witness to Wisdom. Likewise, the identification of Wisdom with the book of the covenant, or the Torah, in Sir. 24:23 demonstrates an implied fusion of different texts. Dt. 4 and 30, in their original settings, are related by the common theme of the "nearness" of the Torah. Only chaps. 4 and 32 associate the Torah with *wisdom*, and only chap. 30 speaks of the "nearness" of the Torah in terms of a *book*.

By citing Dt. 33:4, the writer of Sir. 24:23 keeps this equation in the context of Deuteronomy and the Law of Moses. Only the unusual combination of key words signals the implicit synthesis of the original biblical texts.

c. By a free combination of paraphrase, allusion, and key words. In the case studies one frequently finds a calculated set of statements that appear to summarize, in short form, the essence of several traditions taken together. For example, Sir. 24:8 has the unusual title, "Creator of all things," which is reminiscent of Jer. 10:16 (= 51:19); yet, in a manner foreign to Jeremiah, it serves to introduce God, who gives the *command* to find *rest* and *inheritance* in Zion (cf. Dt. 12). Moreover, the continuation of this theme in the movement of the sacred tent to Zion, in Sir. 24:10–11, as well as the command to "take root," reflects a learned synthesis of related OT passages, such as Nathan's oracle and Ps. 78 and 132. Sir. 17:11–14 illustrates the arranging of individual phrases from different texts which relate the giving of the Law at Sinai. For example, the covenant is called the "Law of life" (cf. Dt. 33:15, 19) which is "set before them (cf. Dt. 4:44). As at Sinai too, the people "beheld his glorious majesty" (cf. Ex. 24:16–17) and "heard his glorious voice" (cf. Ex. 19: 19, 20; Dt. 4:12; 5:4; 30:2, 10, 20). Although this language shows fidelity to the very words of the sacred tradition, the entire epitomization far exceeds the witness of a single text or tradition and encompasses rather the larger context of the related Scripture taken as a whole.

2. The anthological style as one of collecting and reemploying words and phrases gleaned from a variety of different texts and presumed to be linked by a common theme or subject matter.

Sir. 24:5–6 articulates the theme of God (now Wisdom) "walking" or "treading" on the various cosmic horizons, and forms a mosaic of the various passages in the book of Job which share this same concern (cf. Job 9:8; 22:14; 38:16). Furthermore, a conflation of these Job passages supplies a reference to the four corners of the universe, and accounts for Sirach's claim that Wisdom (like God) walks "alone" (see Job 9:8). Similarly, the attributes of created humanity are listed in Sir. 17:1–4, just as they are found in the opening chapters of Genesis [cf. Gen. 2:7; 3:19; 6:3(?); 1:26b, 28b; 3:21(?); 1:26a, 27a (see 9:6b); 9:2]. Yet, distinctions between characteristics before and after the Fall are not observed. While the elements of the Sirach anthology are dictated by a selective recollection of the sacred text, the arrangement is left to the author's imagination. Thus, the last element, "good and evil" (v. 7b) is the high point, and introduces an expanded eulogy on humanity's power of perception. This same method of interpretation is applied to the giants in Bar. 3:26–27a. Each descriptive adjective is drawn either from the antediluvian account of Gen. 6:1–4 or from the depiction of the warrior giants, who were defeated during Israel's conquest of the Land.

3. Selective alterations in the citation of a text that changes its original meaning.

Bar. 3:29–30 provides the best example. Here, although Dt. 30:12–13 is quoted directly, the writer carefully omits certain prepositional phrases and verbs. In their place, additional material, reminiscent of Job 28, has been inserted to complete each thought. The result is a reworking of Dt. 30:12–13, which alters it from a statement concerning the heavenly origin of the Torah to a similar statement regarding the way of Wisdom. In a less dramatic form, Sir. 24:15 excerpts all of the named ingredients for perfumed anointing oil from Ex. 30:23, even as Sir. 24:15b does those for incense from Ex. 30:34. Although each list of elements in Sir. 24:15 retains its original relation to "perfumed scent" and "incense," all the quantitative instructions for mixing the ingredients have been deleted. Consequently, these lists provide, in the context of Sir. 24, an enumeration of spices to complement the naming of flora in vv. 13–14, 16–18. This combination of flora and spices recalls the familiar biblical portrait of a paradisaical garden, from which a woman beckons her lovers. In this instance, the woman is Wisdom, whose appeals to her students are similar to those found in the Wisdom Songs of Proverbs.

4. Texts or traditions pertaining to one agent or subject now identified as pertaining to another.

a. Biblical language descriptive of God and his activity is appropriated to describe Wisdom. Examples of this use of biblical texts occur most frequently in Sir. 24. Even as in the OT God "dwells" "on high" or "in the heights," so Wisdom in Sir. 24 "encamps" or "dwells" "in the high places" (v. 4a). In addition, Wisdom is assigned a throne, like that of God (v. 4b), and all the language in Job about God walking on the cosmic horizons is taken up anthologically and attributed to her (vv. 5–6). Indeed, Wisdom, like God, is depicted as enduring forever (v. 9b, cf. Ps. 90:2; 103:17).

b. Biblical symbols of divine presence within Israel are identified with Wisdom. On two occasions in Sir. 24, these identifications are linked by the formal pronouncement that Wisdom is "as" (ὡς, prob. כ) a particular OT object or activity. Thus, she is identified as the "misty cloud" (ὁμίχλη, prob. ערפל) in v. 3 b, and as the smoke of incense in the tabernacle in v. 15. She is linked also with the divine throne and the pillar of cloud in v. 4. As with her identification with the ministry and the cult objects of that priestly service, these associations are apparently predicated on a similar alignment of Wisdom with the symbolism of divine participation in the life of ancient Israel.

c. Various biblical traditions of priesthood are identified with Wisdom. Wisdom "ministers in the holy tabernacle" and is "established," like the sacred sanctuary, "in Zion" (Sir. 24:10). Sir. 24:11 may signify that she exercises *priestly* "authority" from Jerusalem. In v. 12 she obtains an inheritance like that of the priests and Levites "in the Lord's portion" (cf. Sir. 45:22; 17:17). In v. 15 she is identified with the ingredients of the holy anointing oil and the "smoke of incense" used in the worship ceremonies of the tabernacle. Finally, in Sir. 24:13–14, 16–17, Wisdom is assigned floral metaphors of growth similar to those found in Ben Sira's later description of Aaron and Simeon, the high priests (see Sir. 45:6–22; 50:5).

d. By means of key words, certain historical traditions regarding Israel are re-applied to describe the history of Wisdom. In Sir. 24 the entire scenario of Israel's exodus, wandering and appointment to Zion is found applied to Wisdom. As in Israel's flight from Egypt, she, too, "goes forth from" a place, "encamps," then "causes her tent to rest," while "circling" and "walking" about in "search" of "rest" and "an inheritance," which God eventually "commands" for her "in Zion." Likewise, the land she enters is described as a paradise (cf. Dt. 8:7–10), which the writer of Sir. 24 embellishes with key expressions from the Genesis portrait of Eden. The selection of key words is impressive for its accumulation of detail, its close adherence to a sequential pattern, and its direct dependence upon the very language of the respective OT texts. It is noteworthy that, with the exception of naming the city of Zion, the pattern of key words and phrases is restricted to the limits of the same story in the canonical Torah. Hence, there is no interest in the minutiae of the conquest or the later period of monarchy.

e. The Torah is identified with Wisdom or the way of wisdom. The literary canonical aspect of this identification is suggested by the specification of "the Torah" in Sir. 24:23 as "the book of the covenant" and in Bar. 4:1 as "the book of the commandments." Each of these conclusions makes explicit a relationship that is assumed in the particular discourses which it brings to a close. Each attests to the function of the

Torah as a literary resource for sapiential reflection. Hence, it is not surprising that some OT statements originally indicative only of the Torah are re-applied to describe wisdom. For example, see the use of Dt. 30:12–13 in Bar. 3:29–30.

5. The synchronic juxtaposition of diachronically related narrative texts or traditions.

By a selective use of key words, phrases and allusions to the Genesis narratives, Sir. 16:24–17:4 provides, in general, a sequential synopsis of creation. The last four verses consist of an anthological sketch of created humanity, followed by short excursus on the knowledge of good and evil in 17:6–10. Without any temporal transition, 17:11–14 appends a summary of God's giving the Law as at Sinai. As shown in the case study, the language is borrowed directly from the accounts of the Sinai event in Exodus and Deuteronomy. There is perhaps a thematic link between the presentation on creation and that on the giving of the Law in that the senses (tongue, eyes, ears, heart), which are instrumental in surveying the works of creation in 17:10, are similarly employed in the recognition of the Sinai theophany (see vv. 12–13). In any case, the synchronic juxtaposition of tradition avoids blurring either biblical tradition, although the new relationship itself implies some essential link between them. As in Sir. 24 the connection seems clearly to be that wisdom, which is given to humanity at creation, is likewise made the possession of Israel through the giving of the Torah at Sinai (see pp. 82–83).

6. A key word or phrase may recall a distinct biblical context or tradition and at the same time allow the interpreter to elaborate that context using expressions indicative of some other scriptural tradition or outside source.

In Sir. 17:7b the key phrase "good and evil" is the only link within 17:6–10 to the Genesis context of humanity's knowledge in the garden. Nevertheless, Ben Sira fills out this context with an imaginative eulogy on the various senses that can perceive the works of God and praise him. By this means, the connotation of the phrase, "good and evil," has been shifted from an usurpation of divine knowledge to an honorable feature of the human intellectual capacity for investigation the cosmic orders. This change involves an oblique interpretation of the phrase to signify how one attains knowledge and wisdom through perceptive observation of the universe.

The phrase "the Creator of all things" in Sir. 24:8 perhaps recalls Jer. 10:16 (= 51:15) of the Sirach passage. If so, the reference in the

Jeremiah passages to "Israel ... the tribe of his inheritance" is picked up again in Sir. 24:8b, however, it is there elaborated in terms of the wilderness traditions and the command that Wisdom "make [her] dwelling in Jacob and receive [her] inheritance in Israel."

7. Mimesis of a familiar type of biblical literature which has been, nevertheless, altered for peculiar purposes of its later interpretation.

An obvious example is the entire structure of Sir. 24:1–22. Scholars have often noted the many similarities, including some direct dependence, between Sir. 24:1–22 and the Wisdom Songs in Proverbs.[1] The many parallels in style and content suggest that the writer modeled his composition directly after that of its biblical counterparts. Since the Proverbs Wisdom Songs provided the principal examples which the writer of Sir. 24:1–22 followed, it is significant to observe how the writer incorporated other material from the narrative and prophetic traditions into this Song. For instance, the close relation between Wisdom and creation originally found in Prov. 8, is consequently exceeded in Sir. 24, by a detailed account of Wisdom's origin and activity in terms taken directly from Israel's historical traditions. Likewise, Sir. 16:24ff. and Bar. 3:9ff. each begin with a summons to hear that is reflective of the same type of didactic introduction found in Proverbs (cf. Prov. 4:1f. and 4:10f.), although the literature that follows draws on narrative traditions unparalleled in Proverbs.

8. The extension of familiar biblical themes, metaphors, or motifs to other related subjects.

The naming of the Pison and Gihon in Sir. 24:25–29 adds by extension a specific recollection of Eden in the portrait of Palestine as a land of paradise. The identification of wisdom in the first Eden with the "knowledge of good and evil" (Sir. 17:6–10) makes logical this use of other specific Genesis language in describing the land of Israel, in which the Torah resides as wisdom. Likewise, the metaphors in Sir. 24:13–14, 16–18 of tree-like growth which are familiar from the depiction of the righteous in the prophetic literature, apply in Sir. 24 to those who attain wisdom.

Before concentrating on unique factors in those examples which specifically demonstrate wisdom interpretations, it is appropriate, first of all, to describe factors which these examples have in common. Rather than sketching an arbitrary or encyclopedic portrait, this description will

[1] See Smend, op. cit., pp. 214–16 and Marböck, op. cit., pp. 55–6.

focus on the canonical function of the OT literature exploited by these authors. The advantage of starting with the canonical issue is that the definition of wisdom interpretation given at the outset of this investigation is cast in those terms. Also, by concentrating on redactional alterations in the post-exilic re-application of OT text, it is possible to attain some general insights into the canonical function of the sacred text before raising the question of wisdom interpretations.

The Factor of Canon in These Interpretations

As evident in the book of Sirach, the Torah is a canonical collection and the prophetic literature is distinct from it. The reference in Sir. 49:10 to The Twelve actually demonstrates a closed minor collection within the prophetic literature, although the exact nature of a larger collection of the Prophets can be debated. Admittedly, there is no unequivocal evidence of a distinct collection of canonical wisdom books or of a precise wisdom division within the canon of Ben Sira. However, this judgment does not preclude the function of Proverbs, Qoheleth and Job as canonical books, regardless of the lack of any definitive canonical order. This estimate of Ben Sira's canon is confirmed by Leiman's recent study, despite guestions raised by his uncritical use of tradition history.[2]

Sir. 24:23 and Bar. 4:1 conform to this assessment of the canonical situation, for each speaks of the Torah as a "book" while Wisdom or the way of wisdom remains an extra-literary category. In neither case, nor in the balance of Sirach, is the book of the Torah explicitly described as the five books of Moses. That this is indeed the assumption can, nevertheless, be argued from the selectivity in use of the historical motifs in Sir. 24. Moreover, it is likely that by the time The Twelve was recognized as a canonical collection, the Torah enjoyed a similar status. Furthermore, the admonition to sages in Sir. 39:1 notes "the Torah of the Most High" in a manner that suggests a distinct literary canonical entity. Consequently, there is general agreement among scholars that the references in both Sirach and Baruch are undoubtedly to the five-book Torah familiar in later periods.

In the light of this evidence, it is perhaps helpful to think, in the language of I.L. Seeligmann, of "canon consciousness" as a factor in biblical interpretation.[3] By this term it is not meant that Scripture is a

---

[2] See pp. 14–16, and Leiman, op. cit., pp. 28–31.

[3] I.L. Seeligmann, "Voraussetzungen der Midrashexegese," *SVT*, 1 (1953): 152.

closed set of sacred books with a rigid set of divisions. Rather, as Leiman has suggested, the concept of a canonical literature, even if its limits are not defined absolutely, demands the use of a given sacred literature as a normative guide to faith and practice.[4] Canonical literature, therefore, exercises a special function in religious discourse and is distinguished intuitively by the interpreter from other more general and less authoritative resources.

Under the aegis of "canon consciousness," Seeligmann attempts to sort out aspects of the inner logic, which define the relationship of the interpreter to the canonical text, in order to shed light on the pre-critical exegetical activity itself. Similarly, based on the case studies in Sirach and Baruch, this writer will consider three aspects of the canonical function. Although a full history of canon consciousness as a factor in pre-critical exegesis would be ideal, the limits of the evidence in these studies make such a goal impossible. For the purposes of this investigation it is sufficient to demonstrate the general significance of canon for understanding the use of OT in these case studies. Finally, this discussion will highlight the circumstances from which wisdom interpretation arise.

The Text as the Medium of Interpretation

The authors of the case studies are obviously conscious of some fixed texts before them, which they interpret periodically in the course of their own compositions. Unlike the later midrash, the biblical text is not set apart from the commentary upon it. Instead, text and interpretation are joined together. The sacred text can, therefore, retain its identity only by its intrinsic familiarity to the readers. In this sense, the biblical texts or traditions involved can be "marked" in various degrees within the interpretation by the use of language particularly distinctive of a familiar scriptural passage, by the construction of a recognizable series of related expressions, by lengthy quotation, and by other such devices. Since the author's imagination plays a constitutive role in deciding the structure and theme of the composition, only the contrived context and choice of language informs the reader that a given text or tradition is being interpreted.

As Seeligmann has suggested, the relationship between the interpreter and the sacred text is often one of both flexibility and contextual restriction.[5] The case studies in Sirach and Baruch amply illustrate this point. On

---

[4] See p. 15, n. 61 and Leiman, op. cit., p. 14.

[5] Ibid., pp. 151 ff.

the one hand, by word plays, logical extension, loose allusion, and free imagination the sacred text can prove to be a relatively plastic medium that conforms to almost any outside intention. On the other hand, these authors often show all the signs of providing a learned, detailed, and tightly-controlled rendering of sacred texts. The surprising discovery, in addition to the liberty of expression, is the high degree of selectivity in the meticulous interweaving of key words, paraphrase, and literary motifs from specific biblical texts or traditions. Such a disciplined refraction of the biblical texts clearly indicates that the interpreter possesses an equally profound inner logic which recognizes certain proprieties in the exposition of canonical writings.

To account for this combination of freedom and restraint in the use of biblical literature, Seeligmann proposes that the writers found a mandate in the affirmation that this literature has become the one sacred Word of God.[6] Although his explanation is vulnerable, because of its use of anachronistic dogmatic phraseology, the transition from a pedestrian to a canonical literature certainly entails a change in the appraisal of its meaning and significance. If a distinction exists between "inspired" and "uninspired" canonical literature, as Leiman proposes, then one must ask if this quality Seeligmann seeks to articulate resides in the canonical or in the inspired characteristic of the literature.[7] In any case, inspired canonical literature definitely has a density and immediacy for the pre-critical exegete, in as much as the whole concept of its religious function implies a direct source of divine authority for the living interpreter.

Synthetic Modes of Interpretation

The anthological type of interpretation (#2) may be described as a prime example of a "synthetic" account drawn from Scripture. All of the biblical passages deemed correlative within the limits of an explicit theme form a new independent statement of it. On the one hand, the result of this new synthesis is a rather conservative literary presentation. The very procedure of listing citations or paraphrases of key words and expressions highlights the writer's confidence in Scripture's self-sufficiency and authority. On the other hand, the actual selection, wording, and ordering of its literary elements allow modest but sufficient latitude for the subtle exercise of the interpreter's genius.

---

[6] Ibid., pp. 152, 176.

[7] Leiman, op. cit., pp. 112ff.

In addition, the anthological interpretations illustrate the use of a limited "canonical context" in which the exegesis is carried out. To illustrate, the writer in Sir. 24:5–6 restricted the collection of representative elements to the book of Job. Likewise, the resources of Sir. 17:1–4 are limited to the opening chapters of Genesis. Those of Bar. 3:26–28 are drawn from references within the Torah, although the writer may have included the Former Prophets within the periphery of his search. The approach consequently can be called holistic within the confines of a given book or a canonical division. The restriction to a book, a part of a book, or a division–despite the availability of complementary information in other accessible parts of Scripture and similar information outside of Scripture–exemplifies literary conformity to the dimensions of the canonical context for the sake of an authoritative interpretation.

Finally, the synthetic approach often allows a synchronic appropriation of the biblical texts without adherence to a history-like sequence. This practice may well reflect a conviction that all inspired Scripture shares in the same ontological reality. For instance, the anthological list of Sir. 17:1–4 ignores the original sequence of elements borrowed from the Genesis narrative. Rather, the order of the elements turns on a theological evaluation of their significance. The last element, the gift of knowledge, is the culmination of the anthological series and receives extensive elaboration. Conversely, the order of the elements descriptive of the giants in Bar. 3:26 simply follows that of the canonical order. The first elements derive from Gen. 6 and the rest from the later books. While the canonical context restricts the nature and the number of these elements, the order of their appearance in an anthological list may or may not be governed by a theological concern rather than by their original sequence in Scripture.

Other less complex methods of interpretation share the same tendency toward a synthetic approach within the context of the canon. For example, under the creation theme of Bar. 3:32–35 the writer combines an imaginative paraphrase from parts of Job 28 and 38 with language drawn from the Genesis creation narratives (#1a). Similarly, individual features from the two creation stories of Gen. 1 and Gen. 2 are intermeshed into a single, smooth synthesis in Sir. 16:24ff. (#1a). Sir. 24:3b further illustrates the function of these two chapters of Genesis as commentaries on one another. All of these examples illustrate the assumption that the two creation narratives in Genesis, together with all other scriptural references to creation, stand within a common canonical context as diverse witnesses to one divine creation. It is the proof of good interpretation when the holistic synthesis can be accomplished without violence to the self-sufficiency of the individual scriptural passages upon which it depends.

Beyond these synthetic readings around the theme of creation there are numerous other singular moments of interpretation around various themes. The combination of "throne" and "pillar of cloud," like that of the "book" of the Torah and "Wisdom," is predicated on contextual correspondence between the various passages from which the key words derive. Similarly, the themes of wilderness wandering, election, and entering the Land are developed by a selective and sequential use of a pattern of key words from the Torah. The language of a search for rest and inheritance in Deuteronomy enriches the Exodus traditions of the wilderness pilgrimage and the guiding pillar of cloud. These examples adequately demonstrate that the joining of texts and traditions into a fresh thematic synthesis is one of the most central modes of interpretation within these case studies.

In order to appreciate the literary expertise involved in such interpretation, additional consideration must be given to the thematic links or literary structures that allow for a creative synthesis of biblical information. Admittedly, the term "thematic" is somewhat vaporous and ideological; however, evidence within the case studies usually demonstrates a far more sophisticated literary connection between the underlying passages than appears on the surface. A more precise accounting, perhaps, would be to speak of a degree of correspondence between two or more texts, each of which exists as a distinct configuration of meaning. Linguistic points of resemblance between these respective configurations of meaning are exactly those which invite an interpenetration of language and ideas. Only by the skillful use of patterning or identification between selected key words can the relative correspondence be properly exploited. Only then will the respective texts appear to be illuminated by the new composition of the interpreter. Ideally, too, the mixing of familiar phraseology from different texts must be handled with an intricacy that appears to enhance rather than to detract from the meaning of the respective passages in their original canonical contexts.

Evidence for such close attention to literary nuance has already been shown repeatedly in the case studies themselves. For that reason, only one such example (#1a) will be developed to illustrate this point. Bar. 3:33–35 reflects interest in a common theme between Job 38:35 and Gen. 1, namely, that God is Lord and Creator of the cosmos. Here the author of Baruch has shifted the term "lightnings" from Job 38:35 to "light" in conformity with the creative command of Gen. 1:3. Likewise, the response of the lightnings in Job ("Here we are!") is assigned to the "stars," reminiscent of Gen. 1. In this way, the verbal response of the lightnings to the commission of God in Job 38:35 is seen in resemblance to the creative commands of God in Gen. 1 over both the light and the stars. The shared semantic range of "lightnings," "light," and "stars" marks the moments in the respective OT texts most open to an interpretation of meaning. Consequently, a general thematic link between these passages is not grounds for an unreflective coalescence of texts. While the potential of thematic correspondence is intensified by the assumption of an ontological union of all canonical contexts, any interpreted synthesis based necessarily on thematic correspondence is also restricted by the actual range of linguistic resemblances found in the texts and developed in the imagination of the interpreter.

In sum, this exegetical exercise operates within the literary and linguistic restrictions of the canonical text and thrives in direct proportion to the artistry and imagination which the interpreter can bring to the task. Within this perspective, Scripture interprets Scripture. Consequently, in these case studies this ideal is realized by the tangible synthesis of texts and traditions which may be counted as hermeneutical advances in the understanding of Scripture's common witness to religious reality. Because such a synthesis builds upon thematic correspondence between texts and traditions within the context of the canon, it is logical to describe the literary technique as a canon conscious method of interpretation.

A Shift in the Identification of Subject

For these studies, as has been shown, canon consciousness carries a special conviction regarding the religious authority of a sacred literature, presupposes an ontological unity in the literature as a guide to religious reality, and acknowledges the sanctity of certain literary and contextual dimensions that define the canonical domain of its interpretation. It is in regard to the last category that this writer refers to a "canonical context" within which religious interpretation is carried out. Another conspicuous example which illustrates these principles, is the technique of borrowing traditions pertaining to one subject and applying them to another.

Sir. 24 offers a wide range of instances in which a description, contextually applicable to other agents or subjects, is found applied to Wisdom (#4). For example, Wisdom is portrayed in biblical language normally reserved for God. In these writings, she is identified with symbols of divine presence, with the priestly ministry and cult objects, with the rivers, trees, and the revelation of good and evil in the garden of Eden, and with events in the life of Israel from the Exodus to the Promised Land. In Bar. 3:9ff. the forsaking of the way of wisdom is shown repeatedly to be the explanation for the eclipse of the rulers, the rich, the mighty warriors, and the wordly sages as they appear and disappear in the pages of Scripture. Even the narratives of Israel's exile fall within this same pattern. Finally, this critique in Baruch is heightened by an identification, like that in Sir. 24:23, of the way of wisdom with the entire *book* of the Torah.

Certainly these associations are not all on the same level. Even so, one is left with the impression that in these case studies Wisdom (or the way of wisdom) assumes roles which did not originally belong to her in the biblical narratives. There is, however, a logic to this adaptation of Scripture. For instance, Wisdom in Sir. 24 is a quasi-divine figure and for that reason borrows aspects of divinity usually retained for God. In other words, although Wisdom is never called a goddess and is always subordinate to the Creator, she is, nevertheless, a divine figure and language about God and his activity is taken as ambiguously inclusive of her nature and activity as well. Probably the fullest potential for identifying wisdom with the priestly ministry and cult objects resides in the ambiguity of the numinous in these tokens of Israel's worship. Similarly, the "spirit," "darkness," and "dark cloud" in the creation narratives, as well as the pillar of cloud in the wilderness traditions, invite a clarification of the divine presence in canonical history.

Moreover, Wisdom appears to share with Israel the same pathos, the same wanderlust, and the same desire for rest and inheritance. However, the author of Sir. 24 always maintains this correspondence at a strict literary level. Wisdom is never depicted as a simple incarnation by which God becomes one with Israel. Rather, she is merely associated with the pillar of cloud, which as a divine theophany, defines her place in the mystery of God's presence in the wilderness. Similarly, Wisdom's wandering is like that of Israel, though it occurs on a vastly different cosmic plane. In terms of the inner logic of interpretation, Wisdom only provides a partial clarification of the numinous in the experience of Israel. In the description and acts of God she is veiled and given a subordinate function. Likewise, she is hidden with God in the theophanic symbols of presence and in the sacramental objects of priestly ministry. So, the Edenic imagery recalls the circumstances in which God walked and talked with humanity, at a time when the will and Wisdom of God were found in earthy abundance.

In a similar manner, the function of "the way of wisdom" in Bar. 3:9ff. demonstrates, by means of negative examples, that the absence of wisdom is the reason for the downfall of various familiar figures in the biblical canon. Here the way of wisdom is not literarily identified with the external symbols of divine presence, but rather fills in the silence of Scripture or reduces the charge of wickedness or frailty to a single factor which accounts for the fall of the rich and the mighty. In each case, the way of wisdom is shown to be God's gift, a blessing without which no people can survive. Hence, it is more than the worldly wisdom of famous sages, and, as such, is set forth as some aspect of divine guide or instruction tied up with the presence of God himself.

For both Sir. 24 and Bar. 3:9–4:4, this particular technique of interpreting and re-applying parts of Scripture to wisdom has depended upon the availability of acceptable figures within the context of the biblical canon, especially within that of the Torah. Without exploring the full significance of this insight for wisdom interpretation, it is yet obvious that the canonical context not only provides the principal source of the figures selected, but actually defines the limits of the interpretation. For instance, given a logical association of Wisdom with divine symbolism as in Sir. 24, the canonical context restricts the choice of biblical figures within the theme of a wilderness wandering and dictates Wisdom's ultimate identification with the Levitical priests, rather than with the secular tribes. Similarly, the anthological assessment of the giants in Bar. 3:26–28 explains the moral enigma of their destruction, which is left unresolved in the context of the original narratives. Once again, this type of interpretation suggests a vivid consciousness of a canonical literature which critically limits both the selection and the interpretation of the biblical texts and traditions.

Although a more extensive discussion of all the redactional re-applications of OT could be offered, these observations on the nature of the text, synthetic interpretation and the device of shifting the subject of a text suffice to demonstrate the importance of a consideration of canon for these studies. The function of wisdom interpretation can be more fully explored in the light of this evidence.

Wisdom as a Hermeneutical Construct

Evidence of wisdom interpretation, as defined in the introduction, have been presented throughout the case studies. From the standpoint of canon, the Torah serves as the major literary resource consulted by these writers. Naturally, many allusions and citations from other parts of Scripture were detected in the case studies, but the Torah stands out by the degree of close literary attention it receives and even more directly by Wisdom's identification with it in Sir. 24:23 and Bar. 4:1. In both of these last instances, "the Torah" refers to an explicit literary canonical category (a "book"), while Wisdom, or the way of wisdom, is described as only an intellectual concept within the context of Scripture.

Consequently, this distinction between the Torah as a canonical category and wisdom as an intellectual concept indicates that wisdom still lacks a full literary canonical definition as a closed canonical collection of books on a par with the Torah. Rather, these explicit identifications of the Torah with wisdom support a claim that the post-exilic wisdom traditions derive their chief authority from the fixed Torah. Nevertheless, these wisdom traditions do not purport to arise *de novo*, but are depicted in direct continuity with the biblical wisdom books of Proverbs, Qoheleth, and perhaps Job, when the latter is regarded as a wisdom source. This continuity between the biblical and the post-exilic wisdom traditions is marked by the borrowing of distinctive language and the imitation of certain literary styles, especially from Proverbs. For example, Sir. 24 resembles the structure of the Wisdom Songs in Proverbs and in particular has borrowed language and themes from Prov. 8.

It is significant also that the *direction* of interpretation in these case studies moves most frequently from specific texts or traditions in the Torah to an assessment of them in terms of the wisdom traditions, and not *vice versa*. By contrast, K. Hruby argues that the point of departure for the identification of wisdom and the Torah in rabbinic literature is always *the sapiential literature*.[8] At least, this present study shows just the opposite phenomenon and indicates that the identification between wisdom and Torah can lead to either an attempt to assess wisdom literature in terms of Torah, as Hruby illustrates,[9] or just the opposite interpretation as here in Sirach and Baruch. Von Rad noted this aspect of the use of OT in Sirach and cautioned against construing Sirach as simply "legalized wisdom." As a result of his investigation, he proposed,

> Nicht die Weisheit gerät in den Schatten der Großmacht der Tora, sondern umgekehrt sehen wir Sirach damit beschäftigt, die Tora von dem Verstehenshorizont der Weisheit her zu legitimieren und zu interpretieren.[10]

[8] K. Hruby, "La Torah Identifiée à la Sagesse et L'Activite du Sage' dans la Tradition Rabbinique," *BVC* 76 (1967): 67.

[9] Ibid., pp. 67–68.

[10] G. von Rad, "Die Weisheit des Jesus Sirach," *EvTh*, 29 (1969): 118.

Within these case studies, at least, Von Rad's critique is a salutary one. The case studies and the examples of redactional alteration of OT texts repeatedly illustrate interpretations that originate from Torah texts and move to a wisdom assessment. An excellent example of the effect of this movement is found in the use of verses from Dt. 30:12–13 in Bar. 3:29–31. As the nature of the alterations indicated, language suggestive of the wisdom traditions was subsequently introduced. Thus, the Deuteronomy passage was clearly the starting point of the interpretation.

The listing of redactional alterations of OT texts or traditions illustrates the various techniques employed in the interpretation of earlier biblical material. The examples drawn from Sirach and Baruch generally include both wisdom and non-wisdom interpretations. Hence, the techniques are not uniquely wisdom devices. It is only in their application that they may provide evidence of a wisdom interpretation, and the terms of that application require that the direction of interpretation be from the canonical Torah or prophetic traditions to the concerns of wisdom.

The case studies of Sir. 24 and Bar. 3:9–4:4 demonstrate an entire series of such wisdom interpretations prior to the explicit identifications in Sir. 24:23 and Bar. 4:1. Indeed, each of the identifications provides the obvious conclusion to its own independent proof of wisdom's place in the Torah traditions. In Sir. 24, Wisdom is shown to share Israel's narrative history and to reside with her in terms of the biblical symbols of divine presence. In Bar. 3:9 the teaching of the way of wisdom is portrayed as Israel's salvation in the course of her biblical history, and accounts for her survival, despite the downfall of those possessing more earthly wealth and power than she. Each case depended for its strength on the ability of the interpreter to show that such an evaluation of Israel's past was grounded in the preëminently authoritative teachings of the Torah. In each case, too, these writers attempted to prove that the Torah traditions reveal the story of Wisdom or teach the benefits of the way of wisdom in the life of ancient Israel.

Therefore, on the basis of these case studies, this writer must conclude that, while the Torah retains its character as a canonical division of sacred Scripture, wisdom functions for these post-exilic writers as a hermeneutical construct to interpret the Torah as a statement about wisdom and as a guide to Israel's practice of it. Certainly, Proverbs and Qoheleth, which probably had canonical status in this period, provided biblical precedents for the wisdom tradition. However, it remained for Sirach and Baruch to demonstrate that the canonical Torah provides the ultimate justification and source of wisdom in Israel.

Wisdom has now become more than a general theological discipline; it is a rubric under which the authoritative non-wisdom traditions can be evaluated as a guide to practical conduct. Such a hermeneutical function for wisdom was only one of several means used to affirm the complementarity of a diverse biblical canon. Only by grounding wisdom in the interpretation of the superior canonical Torah traditions, could wisdom teachings (both canonical and non-canonical) retain an independent religious significance in any way comparable to that of the Torah in the post-exilic period. Conversely, these wisdom interpretations legitimate the Torah and its claim to pervasive authority by demonstrating in practical terms how Torah narrative directly informs the concerns of wisdom.

Chapter VI

Evidence of a Similar Phenomenon in the OT

Preface to the OT Investigation

In the last three chapters one particular type of post-exilic wisdom interpretation has been described. It appears to have been a canon conscious phenomenon of reading the Torah narrative, or even prophetic traditions, as a guide to wisdom. The occurrence of such wisdom interpretations in two different early Jewish compositions suggests that this approach was probably a common one, well known to a broad spectrum of the post-exilic community.

Although one could explore the implications of this mode of interpretation for understanding the later moralizing of the sacred text (e.g., see James 5:7), the present study is concerned rather with roots it may have in the prehistory of the Hebrew Scripture. Even as distinct themes and phrases from familar canonical books were incorporated redactionally into the interpretive context of Sirach and Baruch, so the biblical redactors provided a theological assessment of fixed traditions by means of editorial arrangement and addendum. Consequently, the results of the preceding investigation offers some analogous criteria to inform a search for a similar religious use of sacred traditions evidenced in the late redactional history of the OT itself.

Obviously, the only way to test this hypothesis is to examine the literary composition of specific OT books in order to see if such correspondence can be found. The method of inquiry depends on locating redactional layers which evaluate canonically non-wisdom literature in terms of the sacred wisdom tradition, particularly that of Proverbs and Qoholeth. In such a study one must allow, as well, for a possible distinction between the original intention of a redactor and the broader functional significance that the same redaction carries in the latter context of an emerging sacred canon. Indeed, canon contextual analysis can often be distinguished from the older redaction criticism by its consideration of the latter question as well as the former.

The investigations that follow in this chapter are divided into two groups. The first study of Qoh. 12:13–14 explores the significance of the ending of Qoheleth for the identity of the biblical wisdom traditions. The second set of studies pursues evidence of redactions that imply a later wisdom interpretation of non-wisdom traditions. In the first study, it will be argued that the final verses of Qoheleth offer a redactional assessment, not only of wisdom's definition, but of wisdom's role within the context of the canon. Subsequently, the investigations of Hosea, the Psalms, and 1 and 2 Samuel will set forth evidence of redactional layers that, in each case, seem to invite a secondary wisdom assessment of originally prophetic, hymnic, and narrative traditions.

The Epilogue to Qoheleth (Qoh. 12:13–14)

The peculiar features of the ending on Qoheleth have long attracted the attention of scholars. First of all, 12:9–14 breaks off the direct address of the sage and begins with a third person description of Qoheleth (vv. 9–10). Moreover, the viewpoint regarding wisdom in vv. 13–14 does seem to differ from that of Qoheleth's earlier statements. For this reason, Podechard postulated a later *ḥāsîd* who attempted to ameliorate the cynicism of the earlier sage.[1] Roland Murphy finds in these verses a "safe interpretation" and concludes, "In reality, God's 'judgment' (v. 14) is much more mysterious for Qoheleth than it is for this writer, who uses it in the traditional manner of the sages."[2] While these redactional observations advance the current understanding of the literature, the larger canonical implications for interpreting Qoheleth remain relatively unexplored. This study is addressed to that neglected issue.

The entire postscript has been attributed to the work of two (e.g., Podechard, Galling, Zimmerli),[3] three (e.g., Hertzberg),[4] or even as many as eight redactors (e.g., Jastrow).[5] While the following analysis presup-

---

[1] E. Podechard, *L'Ecclésiaste* (Paris: Libraire Victor Lecoffre, 1912), pp. 160–62.

[2] Roland E. Murphy, "Ecclesiastes (Qoheleth)," in *The Jerome Biblical Commentary*, ed. Raymond E. Brown, et al. (New York: Prentice-Hall, 1968), p. 540.

[3] Podechard, op. cit., pp. 151–70, 472; K. Galling, *Die Fünf Megilloth*, 2nd ed. (Tübingen: J.C.B. Mohr, 1969), pp. 124–25; W. Zimmerli, *Prediger*, 2nd ed. (Göttingen: Vandenhoeck & Ruprecht, 1967), pp. 249–51.

[4] Hans Wilhelm Hertzberg, *Der Prediger* (Gerd Mohn: Gütersloher Verlagshaus, 1963), pp. 217–21.

[5] M. Jastrow, Jr., *A Gentile Cynic* (Philadelphia: J.B. Lippencott Co., 1919), pp. 71 ff.

poses the epilogue, especially vv. 12–14, to be redactional, it does not depend on a precise resolution of this question. For the present purposes, the verses can be divided *descriptively* into four parts: (a) the description of Qoheleth as a teacher and a collector of wisdom sayings (vv. 9–10), (b) a generalization in the form of a mashal about the "words of the wise" and the integrity of wisdom collections (v. 11), (c) a warning about generating more wisdom collections on grounds that the purpose of them has already been amply fulfilled by "these" (v. 12), and (d) a statement expressing this purpose in terms of law and divine restitution (vv. 13–14).[6] However, K. Galling has shown that the most decisive issue is the relation between the first "thematizing" of the book (whether by Qoheleth or a redactor) in 1:2 and 12:8 under הבל הבלים and the later thematizing of it by the epilogue in vv. 13–14.[7]

In order more fully to explore this redactional function of the epilogue, it is necessary to examine, first of all, the correspondence in content between the last portion of the epilogue (vv. 11–14) and the books of Proverbs, Qoheleth, and Sirach. Furthermore, in the case of Proverbs and Qoheleth all the possible redactional connections between their respective contents and that of the epilogue must be considered.

Hitzig, Wildeboer, and Barton have each proposed that the mention of Qoheleth's selecting and assembling משלים in v. 9 is a reference to the canonical book of Proverbs.[8] This possibility assumes that a later redactor has fully identified Qoheleth with Solomon (cf. 1:1; 1:12–2:26) and now speaks of his earlier work. Wildeboer thinks the redactor may, in addition, wish to restrict Solomon's participation in writing Qoheleth to the משלים within it.[9] However, Haupt considers the comparisons in v. 11 to be between the disjointed saying in Proverbs and the more strictly ordered

---

[6] I think that Hitzig, in *Der Prediger Solomon's* (Leipzig: Weidmann'sche Buchhandlung, 1847), pp. 221, is convincing in his insistence that סוף is, in the strictest terms, neither "Summe" nor "Endresultat," but simply "Ende" (cf. 3:11; 7:2) or the "goal" to which the previous literature is said to be directed. This interpretation well suits the argument in v. 12 that these books are sufficient to communicate the ideals that follow in vv. 13–14. However, it must be admitted that the goal is not divorced from its presupposition of wisdom's essential content. In that sense, it is inevitably both at once a goal and an estimate of what sacred wisdom actually is.

[7] Galling, op. cit., pp. 124–25; cf. his "Koheleth-Studien," *ZAW*, 50 (1932): 279–80, 282.

[8] F. Hitzig, op. cit., p. 217; D. G. Wildeboer, *Die Fünf Megillot* (Tübingen: J. C. B. Mohr, 1898), p. 166; G. A. Barton, *The Book of Ecclesiastes* (New York: Charles Scribners, 1908), pp. 197–98.

[9] Wildeboer, op. cit., p. 166.

sayings of Qoheleth.[10] The old *baraita* of *Baba Bathra* 14b, 15a sets the canonical order of Proverbs before Qoheleth, and one could perhaps conceive of this order as an early constant.[11] It must be considered, then, whether the epilogue has Proverbs in view when it concluded Qoheleth, or even if, as an extreme possibility, the epilogue was added in order to lock Proverbs and Qoheleth together in an early canonical sequence. The latter possibility would definitely require an overt redactional link by the epilogue to Proverbs.

Most commentators doubt any direct redactional relationship between the epilogue and Proverbs. An interpretation which takes v.9 to mean Qoheleth was "not only" wise to himself, but that he "also" (עוד) taught knowledge to the people and collected choice משלים, need not presume a reference strictly to Proverbs or pit Proverbs over against Qoheleth. Qoheleth contains a large number of משלים and cannot fairly be portrayed as merely solipsistic or elitist in contrast to the teaching of Proverbs.[12] Moreover, the עוד should probably be taken to mean a repeated action, as in Qoh. 3:16, and not a distinction between Qoheleth's private wisdom and his research and teaching.[13] The משלים in v.9 refer to a general literary category intrinsic to Qoheleth and cannot plausibly be a *Stichwort* to the title of Proverbs. Similarly, דברי חכמים in 12:11 is not a convincing play on Prov. 1:6 in which the same construct phrase occurs among other expressions for wisdom. The phrase occurs elsewhere as a general expres-

---

[10] P. Haupt, *Koheleth oder Weltschmerz in der Bibel* (Leipzig: J.C. Henrichs'sche Buchhandlung, 1908), p. 33.

[11] For a discussion of this earliest extant reference to Qoheleth's place in a canonical order, see Podechard, op. cit., pp. 2–20. It is worth noting that the *Baba Bathra* passage cannot be dated with precision, and it cannot be used uncritically. For instance, the order it ascribes to the prophets–Jeremiah, Ezekiel, Isaiah, and the Twelve–differs from that of Isaiah, Jeremiah, Ezekiel, and the Twelve suggested by the sequence in Sirach's Praise to the Fathers (cf. Sir. 48–49). There is no indication that Proverbs and Ecclesiastes ever existed on a single scroll like the Torah and the Twelve. The relative independence of Ecclesiastes is, furthermore, shown by its later movement along with the Song of Songs into the Megilloth.

[12] Sir. 37:22–23 is not an adequate parallel to this type of interpretation because the contrast there is best seen between one who uses wisdom for his own gain or private ambition and one who instructs the people for their own benefit as well. At the outset, Qoheleth is not portrayed as one making private gain by his wisdom. His teaching addresses the universal condition of humanity and routinely offers constructive advice to his audience. For examples of Qoheleth's advice, see Addison G. Wright, "The Riddle of the Sphinx: The Structure of the Book of Qoheleth," *CBQ*, 30 (1968): 334.

[13] Galling, op. cit., p. 124. Hertzberg (op. cit., pp. 217–28) similarly proposes translating עוד to mean "fortwährend, dauernd" and discusses the contrary position of Gordis.

sion for wisdom in both Prov. 22:17 and Qoh. 9:17, and, therefore, is not only indicative of Proverbs but of wisdom literature in general.[14]

Even more significantly, the purpose of wisdom in vv. 13–14 cannot be seen simply as a corrective to the skepticism of Qoheleth from the content of Proverbs. A number of features weigh against such a conclusion. For example, Proverbs always uses יהוה (never אלהים) as the object of the verb ירא, "to fear,"[15] or as the *nomen rectum* to יראת (i.e., "the fear of *YHWH*").[16] Qoheleth, however, always uses אלהים [cf. 5:6(7); 7:18; 8:12, 13; 12:13]. The specific combination "fear God and observe his commandments" does not occur elsewhere in a similar formula either in Proverbs or in Qoheleth. Instead, the idiom in Proverbs is "fear Yahweh and *turn away from evil*" (סור מרע; 3:7; cf. 14:16; Job 1:1; 2:3). Furthermore, the use of a personal pronoun with a plural noun "commandments" is never employed in Proverbs explicitly of God's commandments, but this term stands in the context of a father's precepts to his son. The usual expression in Proverbs is "my son, obey *my* commandments." That these wisdom sayings in Qoheleth are associated explicitly with *God's* commandments is an important difference in orientation, one which will be considered again in the later course of this study. At least it is apparent that the redactional statement regarding the goal of wisdom in vv. 13–14 exceeds the usual understanding of wisdom in Proverbs. The general implications about Qoheleth's prolific activity (vv. 9–10), the public presence of valuable wisdom collections (v. 11), and the warning against making more books (v. 12) probably carry an inclusive reference to Proverbs. However, this possible association does not depend on any manifest intention specifically to link Proverbs and Qoheleth together in an *exclusive* canonical relationship.

The parallels in vocabulary and content between the epilogue and the body of Qoheleth vastly exceed the above-mentioned correspondences with Proverbs. For example, the admonition to fear אלהים is alien to Proverbs, although common to Qohelet. The verb זהר, not in Proverbs, occurs again in Qoh. 4:13. Furthermore, the theme in v. 14 of an appointed time

---

[14] The argument that this phrase is the most general expression among the more technical categories of wisdom listed with it in Prov. 1:6 is still faulted by its incidental occurrence in the list. There are no signs within Proverbs that this construct phrase maintained a special descriptive status for the wisdom of this particular book.

[15] Prov. 3:7; 14:2; 24:21; 31:30.

[16] Prov. 1:7, 29; 2:5; 8:13; 9:10; 10:27; 14:26, 27; 15:16, 33; 16:6; 19:23; 22:4; 23:17; 31:30.

when God will at last establish his justice, a theme not explicit in Proverbs, has virtually an exact parallel in Qoh. 11:9:

11:9 ודע כי על כל אלה יביאך האלהים במשפט

12:14 כי את כל מעשה האלהים יבא במשפט

11:9 Know that concerning all these things God will bring you into judgment.

12:14 God will bring every deed into judgment.

Another clear example of interdependence between the body of Qoheleth and its epilogue concerns a common moral dilemma. This problem is articulated in Qoh. 9:1–3 as the blurring of consequences despite one's good or evil behavior, a condition presupposed in the same terms by the epilogue. Qoh. 3:16–17 anticipates the same problem and reckons with an appointed time when God will judge according to every matter (חפץ) and every work (מעשה). Once again, there is parallelism in language. Like the epilogue, this stress on a time of restitution is not simply tied up with eschatology, as though everything waits for a "day" of final judgment. The hope rests more ambiguously in the relativity of time between God's realization of his משפט and the concrete human experience of amoral inequity. Therefore, the depiction of wisdom in the epilogue speaks directly to a central dilemma contained in Qoheleth with a traditional assurance, likewise contained in the book itself. It effectively conditions the hearing of the book precisely because of these points of literary continuity. In this respect, one can justly speak of its function as that of an adaptive commentary on Qoheleth or, as Galling has suggested, a thematizing of the book.

Consequently it is apparent that this second thematizing of the book, like the first one in 1:2 and 12:8, is not utterly foreign to the literary content of Qoheleth itself. Each thematizing has seized upon a particular dimension *within* the plastic structure of sayings and responses which cluster together in loose units throughout the book. Each is an oversimplification and a judgement concerning the essential intent of the entire complex of sayings. Certainly, the presence of *two* such divergent orientations for Qoheleth's contents must witness strongly against a reduction of the book as literature to any single, harmonized intention in the mind of the original anonymous sage. The reader is given some emphatic guides to the book's interpretation without a flattening or trivializing of its contents.

Despite their functional similarity the two thematizing rubrics prove to be distinct in one important respect. The first rubric, even if it is original to the primary collector, abstracts from the concrete depictions of moral despair a maxim more bloodless and doctrinaire than the book itself.[17] However, it is still conceptually restricted merely to the amplification of a discrete theme in the book. The second epitomization includes, as shown above, a theme within Qoheleth's composition, but it ventures a synopsis of wisdom in terms broader than Qoheleth and unlike that of Proverbs. In fact, it can be demonstrated that, although the statement in v. 13 in connection with v. 14 is conceptually foreign to Proverbs and Qoheleth, these verses express an ideology of wisdom like that in Sirach!

With the discovery and publication towards the end of the nineteenth century of several Hebrew fragments of Sirach, a new enthusiasm emerged to examine Qoheleth's relationship to that book.[18] The epilogue offers several interesting parallels. For instance, an editorial device like that in v. 13 occurs in Sir. 43:27, "More than this may not be concluded, the end of the matter, 'He is all in all'" (עוד כאלה לא נוסף וקץ דבר הוא הכל). One finds not only the internal theme of Qoheleth regarding a time of restitution, but, like the epilogue and unlike the body of Qoheleth, this conceptuality entails specifically the relevation of the secret (נעלם) works (מעשה) to be rewarded according to divine justice (משפט). Furthermore, Sir. 17: 6–15 even casts this same assumption in terms of exposing "good and evil" as in Qoh. 12:14b.

Furthermore, it is noteworthy that neither Proverbs nor the body of Qoheleth offers a parallel to the epilogue command, "fear God and observe his commandments" (v. 13), much less one in combination with the theme of restitution in v. 14. By contrast, both elements of this dual injunction, and the one that follows it, are found in the first chapter of Sirach! Sir. 1:1ff. opens with a statement that all wisdom comes from God (cf. Qoh. 12:11b), and then emphasizes the fear of God as the main credential of such wisdom (cf. 1:9, 10, 11, 12, 14, 16, 18, 22, 24, 25, 29). Here, in vv. 26–30, occur all the same essential elements that are in the clarification of wisdom's goals at the end of the Qoheleth epilogue:

> If you desire wisdom, keep the commandments, and the Lord will supply it to you. For the fear of the Lord is wisdom and instruction, and he delights in fidelity and meekness. Do not disobey the fear of the Lord; do not approach him with a divided mind. Be not a hypocrite in men's sight, and keep watch over your lips. Do not exalt yourself lest you fall, and thus

---

[17] So, Galling, op. cit., pp. 124–25.

[18] For examples of correspondences between Qoheleth and Sirach, see Johann K. Gasser, op. cit., pp. 235–36; A. H. McNeile, *An Introduction to Ecclesiastes* (Cambridge University Press, 1904), pp. 34–37; and Th. Middendorp, op. cit., pp. 35–90.

bring dishonor upon yourself. The Lord will reveal your secrets and cast you down in the midst of the congregation, because you did not come in the fear of the Lord, and your heart was full of deceit (RSV).

Besides additional examples of the parallelism between fearing God and obeying his commandments (e.g., 23:27; 10:19), another related expression appears in Sirach. Sir. 2:16 is exemplary, "Those who fear the Lord disobey not his words; those who love him are filled *with his Torah*" (cf. 15:1; 19:20). In Sirach, there is a conscious relationship between the tasks of wisdom and the authority of the Torah. If the same early viewpoint of Scripture implicit in Sirach (e.g., Sir. 24) and Bar. 3:9–4:4 persists in these other instances, then the above-mentioned formula in Qoh. 12:13–14 represents a fairly sophisticated theological interpretation of sacred wisdom in relation to an authoritative Torah.

In sum, only Sirach has exactly the same ideology as Qoh. 12:13–14, a perspective not expressed in the body of Qoheleth itself. It is, therefore, probable that the redactor of Qoh. 12:13–14 either knew of the book of Sirach or shared fully in a similar, pervasive estimate of sacred wisdom. Moreover, this later formulation offers an interpretation of the relationship between biblical wisdom and the commandments of God in the Torah. The minimal effect redactionally is to place Qoheleth in the domain of the biblical wisdom which has itself become a developed theological construct already functioning as an interpretive idiom in the context of a nascent Scripture. In other words, Qoheleth has been thematized by the epilogue in order to include it fully within a canon conscious definition of sacred wisdom, one that is remarkably close to that of Sirach and Baruch.[19]

In my opinion, this evaluation of Qoheleth's epilogue still leaves room for another more adventurous possibility. The description of Qoheleth in vv. 9–10 is followed by a wisdom saying which governs the activity of biblical wisdom in general. The next verse (12) warns against any preoccupation with books beyond "these" (מהמה). If בעלי אספות is taken to signify "overseers of the collections," then the antecedent to "these" must be those same collections or "the words of the wise," that is, a reference to a set of existent collections or books inclusive of, but larger than, Qoheleth. Hence, the particularity of focus on Qoheleth is loosened by the generalization on the nature of wisdom in v. 11 and this statement is made

[19] See pp. 182 ff. Regarding the recognition of the relation of the epilogue to the process of canonizing Qoheleth, see Hertzberg, op. cit., pp. 220–21. Also, cf. Judah Goldin, "The End of Ecclesiastes: Literal Exegesis and Its Transformation," pp. 135–58, in *Biblical Motifs: Origins and Transformations*, ed. by A. Altmann, (Cambridge: Harvard University Press, 1966).

in reference to a broader category of literature, of which Qoheleth is presumed to be a part. The admonition in v. 12 has "books" for its concern and warns against the production of more. The force of the argument is that "these" are sufficient to communicate the goal of wisdom as given in vv. 13–14. Other wisdom books would only weary their readers when the purpose of sacred wisdom is already achieved through "these."

One cannot avoid two possibilities. On the one hand, the writer seems to have some specific set of wisdom books in mind at the time he adds the epilogue to Qoheleth. He speaks of "these" as though he can assume a recognition of their identity by his readers. The assumption is suggestive of some early canonical division of wisdom books, perhaps containing only Proverbs and Qoheleth.[20] On the other hand, the wisdom books are traditionally known by their assignment to Solomon. Since Qoheleth is identified with Solomon by implication in the title (1:1) and in the autobiographical prose of 1:12–2:26, one may suspect that the redactor presumes the requisite wisdom books are simply those bearing Solomon's name in their titles. Perhaps Proverbs, Qoheleth and even the Song of Songs fall together in a recognized division of sacred wisdom books. Once the ending was appended to Qoheleth there would logically be considerable difficulty for other books, like Sirach, to find a full place among these Solomonic books. Likewise, Ben Sira in 39:1 may casually refer to a collection of sacred wisdom books without listing them. In either of the above possibilities the epilogue to Qoheleth would not only thematize that book but apply as well to some larger biblical collection of sacred wisdom. In effect, it would give all of biblical wisdom a singular theological focus in the context of the emerging canon of Scripture.

With its epilogue, Qoheleth has been overtly thematized according to a particular theological understanding of wisdom which closely resembles that in Sirach and Bar. 3:9–4:4. Therefore, the epilogue provides a rare glimpse into a comprehensive, canon conscious formulation concerning the theological function of biblical wisdom. When the assumed ideological coherency of the wisdom books is clarified in such a manner, the comple-

[20] The question of Job's placement in or outside the wisdom books is a difficult one. Sir. 49:9 mentions it after Ezekiel and before the minor prophets, although this occasion may simply be triggered by Ezekiel's own reference to Job (cf. 14:14, 20). Job is never assigned to Solomon; nevertheless, the LXX places it after the Song of Songs and before the Wisdom of Solomon. The canonical placement of a book in or outside the wisdom collection is at least as much a theological decision as a literary assessment. The equivocal place of Job in the early Palestinian canon is both a witness to the openness of the literature to a multisided reading and a warning against the assumption that biblical divisions are always closed or determined by genre distinctions alone.

mentarity between the canonical function of the biblical wisdom books and the function of certain other inner-biblical sapientializing redactions becomes all the more obvious and compelling. The studies that follow offer three probable instances of this latter phenomenon.

The Ending of the Book of Hosea (Hos. 14:10)

The last verse of Hosea reads:

מי חכם ויבן אלה
נבון וידעם
כי ישרים דרכי יהוה
וצדקים ילכו בם
ופשעים יכשלו בם

Who is wise that he understands these things?
[Who is] discerning that he knows them?
Indeed, the ways of the Lord are right,
and the righteous walk in them,
but rebels stumble in them.

Unlike Isaiah and Amos, Hosea has attracted little interest in the recent wisdom influence discussions. The language of the book is suited to the prophet's confrontation with the Canaanite fertility cults and lacks any specialized wisdom vocabulary. Consequently, the last verse is a remarkable exception to this lack of wisdom orientation within the book as a whole. Pre-critical commentary found in it a pious call to the reader for careful interpretation of the preceding book and a play on the admonition in Dt. 32:4, "The Rock, his work is perfect, for all his ways are justice ..." However, with the rise of form-critical analysis the last half of the verse was clearly identified as a proverb reminiscent of sayings within the biblical wisdom books of Proverbs and Qoheleth. In the light of this evidence, the traditional recognition that the second half of the verse summarizes the content of the book of Hosea heightens the question of how and for what purpose the contents of a fundamentally prophetic book, which offers virtually no internal evidence of wisdom influence, can be summarized by a didactic proverb, which is typical of biblical wisdom literature.

In the composition of the book, Hos. 14:10 appears as a secondary editorial appendage to the already appropriate ending of the book (cf. v.9). Furthermore, its character as a later commentary on the original book is evident implicitly by the style of editorial detachment in a third person address to the readers and explicitly by the retrospective demonstrative pronoun ("these things") which is picked up again in the suffix of וידעם. This use of the demonstrative pronoun is a literary device similar to that found in Sir. 24:7, 23 and Bar. 4:1. In each of these cases, a near demonstrative pronoun refers abstractly to the essential contents of the whole preceding literary unit. By this means, the author-redactor can draw attention to the preceding narrative as a whole in order to generalize upon it. Hos. 14:10 is further distinguished from the previous prophetic oracles by a vocabulary and manner of expression foreign to the rest of the book and strongly reminiscent of the canonical wisdom traditions (cf. Prov. 10:29; 24:16). Although critical commentators readily acknowledge that this verse offers a didactic epilogue to the book of Hosea and shares uniquely in the language and style of biblical wisdom, the same commentators are less sure of its implications.

As the outset, the parallel stichoi beginning what מי present a problem for translating the verse. It is possible to take the מי as a relative pronoun, "whoever is wise will understand this;" however, Hebrew grammar lends greater support to the use of the interrogative.[21] The LXX and Vulgate, also, assume this to be a question. In addition, the phrase itself must *not* be understood to suggest that the book Hosea is impenetrable as, for example, "who could be so wise as to comprehend this?" The proverb that follows (v. 10b), contradicts such a presupposition.[22] Rather, this phrase belongs among the examples S. R. Driver provides in his discussion of the מי clause in 1 Sam. 11:12, and can, therefore, be identified as an idiom or formula common to the OT.[23] Jud. 7:3, for example, reads מי ירא וחרד ישב and may be translated literally as, "Who is fearful and trembling? let him return" or more dynamically, "*Whoso* is fearful and trembling, let him return." Consequently, this formula, "invites attention to a person of a particular character, in order afterwards to prescribe what he is to do (or what is to be done to him), or to state how he will fare."[24] Although a translation like that of the *RSV*–"Whoever is wise, let him understand these things"–communicates the right idea, the formula itself consists technically of an interrogative of address with a jussive or infinitive ab-

---

[21] See the discussion in Hans W. Wolff, *Dodekapropheton: Hosea*, 2nd ed. (Neukirchener Vluyn: Neukirchener Verlag, 1965), vol. 1, p. 310.

[22] Cf. Wilhelm Rudolph, *Hosea*, Kommentar zum Alten Testament (Gütersloh: Gütersloher Verlagshaus, 1966), p. 253.

[23] S. R. Driver, *Notes on the Hebrew Text and the Topography of the Books of Samuel*, 2nd ed. (Oxford: Clarendon Press, 1913), p. 87.

[24] Ibid.

solute specifying directions or consequences. Hence, in Hos. 14:10 "the wise" and "the discerning" among readers are singled out and invited to acquire a full understanding of the book.

The type of formula found in Hos. 14:10a does not occur in Proverbs, although the paired concepts "wisdom" and "understanding," are, of course, idiomatic to the book (e.g., Prov. 1:2; 2:2,6; 3:13,19; 4:5,7; etc.). The same type of formula does, however, have parallels elsewhere in the OT, namely, Jer. 9:11 and Ps. 107:42–43 (cf. Qoh. 8:1).

The occurrence in Jer. 9:11 is part of a disputation against the official counselors and the professional prophets. Both groups fall periodically under Jeremiah's attack throughout his oracles (e.g., Jer. 8:8–12; 9:12–13; 14:14). The formula in Jer. 9:11 follows after a judgement oracle and chides the hearers: "Who is wise, let him comprehend this! Unto whom has God spoken, let that person reveal it!" It is a jeering invitation which mocks the ability of those addressed to have any insight into the matter. Without waiting for a response the prophet offers an oracular explanation in language reminiscent of Deuteronomy. As in Hos. 14:10 the formula in Jer. 9:11 calls for an immediate interpretation of the preceding oracle, but here it is directed to both sages and prophets and the response is not distinctive of wisdom literature.

The occurrence in Ps. 107:42–43, by contrast, comes much closer to that in Hosea. Ps. 107 is a combination of a thank song (vv. 1–32) and a hymn (vv. 32–43).[25] The summons formula ends the hymn, but, unlike that in Hos. 14:10, it is probably not redactional. Nevertheless, the style and content of the hymn is noticeably different from its ending. The hymn itself expresses in timeless, prosaic metaphors the alteration between the judgments and blessings of God. This choice of imagery is not conceptually indicative of biblical wisdom literature, but is more like that of Isaiah (cf. v. 33a, Is. 50:2; v. 33b, Is. 35:7; v. 35, Is. 41:8; except v. 40a, Job 12:21; v. 40b, Job 12:24). Only the antithetical proverb in v. 42 offers a gnomic wisdom assessment, "The upright see it and rejoice, and all wickedness closes its mouth" (cf. v. 42a, Job 22:19, v. 42b, Job 9:16).

Paralleling the Hosea ending, there follows a summons for the wise among those hearing the psalm to reflect upon the profound dialectic of God's grace and steadfast love (חסד) extolled in the hymn. In this way, the hymn depicts the unresolved tensions between wrath and grace, which precipitate a final wisdom evaluation and an invitation to seek further

[25] H. Gunkel, *Die Psalmen* (Göttingen: Vandenhoeck & Ruprecht, 1926), pp. 470, 472–73.

understanding. It is this perception of the literature that leads Gunkel to call the ending of the psalm "a theodicy," an incisive description which may, nonetheless, overinterpret its actual function.[26]

While the ending of Hosea is similar to that of Ps. 107:42–43, it was not originally a part of the composition and placed, as it is, at the end of a prophetic book, represents a dramatic redactional and hermeneutical shift. J.L. Mays summarizes prevailing opinion regarding the redactional function of Hos. 14:10, "Its author sees in the book of Hosea a witness to the ways of Yahweh which the wise may interpret as a guide for a righteous life.[27] This commonly recognized position can be refined in several directions. First of all, the function of v. 10b, in relation to both the summons in 10a and the book of Hosea as a whole, merits further examinations. Recognizing this, Wolff is probably correct in viewing the כי between the summons and the statement in v. 10b as a deictic particle, one which occurs frequently in the body of Hosea.[28] In that case, v. 10b would not supply the reason for v. 10a. Its function is rather to offer, immediately after the summons, an example of the type of interpretation which the summons calls for. This arrangement of a proverb complementing a summons to interpret a literature sapientially is paralleled in Ps. 107:42–43, although here the order is reversed.

A second factor of importance is the relationship of the concluding proverb in Hos. 14:10b to the content of the preceding book of Hosea. The precise nature of the relationship remains virtually unexplored. First, as scholars have already noted, the customary antithetical parallelism of the righteous and the wicked (רשע) has been changed to that of the righteous and the rebels (פשע). This latter parallelism never occurs in Proverbs and appears artificial. Moreover, the change is highly significant because it reflects a preference for the same key pejorative term which occurs in Hos. 7:13 and 8:1. The decision to alter slightly this particular antithetical pair may also be conditioned by the circumstance that the difference between the nouns is only, orthographically, a single consonant and the new term still retains assonance with the old. A second noteworthy feature of the wisdom saying is that the typical Hoseanic verb, "to stumble," is strategically employed. As a key descriptive term in Hosea for wayward Ephraim and Judah (5:5, cf. 4:5–9), it is the leading metaphor for Israel and is used in the book's final appeal for repentance.

---

[26] Ibid., p. 473.

[27] James L. Mays, *Hosea*, Old Testament Library (Philadelphia: Westminster Press, 1969), p. 190.

[28] Wolff, *Dodekapropheton: Hosea*, op. cit., p. 310.

A third feature in the relation between the wisdom saying and the book appears upon an examination of proverb's learned play on a particular complex of words and ideas expressed throughout the book. The proverb declares initially, that "the ways of the Lord are right." The choice of ישרים allows for an inclusive interpretation of both "just" and "straight." An interpretation of the ways as "straight" carries implicitly over to the first stichos of the antithetical phrases, namely, "the righteous walk [straightforward] in them." By implication, the ways of the Lord portend opposing consequences for the righteous and for the rebellious. The righteous will walk forward in them, while the rebels will stumble. From the standpoint of redaction, this wisdom saying offers a retrospective commentary on the alternation in human experience between divine destruction and blessing, as already portrayed in the prophetic book. Hence, one finds that the vocabulary of "ways," "walk," "rebel," and "stumble" in the final wisdom saying corresponds clearly to the particular language and depiction of the book itself.

For example, in 5:5–7 the key word "stumble" is repeated twice with the assertion that this stumbling occurs even when Israel and Ephraim walk (< הלך) with their flocks and herds "to seek the Lord." To their surprise, the very God they seek withdraws himself, and they cannot find him. Because they have been faithless, he allows them to be devoured. The proverb seizes upon this same enigma that even when the rebellious attempt to walk in the ways of the Lord, he, being weary of their wickedness, will hide from them and cause them to stumble in their guilt (v. 5).

Likewise, in Hos. 9:7–9 and 13:5–8 this same imagery is again applied to Israel. According to Hos. 9:7–9 the typical northern prophet, "the watchman of Ephraim," has corrupted himself because of iniquity and hatred. Consequently, God will remember his sins and "set a fowler's snare on all his ways" (v. 8). So, also, in Hos. 13:5–8 God recalls the wilderness wanderings and how he sustained the people of Israel when they had neither food nor drink. In spite of God's beneficence to them, their hearts "were lifted up; therefore they forgot me" (v. 6b). For this reason, God will now, like a lion or a leopard, "lurk beside the way" in order to devour them. A comparison is drawn, therefore, between the Hebrew people sustained by God during their wilderness journey and the current rebellious generation who will confront God only as a wild beast which stalks its prey along their paths.

What further makes this generalization in the proverb true of the book as a whole is its ability to function as a gnomic critique of the central historical paradigm in Hos. 1:2–3:5. The proverb picks up the imagery of the "way" (דרכה, 2:8) which the adulterous woman takes (< הלך, 2:7, 9, 15, 16) and the manner in which her husband seeks to manipulate her paths. Hos. 2:6 is typical, "Therefore, I will hedge up her way with thorns, and I will build a wall against her so that she cannot find her paths." Being a rebel, she takes her own paths and finds in them perpetual stumbling. The proverb in v. 10b, consequently, is a literal assessment of the content of the book. The admonition in v. 10a to read Hosea as a guide to the righteous life is reinforced by this tangible example in 10b, which proverbializes the central enigmatic theme of the book.

This conclusion significantly effects the interpretation of the entire book. Originally Hosea prophesied only against the northern kingdom, yet the later work shows many indications of Judean interpolations (e.g., 4:15; 5:5, 10, 12, 13, 14; 6:4; etc.). The introductory verse even lists the kings of Judah before those of Israel. A collection of oracles which once applied only to the northern kingdom is, thus, generalized so that it becomes a religious address to the southern kingdom as well. In continuity with this redactional tendency the proverb has the effect of relativizing even further the original particularity of address. The reader is offered a timeless axiom that transcends the national identities of pre-exilic Israel and Judah. Its teachings are thus extended *to individuals* and now apply to the righteous and the rebellious of every generation who venture upon the paths of Yahweh.

Furthermore, this call for a wisdom interpretation of Hosea may already be predisposed by the unique assertion in Hos. 12:10 that God gave "parables" (אדמה) through his prophets. Indeed, the narrative portions in the first three chapters can easily be taken as a parable on the relationship of God and his elect. This viewpoint is, in fact, the common one in the history of interpretation and has the effect of stressing the *realia* of the narrative, while checking any attempt to reconstruct the psychology or historical circumstances of the prophet and his adulterous wife. Hence, the proverb in Hos. 14:10b complements the summons in v. 10a by providing a wisdom interpretation which checks any attempt merely to historicize, in terms of the prophet's original ministry, the profound tension between God's wrath and grace toward a profligate people.

An additional refinement to the scholarly discussion of this editorial ending lies in the direction of canon consciousness. The ending was probably an afterthought added to the self-sufficient collection of Hoseanic oracles, and most scholars suggest an exilic or post-exilic date. In one of the more cogent explanations of its origin, Ina Willi-Plein offers:

> ... man die Worte nicht mehr in ihrem ursprünglichen Rahmen der Zeitgeschichte vernimmt, sondern sie für die Hörer und Leser in die Gleichzeitigkeit und Einheit des kanonischen Gotteswortes gefaßt sind (s.o. S. 10). Gericht und Verheißung, Verwerfung und Begnadung, Tod und Neubeginn für das eine Israel – wie ist das zu verstehen?[29]

Here she recognizes the manner in which this redactional ending highlights the function of the Hoseanic corpus as an enduring sacred word to the later Jewish community.

However, the argument that the ending arises simply as an isolated gesture to actualize an ancient and static text, one which no longer speaks relevantly to the post-exilic community, is totally unconvincing. Even without the ending, the book of Hosea has a shape that allowed for an edifying reading in the exilic and post-exilic communities. The oracles, for instance, are no longer securely anchored to their original and particular historical settings. They have been blurred together and reworked so that some of the original form critical distinctions have been lost. They can now be read topically through the prefaced paradigm of the prophet and his profligate wife. In addition, the salvation oracles are predominantly eschatological and continue to promise a future far surpassing the experiences of the people after their return from exile. In fact, the message of Hosea, more than being merely contemporary, is truly prophetic to later generations who have not yet realized these promises.

The ending of Hosea, therefore, complements these other features and, together with them, indicates a long history in the shaping and in the religious usage of the Hoseanic traditions. Nevertheless, in distinction to these other features, this final verse offers an assessment to a book which has already acquired its essential shape. The nature of this appendage, as a second conclusion to the book, suggests that its author views Hosea as a fixed literature which already exercises religious authority within a Jewish community. In this sense, the ending presumes a canonical function for the prophetic book and calls for a reading of Hosea as a guide to wisdom.

If one compares the hermeneutical techniques used in this addition to Hosea with those identified in the Sirach and Baruch studies, a number of similarities appear. Both the unique antithetical parallelism of the righteous and the rebels and the use of other key terms from the book of Hosea (e.g., "stumble") suggest that the proverb is artificially constructed or at least revised from an older proverb for the express purpose of inter-

---

[29] Ina Willi-Plein, *Vorformen der Schriftexegese innerhalb des Alten Testaments*, BZAW, 123 (1971): 235.

preting the book. Therefore, in a strict form critical sense the wisdom saying of Hos. 14:10 is probably not a proverb with an oral history, but a literary creation specifically written for the purposes of interpreting the book. The literary imitation of Prov. 8 in Sir. 24 for the purpose of interpreting the Torah narrative may be viewed as a parallel phenomenon.

Other parallels in techniques can be found between the ways Sirach and Baruch passages interpret the Torah narrative and the way this wisdom saying assesses the book of Hosea. Like the second century examples, the wisdom saying makes reference to the previous literature both by means of key words and by allusion to a set of words and concepts. Even as the reference to "rest" and "inheritance" in Sir. 24:7 recalls the same technical terminology in Deuteronomy, so the mention of "rebels" who "stumble" in Hos. 14:10 links the wisdom saying to the preceding text by means of a shared distinctive vocabulary. However, the wisdom saying also describes a pattern of activity and consequences which alludes to corresponding patterns in the text. Here the connection between text and interpretation depends more on semantic agreement than on lexical repetition. So, the depiction of Israel on a "path" which leads to destruction because of her disobedience is a recurring pattern in the book of Hosea which is picked up and given a definitive interpretation by the wisdom saying at the end. Similarly, the Sirach and Baruch studies alluded to Israel's pilgrimage from the Exodus to her settling in Zion in order to apply this same pattern to Wisdom as well.

On the basis of this evidence, the ending of Hosea clearly parallels the type of wisdom interpretation described in the Sirach and Baruch studies. Hence, the last verse is suggestive of a canon conscious addendum which offers a hermeneutical judgment on the reading of this fixed prophetic tradition. While there is little intrinsic evidence from which to suggest a late date, this redaction belongs to the last stages in the formation of the book, perhaps in the exilic or post-exilic period. The similarities with Sirach and Baruch provide indirect evidence of a similar hermeneutical device, unusual for pre-exilic inner-biblical interpretation. The ending probably affirms in editorial fashion a function which the book has already attained, namely, the use of it to gain practical religious advice like one finds in the sacred biblical wisdom literature assigned to Solomon.

The Preface to the Psalter (Ps. 1 and 2)

Ps. 1 has been described as either a "wisdom" or a "Torah" psalm. Each of these designations betrays the same unsolved form critical problem. While other form critical designations carry an implicit assessment of sociological function (e.g., individual lament, thanksgiving song), these two categories seem to reflect only an estimate of the supposed content or subject matter of a psalm. Ps. 1 illustrates why confusion results from the use of this criterion. On the one hand, it is acknowledged that the style and certain expressions in Ps. 1 are idiomatic to wisdom literature. On the other hand, the Torah seems to be its principal object of concern and it, not the wisdom literature, is commended for study.

Mowinckel has pressed the form critical problem and concluded that the so-called "wisdom psalms" must have functioned in wisdom circles. According to his analysis, their setting was non-cultic, associated with private and learned piety. The function of such a literature was principally to praise God in worship and to teach the younger participants the art of prayer.[30] For this purpose, the sages frequently borrowed a particular type of a hymn or used a general psalmic style.[31] However, both Roland Murphy and Erhard Gerstenberger question this presupposition of a non-cultic life setting.[32] Certainly evidence from the case study of Sir. 24 works against the analogous non-cultic characterization that Mowinckel assumes for the wisdom of Ben Sira.[33] The priests are, in fact, portrayed in Sir. 24 as the bearers of heavenly wisdom that travels with the tent shrine to Zion where it is represented by the sacred incense and anointing oil.[34]

In any future attempt to resolve the form critical problem, it is, consequently, extremely important that the linguistic function of the alleged wisdom features of these psalms be carefully evaluated. The key issue in Ps. 1 turns on the contextual use of the wisdom doctrine of the two ways.[35]

[30] S. Mowinckel, "Psalms and Wisdom," *Wisdom in Israel and in the Ancient Near East*, *SVT*, 3 (1955): 205ff.

[31] Op. cit., pp. 208, 211.

[32] Roland Murphy, "A Consideration of the Classification 'Wisdom Psalms,'" *SVT*, 9 (1962): 161; Erhard Gerstenberger, "Psalms," *Old Testament Form Criticism*, ed. by John H. Hayes (San Antonio: Trinity University Press, 1974), pp. 220–21.

[33] Mowinckel, op. cit., pp. 210–11.

[34] This priestly orientation for Wisdom is complemented by the extended eulogy to priests in the Praise to the Fathers, Sir. 44ff. Mowinckel's distinction between cultic and ritual performance is not entirely clear. Even if the sacrificial system appears to have fallen away in the time of Sirach, this factor does not necessarily suggest a distinctive movement toward inward and privatistic piety in the period. This criticism is valid because a change in the nature of cultic observance would not inevitably diminish the communal and institutional forms of worship. That Sirach contains numerous psalms of the same form critical type as those of the earlier Psalter suggests a continuing institutional context with deep roots in the cultic past.

[35] In addition to ideological similarity with the wisdom traditions, some of the phraseology in Ps. 1 is distinctive of Proverbs. For example, the use of "the way of sinners" (cf. Prov.

In this regard, it should be observed that the psalm does not, in the strict sense, *teach* the doctrine, even though it is assumed and is used to express the results of studying Torah. Precisely the Torah, not wisdom, is the literary source for an understanding of the ways of the righteous as opposed to the ways of the wicked. Nevertheless, this function of the Torah entails a guide to wisdom like that claimed by the wisdom traditions. The latter assumption recalls a similar view of the Torah demonstrated in the case studies of Sirach and Baruch. In the light of this possible correspondence, a consideration of the redactional function of Ps. 1 in relation to the rest of the Psalter is particularly important.

In his brief but penetrating re-investigation of the collection of the Psalter, Westermann suggests a redactional relationship between Ps. 1 and 119. Both are no longer to be regarded as psalms in any real sense.[36] Rather, they are the preface and conclusion which frame an earlier collection of psalms.[37] From this proposal Westermann evaluates the new function for Ps. 1 within the tradition history of the Psalter.

> Dieser Rahmen wiederum bezeugt ein wichtiges Stadium auf dem Traditionsweg des Psalters, in dem der Psalter als *Sammlung* nicht mehr primär kultische Funktion hatte, sondern sich auf dem Weg gesetzesfrommer Überlieferung bewegte. Die Psalmen sind Gotteswort geworden, das gelesen, studiert, meditiert wird [in footnote: "Genau wie es Ps. 1 beschreibt!"].[38]

He observes that the same holds true for the ending of Hosea (14:10).[39] Hence, one finds here, as in Hos. 14:10, a case for a canon conscious redaction of fixed biblical tradition which commends an interpretation in terms of wisdom. However, the precise function of Ps. 1 with its concern for Torah and wisdom must be further examined to show how it relates specifically to the reading of the Psalter.

Initially, the suggestion by Mowinckel and others that Ps. 1 was composed by the last redactor, as a motto or a preface to the Psalter after reflection on Jer. 17:5–8, must be questioned.[40] Besides the factor of a continuing debate over Ps. 1 in relation to Jer. 17, the psalm itself explicitly charges its readers to study "the Torah," not the following psalms.[41] If its

1:10–15), "the way of the wicked" (cf. Prov. 4:19; 15:9), and "the way of the righteous" (cf. Prov. 4:18; 12:28).

[36] Claus Westermann, "Zur Sammlung des Psalters," *Forschung am Alten Testament* (München: Chr. Kaiser Verlag, 1964), p. 338.

[37] Op. cit., pp. 338–39.

[38] Op. cit., p. 339.

[39] Ibid.

[40] S. Mowinckel, *Psalmenstudien*, 6 vols. (Kristiania: Jacob Dybwad, 1924): 6:33.

[41] Cf. Hans-Joachim Kraus, *Psalmen*, 2 vols. (Neukirchener Verlag, 1960): 1:3.

composition were entirely conditioned by its function as a motto or introduction to a given collection, one would expect a bold and direct acknowledgement regarding the purpose of the literature that follows it.[42] Likewise, "the Torah" cannot be easily generalized to mean "Scripture."[43] Therefore, the introductory function of the psalm to the Psalter was probably the result of the later redactional positioning rather than the free composition of the final redactor.

Other features strongly suggest a secondary redactional association between Ps. 1 and 2.[44] Although the *Gratulationsformel* at the beginning of Ps. 1 is original to it, the one following Ps. 2 is probably secondary.[45] The two formulae now provide an *inclusio* around the two psalms and set them apart from the larger collection of psalms that follow. This intended distinction for the first two psalms is further substantiated by the absence of titles for either psalms. Titles begin only with Ps. 3. In this regard, it is striking that Ps. 2 lacks a title because, unlike most psalms, it presumes Davidic authorship by internal evidence. The statement, "the Lord said *to me*," and what follows recall the oracle of Nathan to David. Furthermore, the absence of a title for Ps. 2 is highly significant because it offers internal evidence to invite such a titular designation, even during a time when untitled psalms were progressively gaining them. It is quite possible that an original title to Ps. 2, in a time when it, perhaps, stood as the lead psalm of a smaller collection (e.g., Ps. 2–41), has been removed as a part of

---

[42] Mowinckel's use of the term "motto" reckons with the problem, but it lacks a sufficient form critical dimension to establish the identity and function of such a nuanced literary form.

[43] Kraus (op. cit., p. 9) observes, "Diese תורה aber ist nicht der tötende νόμος, sondern die lebensbringende, heilsame Offenbarungsgröße der damals vorliegenden Heiligen Schrift (vgl. Ps. 119)." For a criticism, see Gerstenberger, op. cit., p. 219.

[44] For an attempt to view these associations as evidence for the use of the combined psalms in a single life setting, see W. H. Brownlee, "Psalms 1–2 as a Coronation Liturgy," *Bib*, 52 (1971): 321–35.

[45] It follows the psalm and is not essential form critically. Nevertheless, Gunkel (op. cit., p. 12) can show that the argument from imbalance metrically or from its unusual character may not be conclusive. Such a formula occurs elsewhere at the end of only four other psalms, viz., 84, 127, 137, 144. However, it is difficult to determine the function of the formula at the end of some of these and at the end of Ps. 2. If Gunkel is correct in seeing this as original to the composition of the psalm, then its selectivity seems to be conditioned by this factor. I would prefer to regard the content of the psalm to be the decisive factor in its selectivity and ordering after Ps. 1. In that case, the arbitrary occurrences of the formula in random types of psalms makes less probable the chance that the psalm would both have the desired compatibility in content with Ps. 1 *as well as* the necessary formula to create an *inclusio* about the two.

the same redactional effort behind the addition of the concluding formula.

To this evidence for a redactional framework can be added a high degree of correspondence in the substance and sequence of these two psalms. Here there appears a decisive complementarity of content. What Ps. 1 sets forth as a didactic generalization is modeled in historical terms by Ps. 2. The psalms constructively interpret each other by means of several parallel literary features:

a. Ps. 1 oscillates between a depiction of the person who walks in the way of the righteous (vv. 1–3) and of the person who walks in the way of sinners (vv. 4–5). The last verse summarizes the intended lesson, "the Lord knows the way of the righteous, but the way of the wicked will perish." The beginning of Ps. 2 seems to pick up the theme of this last stichos, i.e., "the wicked," but spells it out in terms of nations and their rulers. These stand in bold relief against the divinely appointed king (vv. 6–9), before the subject reverts back again to a summarizing admonition. Thus, the reader moves easily from Ps. 1 to Ps. 2 following one general theme related to similar contrasted subjects before reaching the concluding admonition.

b. The righteous in Ps. 1:2 *meditate* (יהגה) upon the Torah day and night. Conversely, the apostate nations and rulers in Ps. 2:1 *meditate* (יהגו) in vain against God. In contrast to the concise language describing intellectual activity in Ps. 1, there is in Ps. 2 a piling up of noetic vocabulary for the plotting of the nations and rulers. Not only do they ponder vain plans, but they "conspire" and "counsel together." Despite all this effort, they are no match for God. Thus the conclusion seems to recall the either-or character of Ps. 1 in its lines, "Now therefore, O Kings, be wise [השכילו] ... serve the Lord with fear."

c. Ps. 1:1b identifies the wise man as one who does not sit (ישב) in the seat of scoffers (לצים). This expression now stands in contrast with the imagery of God's reaction to the foolish world leaders who plot and counsel together: "He who sits [יושב] in heaven laughs [ישחק]; the Lord has them in derision [ילעג]."

d. The next to the last phrase at the end of Ps. 2 closely resembles that at the end of Ps. 1:

1:6 ודרך רשעים תאבד

2:11b פן יאנף ותאבדו דרך

1:6 but the way of the wicked will perish.

2:11b lest he be angry and you perish in the way.

The LXX seizes upon this functional resonance predisposed by the redactional association of the two psalms and heightens the effect. In 2:10 the command that the kings "be wise" is followed in the *MT* by the imperative "be warned" (הוסרו). The latter is taken in the LXX as παιδεύθητε, "be instructed." The obscure demand in the *MT* of 2:12 נשקו בר, "kiss his feet [RSV]," is rendered δράξασθει παιδείας, "accept discipline/instruction." This last Greek word is, of course, the common LXX equivalent for מוסר in Proverbs. However, the most conspicuous conformity is the translation of the above mentioned ending of Ps. 2 to read, ἀπολεῖσθε ἐξ ὁδοῦ δικάιας, "you shall perish from *the way of righteousness*." With that alteration all ambiguity is removed and the respective endings stand in stark, verbal symmetry. One can, therefore, interpret Ps. 2 through Ps. 1. The nations and kings who lack "understanding" and "instruction" (v. 10) must accept "discipline/instruction" (v. 12a), or they will forfeit "the way of the righteous" (v. 12b).

Consequently, Ps. 1 and 2, as has been shown, share a common redactional framework. Outside of the texts themselves, an early variant of Acts. 13:33 treats the citation of a few lines from Ps. 2 as from "the first psalm."[46] This should not be viewed as a proof positive that Ps. 1 is a *Prooemium* and that Ps. 2 starts the actual body of the Psalter.[47] Rather, Ps. 1and 2 are so linked redactionally that it is a natural consequence that they may be evaluated *in tandum* as the first psalm of the Psalter. So, too, one finds in the rabbinic literature, and possibly in 4Q Florilegium, a witness to an early tradition of viewing Ps. 1 and 2 as a single psalm.[48] Together they form a joint preface to the entire Psalter.

When Ps. 1 and Ps. 2 are combined redactionally at the beginning of the Psalter, the Torah and probably some wisdom books are recognized as having canonical authority. In this sense, canon consciousness appears evident in the very nature of the redaction of Ps. 1 and 2. What Westermann says of Ps. 1, he applies as well to Ps. 2 in his observation that so-called "royal psalms" have at this time in the collection taken on a messianic force.[49] Hence, the admonition in Ps. 1 probably represents a late redactional assessment of perhaps the exilic or post exilic period. It carries

---

[46] While the *textus receptus* reads, "the second psalm," this reading is found in the Codex Bezae, Origen, etc.

[47] Kraus, op. cit., p. 2.

[48] See Berakoth 9b–10a and *Tractate Sopherim*, ed. by M. Higger (New York, 1937), line 57 and notes. For an estimate of 4Q Florilegium as a midrash on Ps. 1 and 2, see Brownlee, op. cit., pp. 321–33, n. 2.

[49] Westermann, op. cit., p. 342.

obvious canonical ramifications. The Torah, at least by this period, probably signifies the first five books of Moses, though some lesser Torah may be possible. Readers are, therefore, invited to view the Torah as a guide to the righteous life in terms like those of the sacred wisdom books which form another part of the emerging matrix of canonical Scripture.

How, then, does an admonition in Ps. 1 to study *the Torah* in order to walk in the way of the righteous serve with Ps. 2 as a preface to *the Psalter*? By implication the demand to read the Torah as a guide to wisdom is what the redactor presupposes to be illustrated by the Psalter. This presupposition is made even more explicitly by the close relationship between Ps. 1 and Ps. 2. The profane nations and rulers in Ps. 2 are identified with those who walk the way of the sinners and the wicked in Ps. 1. Opposite these, one finds the divine king depicted in the language of Nathan's oracle as one who, by contrastive implication, walks in the way of the righteous. Consequently, David is represented in Ps. 2 both as the author of the Psalms and also as one who qualifies under the injunction of Ps. 1 to interpret the Torah as a guide to righteousness.[50] David's prayers, therefore, are set forth as having an authority derivative from the Torah and as a guide to righteous living like that found in the wisdom traditions.

In sum, Ps. 1 and 2 have been redactionally ordered into a combined prologue to the Psalter. Whether or not they belong at the latest stage in the redactional history or to a smaller collection ending with either Ps. 42 (e.g., Mowinckel) or Ps. 119 (e.g., Westermann), their final role is the same. Ps. 1 and 2 correlate the study of the Torah collection with the goal of attaining sacred wisdom like that found in the wisdom traditions, and perhaps in a set of biblical wisdom books. By his associations with Ps. 2, David, who is, in canonical terms, the chief architect of the Psalter, is identified fully in accord with the ideals in Ps. 1. The entire Psalter, therefore, is made to stand theologically in association with David as a source book of guidance for the way of the righteous. In this fashion, the Psalter has gained, among its other functions, the use as a source for Wisdom reflection and a model of prayers based on such a pious interpretation of the Torah.

A comparison of the way Ps. 1 and 2 interpret biblical traditions with that of Sir. 24 and Bar. 3:9–4:4 shows that they share a similar point of view. At the level of literary structure, Ps. 1 and 2 may be divided into two parts. A didactic instruction in Ps. 1 is followed in Ps. 2 by an inner-

[50] Mowinckel, *Psalmenstudien*, p. 82, regards the implication of David in Ps. 2 as an attribution of authorship to the Psalter.

biblical demonstration of its application and opposing consequences for David and the worldly kings. The same two-part structure is found in Sir. 24 and Bar. 3:9–4:4, only the order is reversed. In Sirach and Baruch, the exhibition of Wisdom's beneficial presence in the Torah narrative and the illustration of the opposing consequences in biblical history for those who knew or did not know "the way of wisdom" represents the demonstration which preceeds a statement of principle in Sir. 24:23ff. and Bar. 4:1ff. Furthermore, the pericope on the way of wisdom in Bar. 3:9–4:4 ends with the assurance. "Happy are we, O Israel, for we know what is pleasing to God." This self-declaration at the end of Baruch is at least structurally reminiscent of the *Gratulationsformel*–"Happy are those who take refuge in him"–which occurs at the end of Ps. 2. Therefore, in its concern to provide both a general claim that the Torah is a source of wisdom and a specific demonstration of it in the sacred traditions, Ps. 1 and 2 established a structural precedent which was followed later in Sirach and Baruch.

Besides this important structural parallel, Ps. 1 and 2 share with the second century literature a similar vocabulary and choice of imagery at certain crucial points. Bar. 3:9ff. claims that Israel was given "the way to knowledge" by divine election (3:27, 36). Conversely, the learned and mighty heros of the nations perish because they do not know "the way of wisdom." Similarly, the redactional effect of linking Ps. 1 with Ps. 2 is to contrast David–whom God has chosen by decree (2:6–7) and who, by implication of Ps. 1, knows "the way of the righteous"–with the wicked kings who take counsel together in vain. Bar. 3:9ff. illustrates repeatedly how the worldly heroes "perished because they had no wisdom" (3:28a), just as Ps. 1 claims "the way of the wicked will perish" (1:6b), a claim which is sustained by the warning to the rulers in Ps. 2, "be wise ... lest he be angry and you perish in the way" (2:10–11). Therefore, the contrast in Ps. 1 and 2 between David, who is chosen to know the Torah as a guide to wisdom, and the rulers of the nations who perish without it, closely parallels the contrast in Bar. 3:9ff. between Israel who is elected to know "the way of wisdom" by her possession of the Torah and the heroes of the nations who perish without it. Finally, Ps. 1 compares those who are wise through meditation on the Torah with "a tree planted by the streams of water (which) yields fruit in its season and (whose) leaf does not whither" (1:3). According to the last stichos of Ps. 1:3, the purpose of the imagery is to show the wise person "will prosper in all that he does." Sir. 24:12–17 draws upon exactly the same milieu of earthly vegetation and precious spices in order to describe Wisdom's fruition in Zion.

At a minimum, this evidence shows that Ps. 1 and 2 establish a basic structure and employ certain imagery which closely parallels the passages in Sir. 24 and Bar. 3:9ff. This comparison is not meant to obscure differences between the passages. Certainly the statement of principle in Sir. 24:23 and Bar. 4:1 is in the form of a revealed identification rather than an advisory admonition to read the Torah in order to know the way of righteousness. Moreover, Ps. 1 and 2 achieve their effect by a redaction which gives a secondary context to once independent psalms. By contrast, the Sirach and Baruch passages are free compositions which offer learned plays on past fixed traditions. Nevertheless, Ps. 1 and 2 clearly represent an earlier canon conscious attempt to relate Torah to wisdom within the formation of the OT, an effort which anticipates the later formal and freely exegetical attempts in Sirach and Baruch.

The hermeneutical implications for reading the Psalter in the context of the canon is not one of restricting its interpretation to the concerns of wisdom. Wisdom interpretation is only one of several means that open the Scripture up to its use by later generations and creates a place for the Psalter among the larger canonical collections. For example, the role of Ps. 1:2 is clearly to place the psalms in the context of the Torah, while the messianic cast to Ps. 2 and other such psalms allows them to be read productively as prophetic to a later community. Moreover, the titles of the psalms allow them to be read as commentary on the subjective side of David, the same David who performs in the secular sphere in the historical narrative of the Former Prophets.[51] Finally, the identification of the psalms as a product of Torah study, which has found there the ideals of the wisdom traditions, allows the psalms to be read as a moral guide to the obedient life. In each of these various ways the Psalter has been closely related in its interpretation to the Torah, the Prophets, and the wisdom books. For the present investigation, the most significant of these has been the use of wisdom as a hermeneutical construct, which finds in the Torah and, by implication, in the Psalter an authoritative source for moral reflection.

The Last Words of David (2 Sam. 23:1–7)

Since the groundbreaking work of L. Rost, form critical studies on the books of Samuel have continued to stress their preservation of an

[51] Cf. Brevard S. Childs, "Psalm Titles and Midrashic Exegesis," *JSS*, 16 (1971): 137–50; F. F. Bruce, "The Earliest Old Testament Interpretation," *OTS*, 17 (1972): 44–52.

original "Succession Narrative (or 'Document')."[52] The close interweaving of precise chronological detail and vivid characterization led von Rad to describe this narrative as representative of a renaissance in historical writing.[53] More recently, the redaction critical issues have been raised into sharp focus. Despite substantial scholarly agreement on the redactional character of the last four chapters (21–24) of 2 Samuel, which interrupt the Succession Narrative and bring the Samuel books to a close, their origin and function in the deuteronomistic history remains only partially explored. Consequently, our analysis will begin with a study of how these chapters are organized and related to the preceding Samuel books, then focus on the role of 2 Sam. 23:1–7 within them, and finally describe the nature of the redaction in the light of the previous studies of Sirach and Baruch.

In redactional investigations there has been sustained scholarly agreement that the last four chapters of 2 Samuel separate the bulk of the Succession Narrative still found in parts of 2 Sam. 6–7, 9–20 from its original conclusion in 1 Kings 1–2.[54] On the one hand, in spite of this evidence of a radical severing of a previously coherent document, one must acknowledge that the interruption is not arbitrary, but judicious enough to maintain its own literary integrity. Even the casual reader of these chapters will recognize that they provide an effective conclusion to the eventful career of David. They follow after a recollection of the Israelite hero's last triumphal deeds, namely, his return from temporary exile to Jerusalem and his annihilation of the rebels Abishai and Sheba through his faithful commander, Joab.

On the other hand, 1 Kings 1–2 offers only the most pathetic portrayal of an elderly David who can no longer keep warm and must stay in his chamber. Compared to Adonijah and the supporters of Solomon, David is inert, uninformed and unresponsive. In the shadow of his death he must be coaxed pathetically into the pivotal political decision to legitimize Solomon's claim to the throne over that of his rival. While this

---

[52] L. Rost, *Die Überlieferung von der Thronnachfolge Davids* in BWANT III/6 (Stuttgart: Verlag von W. Kohlhammer, 1926), pp. 82–139.

[53] For example, see G. von Rad, "Der Anfang der Geschichtsschreibung," *AK*, 32 (1944): 1–42.

[54] See, for example, Karl Budde, *Die Bücher Samuel* (Tübingen: Verlag von J. C. B. Mohr, 1902), p. 304 and R. A. Carlson, *David the Chosen King* (Stockholm: Almqvist & Wiksell, 1964), pp. 194–98. For a detailed summary of the passages of 2 Samuel in which the *Thronfolgequelle* is alleged to be preserved, see Rost, op. cit., pp. 107–8.

vestigial David manages some perfunctory directions regarding the royal anointing ceremony (vv. 32–35), he remains entirely oblivious to all of the crucial military and political strategy necessary in order to implement the succession.

Hence, the effect redactionally has been to separate 1 Kings 1–2, which is concerned most directly with the succession, from the previous 2 Samuel record of David's energetic life. Moreover, the conclusion to the Samuel books (ch. 21–24) does not evaluate the preceding narrative in terms of its original function in a Succession Document, but views the narrative purely in terms of what it says about David.[55] It is this particular redactional relationship of 2 Sam. 21–24 to 1 Sam. 1–2 Sam. 20 that is of greatest significance for the present study.

Concerning 2 Sam. 21–24, K. Budde was the first to point out a threefold pattern of (a) narratives *(Erzählungen)* regarding famine and pestilence in 21:1–14 and 24, (b) enumerations *(Aufzählungen)* of heroic deeds and heroes in 21:15–22 and 23:8–39, and (c) poetic compositions *(Gedichten)* in 22 and 23:1–7.[56] The majority of scholars since Budde have followed his suggestion that these chapters are post-Deuteronomic in origin. However, the investigations of Albright and his students on the style and orthography of 2 Sam. 22 argue against assigning it a late date of composition.[57] Accordingly, while the redactional structure of 2 Sam. 21–24 is still regarded as exilic in origin, Engnell, Hertzberg, Schildenberger, and Carlson consider many of the traditions, especially the psalm and the so-called "last words" in 22:1–23:7, to reach back even to the period of David. Carlson, in particular, mounts a detailed case for seeing these traditions as transmitted from ancient times and redacted by later exilic editors in a Deuteronomic circle, which he calls the "D-group."[58] Furthermore, these same scholars with Carlson stress the chiastic structure of traditions in 21–24 as a clue to their history of transmission.

Carlson offers the following diagram:[59]

---

[55] Only 2 Sam. 22:51 and 23:5 speak of an everlasting throne for David and his descendants. In the course of the present study it will be shown that these statements evaluate David in a way that ignores the impending question of succession.

[56] Budde, op. cit., p. 304.

[57] F. M. Cross, Jr. and David N. Freedman, "A Royal Song of Thanksgiving: II Samuel 22 = Psalm 18," *JBL*, 72 (1953): 15–34; and W. F. Albright, *Archaeology and the Religion of Israel* (Baltimore: Anchor Books, 1946), p. 129.

[58] Carlson, op. cit., pp. 197–98.

[59] Ibid., p. 248.

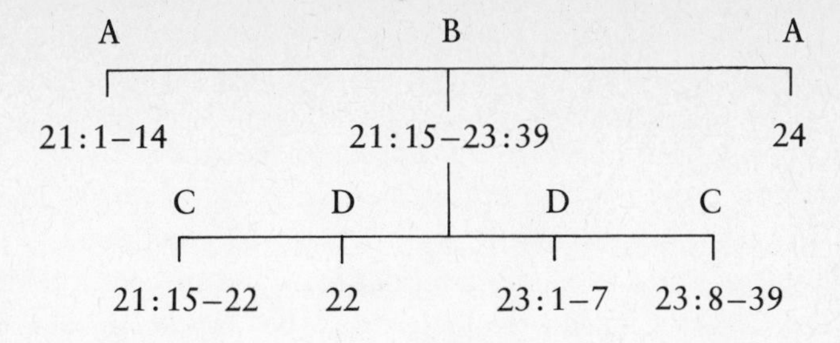

Whether or not Carlson's hypothesis of a D-group is correct, this unified structure conveys quite well the literary aesthetic skill of the editor(s) and a precise intentionality behind this redactional arrangement. The following compositional analysis will concentrate on demonstrating the retrospective character of 2 Sam. 21–24 and on showing how the literary associations between the parts of the chiastic structure point to its singular intent.

That these chapters are generalizations on the preceding David story appears in a variety of ways. For example, although 21:1–14 is historical narrative like the preceding chapters, it departs sharply from their chronological sequence. 21:1–14 looks back to the time of David's earlier triumph over Saul and his response to Saul's remaining associates and relatives. Both 2 Sam. 9 (Mephibosheth) and 16:5–13 (the cursing by Shimei) address the same matter but presuppose a set of circumstances and resulting treatment of Saul's sons different from that given in 21:1–14.[60] The literary purpose of ch. 21 is less one of supplying supplementary historical detail than one of providing a retrospective estimate of David's dealing with the question of inherited guilt and punishment. By an appeal to God, David finds that the reason for the three-year famine is Saul's maltreatment of the Gibeonites. Undoubtedly this recollection provides an apologetic for David's innocence in the matter and, more importantly, acknowledges his subsequent ability to seek God and take the right course of action.

In the parallel ch. 24, the anger of the Lord is said "to continue" (יסף, v. 1) against Israel. God, therefore, incites David to number the people. Afterwards, David recognizes his numbering the people as a sin and repents for his misdeed. In an act of divine mercy the land experiences only three days of pestilence for David's crime. Both passages, 21:1–14 and 24, are paradigmatic of David's reaction to the situation of wickedness and guilt. Both begin with a condition under the wrath of God which David eventu-

[60] Cf. Hans Wilhelm Hertzberg, *Die Samuelbücher* (Göttingen: Vandenhoeck & Ruprecht, 1956), p. 309; Budde, op.cit., p. 304.

ally overcomes through prayer and right action. They point back to the earlier history as typologies of Davidic conduct.[61] Later in this study the function of 21:1–14 and 24:1–25 as a framework around the most central compositions of 22 and 23:1–7 will be explored.[62]

Because the restricted goal of this short study is to examine 23:1–7, a full redaction critical discussion about 21:15–22 and 23:8–39 is unnecessary. Suffice it to say that both recall heroes and anecdotes connected with the Davidic wars against the Philistines. They bracket again the core poetic sections by capturing, in compressed and representative depiction, the glories of the battles which so punctuate the course of David's career.[63]

Both 22 and 23:1–7 are similarly significant for their retrospective connections with the previous narrative of first and second Samuel. The hymn in 2 Sam. 22 is the same as that found in Ps. 18. While it is form critically without any question an individual thanksgiving psalm, an exact

[61] Cf. Carlson, op. cit., pp. 198–222.

[62] Both narratives concern a divine threat to the people and to the land (21:14b; 24:25) for which David is responsible and seeks expiation. Although these narratives are not discussed in R. C. Culley's *Studies in the Structure of Hebrew Narrative* (Philadelphia: Fortress Press, 1976), the close structural correspondence between them can be exhibited by comparing parallel episodes similar to Culley's analysis of other texts:

2 Samuel 21:1–14	2 Samuel 24:1–24
expression of divine anger implicit in famine	expression of divine anger "again" as reason for God's inciting David to number the people
prayer to God	recognition of sin and prayer to God
the Lord answers the prayer with a revelation of the sin which David then seeks to expiate.	the Lord answers the prayer with terms for expiating the sin
act of expiation by handing over the sons of Saul to the wronged Gibeonites	act of expiation by choosing and receiving a divinely ordered form of punishment
surprise interlude necessary for expiation: David's mercy to Rizpah and his burying the bones of Saul and Jonathan in the tomb of Saul's father Kish	surprise interlude necessary for expiation: David's mercy for the suffering people, Gad's order to build an altar on the threshing floor of Arunah, purchase of the temple site and burnt offering for expiation
"And after that God heeded suplications for the land."	"So the Lord heeded suplications for the land, and the plague was averted from Israel."

[63] Hertzberg (op. cit., pp. 327–31) discusses the Egyptian evidence for the significance of the number 30 in the listing of 23:8–39. Moreover, he considers the final listing of Uriah among the heroes as a reminder of God's grace to David despite his sin in that earlier episode.

cultic life setting for it is elusive.[64] Gunkel can speak only generally of a royal *Siegesdankfest*, while H. Schmidt posits a royal enthronement festival.[65] In any case, the antiquity of the hymn can no longer be doubted.[66] Two probable redactional stages in the transmission history of the hymn are significant for the present study. First, the original cultic hymn was given an historically explicit title, which assigned it to the victory celebration of David over Saul. This move historicized the psalm in terms of David's life, and predisposed any future hearing to find in the ambiguity of the hymn's language echoes of the particular Davidic victory recorded in the title.[67] Second, the titled psalm was redactionally placed with 23:1–7 at the center of the complex 21–24 and at the end of the Samuel books. Hertzberg describes well the effect of this literary positioning on the psalm and its semantic function,

> Ja er liefert den theologischen Kommentar zur Davidgeschichte. Im Sinne dieses Psalms soll die Davidgeschichte gelesen und gehört werden. Das ist die Meinung des Endverfassers.[68]

Perhaps the most immediate consequence lies in the literary associations between both the hymn and 23:1–7 with the Prayer of Hannah in 1 Sam. 2, by means of which the beginning of the Samuel books has been united with the end.[69] Additionally, 23:1–7 is connected with the earlier oracle of Nathan (2 Sam. 7) by its statement in v. 5. Whether or not the statement in v. 5 was dependent originally on 2 Sam. 7, the new redactional setting in the literature makes an identification with the earlier passage unavoidable. Only in 23:1–7 does one find the same conceptuality and language as that occurring in 2 Sam. 7 (cf. 2 Sam. 23:5 with 7:16). Hence, the combination of David's hymn and last words seems to recall the earlier narrative and to identify the fulfillment of Nathan's oracle with the events of David's kingship and the future of his dynasty.

Before considering 23:1–7 independently, it is significant to note how various parallels in language between 22 and 23:1–7 predispose them to function *together* as theological commentary on the preceding Samuel narrative. For example, as in the Prayer of Hannah, 2 Sam. 22:3,

---

[64] See Gunkel, *Die Psalmen*, op. cit., p. 62 and Kraus, op. cit., p. 140.

[65] Gunkel, op. cit., p. 67. H. Schmidt, *Die Thronfahrt Jahves* (Tübingen: J. C. B. Mohr, 1927), pp. 21–22.

[66] See n. 57.

[67] See n. 51.

[68] Hertzberg, op. cit., p. 319.

[69] See Carlson, op. cit., pp. 226–27, 246–47.

32, 47 and 2 Sam. 23:3a refer to God by the title, the "rock." Interwoven in David's hymn of 2 Sam. 22 is the refrain that God on high reached down to him (v. 17), secured him on the heights (v. 34b), and exalted him above his adversaries (v. 49). Similarly, 23:1 includes as an epithet of David, "the man who was raised on high." Likewise, 22:51 provides a conceptual bridge between the psalm and the words of David.[70] As in 23:1 David is called "the anointed." There is also the assurance of posterity "forever" (עד עולם), even as the wisdom saying and the comparisons with the natural orders in 23:3b–4 are interpreted by a statement on the "everlasting [עולם] covenant ordered in all things and secure" (v. 5b).

This redactional combination of a hymnic song (22) and last words (23:1–7) at the end of the Samuel books is probably modeled on the occurrence of Moses' Song and Blessing at the end of Deuteronomy.[71] The verbal parallels between the introduction of Dt. 32 and that of 2 Sam. 22, the place of these respective chapters at the end of a book and at the end of a life, as well as other similarities in style and function, make the analogy compelling. Nevertheless, ch. 22 still possesses a title which provides a setting for it at the time of David's triumph over Saul and not at the time of his death. Only the introductory formula in 23:1 suggests by האחרנים that what follows is the "last words" of David. Furthermore, the content of 23:1–7 is not a series of blessings like the other last testaments of Isaac (Gen. 27), Jacob (Gen. 49), or Moses (Dt. 33). Therefore, the positioning of 22 and 23:1–7 in the final complex 21–24 is suggestive of a late redactional interpretation of the two together after the formation of Deuteronomy on the analogy of Dt. 32 and 33. Like Dt. 32 and 33, these chapters are made the final, culminating statement of the principal protagonist at the end of his life's activity.

Finally, it is particularly noteworthy that the most significant shared feature between 2 Sam. 22 and 23:1–7 is the major interpretive theme that lies at the heart of each composition. Twice in the psalm David is seen to formulate the principal factor in his experience, "The Lord rewarded me

[70] M. H. Segal, "Studies in the Books of Samuel," *JQR*, 5 (1914–15): 201, shows 22:51 to be an interpretive link between the Song in 22:1–50 and the last words in 23:1–7.

[71] See Carlson, op. cit., pp. 228–47, for an excellent consideration of the evidence. Carlson is justly cautious about defining precisely the influence of Dt. 32 and 33 upon the formation of 2 Sam. 22 and 23:1–7. He suggests that both were transmitted by the same Deuteronomic group. However, there would also be the possibility that the relationship between 22 and 23:1–7 is purely redactional at a time when Deuteronomy in its present structure was essentially complete. In that case, the post-Deuteronomic redactors chose to provide a combined conclusion in the words of David similar to that of Moses in Deuteronomy.

according to my righteousness [כצדקתי]; according to the cleanness of my hands he recompensed me" (vv. 21, 25). With a strikingly similar point of view the wisdom saying in 23:3b describes the enduring king as the "one who rules over men justly [צדיק]; ruling in the fear of God." Whereas before, in ch. 22, the statement is part of prayerful self-reflection, the wisdom saying and its elaboration in 23:3b speaks to the same issue in general wisdom terms.[72] In sum, 22 and 23:1–7 are linked together redactionally and by repeated and shared themes they emphasize together a similar perspective on the preceding traditions. A specific examination of the wisdom saying in 23:1–7 is required to demonstrate its function.

The text of the wisdom saying in 2 Sam. 23:3b–7 presents a number of serious problems. The difficulty seems to lie at the earliest level of its insertion at the end of 2 Samuel and, therefore, is not simply a result of the later textual transmission.[73] The variants are often a result of trying to make better sense of a text which appears full of *lacunae* in the fashion of a poetic reduction of language. Only enough words are left to sustain the barest intuition of its meaning. The syntactical ambiguity for a later translation is consequently maximized. Despite these serious limitations certain essential lines remain unobscured, and these persistent features are sufficient to support our limited investigation.

In v. 3b one finds a concise wisdom saying in the conventional style of Proverbs. The *MT* offers:

מושל באדם צדיק
מושל יראת אלהים

A number of scholars follow Mowinckel's interpretation of these lines as a temporal conditional clause. This reading is reflected, for example, in the *RSV*: "When one rules justly over men, ruling in the fear of God, [then] he dawns on them like the morning light ..."[74] Hertzberg offers, "Wer

---

[72] See the discussion by S. Mowinckel, "'Die letzten Worte Davids' II Sam. 23:1–7," *ZAW*, 4 (1927): 44–45.

[73] Cf. Mowinckel, op. cit., pp. 41–43. Mowinckel suggests that several words and phrases have been dropped accidentally from these verses. However, it is probably better to view this sparseness of language more in terms of an original tendency towards poetic compression.

[74] Ibid., p. 41. Mowinckel adjusts the *MT* only by the addition of a ב before יראת (see pp. 33, 40). Another possibility is that the באדם in the first strophe is carried over by implication into the next. In that case both צדיק and יראת אלהים should simply by regarded as adverbial accusatives, and Mowinckel's addition of the ב would be unnecessary. On the possibility of a resumptive באדם, see P. A. H. de Boer, "Texte et Tradution des Paroles attribuées à David en 2 Samuel xxiii 1–7," *VTS*, 4 (1957): 46–56. He translates v. 3b, "celui qui

gerecht über Menschen herrscht, wer herrscht in Gottesfurcht."[75] The majority of commentators regard the statement as clearly a wisdom saying. It describes the ideal attributes of a ruler in terms of righteousness and the fear of God. Even the LXX's misreading of the first מושל as παραβολήν confirms the recognition of its obvious wisdom character. Moreover, the parallelism of צדיק with יראת אלהים recalls the ethical religious understanding of צדיק commonplace in the wisdom books.[76]

After the wisdom saying, v. 4 follows and is with v. 6 the most difficult to translate. Only the minimal intention is explicit to the later reader. At least it is obvious that in v. 4 the writer portrays the righteous ruler of the wisdom saying in the imagery of recurring and beneficial natural phenomena. Conversely, vv. 6–7 describe the fate of the wicked. Once again, the conventional wisdom polarities are obvious in style and content. Furthermore, this regularity in style makes the appearance of v. 5 seem anomalous, for the verse interrupts a coherent literary type by introducing a personal application between the usual antithetical comparisons of fates for the righteous and the unrighteous. Here David explicitly identifies his monarchy with the side of the righteous. The "house" of David is supposed to exhibit the very rewards of the righteous as poetically described in v. 4 (see כן in v. 5). So, too, the "everlasting covenant" which God made with David is cast as a realization of the proverb and the elaboration in v. 4. The perpetual character of the natural forces portrayed in v. 4 is thus made to correspond to the "eternal covenant" which is "ordered and made secure" (v. 5). The close connection between the wisdom saying and this secondary interpretation is confirmed further by the association between the rain and herbage in 4b and the claim in v. 5b that every desire of David will come to fruition (יצמיח).

Over against this stress purely on the wisdom character of vv. 3b–4, 6–7, the larger literary setting of 23:1–7 must be considered. The introduction in v. 1 finds close parallels both in the preface to the teaching of Agur in Prov. 30:1 (cf. 31:1) and to the oracles of Balaam in Num. 24:3, 15. Only the opening words in v. 2 succeed in tipping the scales in the

domine sur un juste (ou privilégié); celui qui domine sur la crainte de Dieu" (p. 51). He takes this to mean, "Aussi peu que l'on domine sur un homme craignant Dieu, l'on domine sur un juste" (p. 52). Although his translation is perhaps theoretically possible, it does not fit the context as well as the more conventional proposals. If one takes the באדם (with the *MT* pointing) as definite then the following indefinite cannot serve properly as an adjective to it.

[75] Hertzberg, op. cit., p. 323.

[76] Joachim Becker, *Gottesfurcht im Alten Testament* (Rome: Päpstliches Bibelinstitut, 1965), p. 258.

direction of a prophetic context rather than simply that of wisdom. On the one hand, the nuance that David is not really speaking as an ecstatic, but merely in words that purport to be as inspired as a prophet's, is too fragile a hypothesis. It is insufficient evidence for Budde to conclude, therefore, that 23:1–7 is strictly a *Weisheitsspruch* in its entirety.[77] On the other hand, the later traditional messianic reading should not dominate the interpretation, as with O. Procksch and C. J. Goslinga, at the expense of the obvious wisdom content.[78]

Mowinckel offers perhaps the most impressive analysis of the passage. He acknowledges that the content is not prophecy but that of a wisdom saying together with an elaboration in antithetical parallelism. The prophetic introductions are a *literarische Fiktion.*[79] However, this secondary redactional context does, in fact, cast the passage as a prophetic oracle, and David's personal application in v. 5 now has a futuristic ring to it, as though the wisdom were an omen. Although there would no other examples of prophecy quite like this in the OT, he treats the passage as an artificial mixture of wisdom and prophecy on the analogy with wisdom used in other prophets.[80] Since the analogy is weak, he explores the alleged relation between wisdom and omen literature in support of a prophetic understanding of a wisdom saying.[81] The futuristic meaning lies only *zwischen den Zeilen.*[82] By an extraordinarily subjective approach he has a "feeling" for the syntax of the "*mashal.*"[83] He claims to detect an ominous, veiled staccato quality to it. This mysterious, lapidary style is then alleged to be reminiscent of the symbolism of a vision. Therefore, he concludes that the original wisdom material has been completely overcome in a prophetic setting. He theorizes that the passage probably finds its original setting in the political-religious sphere, namely, as a prophetic guarantee of security, *vaticinium ex eventu*, for the reigns of either Hezekiah or Josiah.[84].

Mowinckel's distinction between the wisdom content and its secondary prophetic function is helpful. Nevertheless, he does not explore the larger redactional context of the passage. His attempt to dissolve the wisdom narrative entirely into a homogeneous prophetic interpretation

---

[77] Budde, op. cit., pp. 315–16. Cf. Hertzberg, op. cit., p. 325.

[78] O. Procksch, "Die letzten Worte Davids (2 Sam. 23:1–7)," *Alttestamentliche Studien, BZAW*, 13 (1913): 118, 122–25; C. J. Goslinga, *Het Tweede Boek Samuel* (Kampen: N. V. Uitgeversmaatschappij J. H. Kok, 1962), pp. 412–28.

[79] Mowinckel, op. cit., pp. 44–45.

[80] Ibid., pp. 48 ff.

[81] Ibid., p. 49.

[82] Ibid., p. 47.

[83] Ibid., p. 51.

[84] Ibid., pp. 52–57.

is faulted by the extravagant ingenuity in interpretive methods and by the lack of a convincing analogy. His argument that Hag. 2:15–19 is an exact parallel in fact, if not in form, fails for the same reason as the example of a wisdom saying in Is. 32:1ff. In these instances, a wisdom saying is a rhetorical device and not clearly deprived of its wisdom character in order to give it a prophetic function. While Mowinckel elsewhere describes the prophetic oracle as only a lightly retouched wisdom saying, he now presses the prophetic framework by extraordinary means in order to obviate completely any remaining ambiguity.[85]

In my opinion, the last words of David must be viewed in a twofold manner which is truer to its composition. On the one hand, the secondary context of the passage given by its introduction (vv. 1b–2) allows the word עולם in v.5 to trigger a strongly futuristic hearing. It is this dimension that Mowinckel exploits in the direction of a prophetic assurance to some specific Davidic king in the later Judean Monarchy. Post-exilic Judaism was to see a messianic promise in it. On the other hand, the style of 23: 1–7 and its redactional placement with 22, in the complex 21–24, allows it to serve another function. As the LXX recognized, although prophetic, it is still a wisdom saying which David interprets in v.5 as a pious commentary on his life as king of Israel.[86]

The retrospective quality is maintained in the Hebrew by the rhetorical questions which David addresses to the readers in v.5. These questions must be answered in the affirmative by those who have read the David story. As with ch. 22, 2 Sam. 23:1–7 exercises a hermeneutical function to interpret the previous literature, but now specifically by means of a wisdom saying reminiscent of Proverbs (cf. Prov. 16:12; 29:4, 14). In other words, the proverb is evaluated in terms of a wisdom assessment of the David story. The criterion of this assessment, "righteousness ... fear of God," is marked by its association with 2 Sam. 22 and the repeated claim to success "according to my righteousness" (see vv. 21, 25). In the light of this use of wisdom in 23:1–7, it is significant that David is elsewhere in the Psalms pictured as one who teaches "the fear of the Lord" by means of proverbs (see Ps. 14:11–14).[87]

---

[85] Ibid., p. 47.

[86] Perhaps the use of a moralizing proverb in the context of prophetic pronouncement is justified by evidence of mixing oracular and moralizing omens in the ancient Near East, and even in Proverbs. Cf. Glendon E. Bryce, "Omen Wisdom in Ancient Israel," *JBL*, 94 (1975): 19–37.

[87] Carlson, op. cit., p. 257. See, also, 11 QPs[a] in which a prose insert follows a citation of 2 Sam. 23:7b. The prose reads, "And David, the son of Jesse, was wise, and a light like the light of the sun, and literate, and discerning and perfect in all his ways before God and

The significance of this sapiential assessment of the Davidic traditions is heightened for the present purposes if the redaction of 2 Sam. 21–24 occurred at a "canon conscious" stage in the formation of the Samuel books. That is to say, the redactors may be conscious of giving the books a definitive shape which reflects their normative, religious interpretation in the context of other sacred books. In that case, one could argue that wisdom plays a theological role in the context of the emerging Hebrew canon.

At the outset, 2 Sam. 21–24 breaks the Succession Narrative, the continuation of which the book of Kings picks up (chs. 1–2). Hence, the redaction is integral to the final, constitutive formation of biblical books. Moreover, 2 Sam. 22 and 23:1–7 are modeled after the last Song and Blessing of Moses in Dt. 32 and 33.[88] This redactional arrangement presumes both the prior recognition of Deuteronomy as an authoritative religious book and a similar religious function and authority for the books of Samuel. Likewise, the formal descriptions of David as one who succeeded according to righteousness recall both the summarizing descriptions of Moses as "the man of God" (Dt. 33:1, structurally parallel to 2 Sam. 23:1!) and the idealization of Moses at the end of Deuteronomy as the prophet *par excellence* (Dt. 34:10–12). By implication, what Moses was to the prophets in Israel, David was to her kings.

The late date of the redaction allows the possibility of canon conscious rather than merely inner-biblical interpretation. The addition of 2 Sam. 21–24 in the course of a redactional reworking of the Samuel traditions would not be likely before the time of Josiah when at least an edition of Deuteronomy was promulgated. One might argue for its origin with a dtr[1] (cf. Cross[89]), during the reign of Josiah, but the parallels with Dt. 32 and 33, which M. Noth takes to be part of the exilic dtr redaction along with the second introduction of Deuteronomy suggest an exilic or post-exilic date. Carlson seeks to explain their origin by appeal to an exilic, Deuteronomic circle, his "D-group," which intended to "lend depth, by (their) description of the ideally 'righteous' king, to the Deuteronomists' criticism of David in these traditions."[90] However, the historical existence

men." Cited and discussed in James Sanders' *The Dead Sea Psalms Scrolls* (Ithica: Cornell Univ. Press, 1967), pp. 134–37.

88 Carlson, op. cit., pp. 228 ff.

89 Frank M. Cross, "The Themes of the Book of Kings and the Structure of the Deuteronomistic History," pp. 274–89, in *Canaanite Myth and Hebrew Epic* (Cambridge: Harvard University Press, 1973).

90 Carlson, op. cit., p. 257.

of such a group is difficult to establish on the basis of compositional techniques; the context of the judgment made of David in 2 Sam. 21 and 24 weakens the defense of such an explicit counter-*tendenz*; and the idealization of David in the deuteronomistic redaction of 1–2 Kings suggests that such a concern for David's righteousness would not *necessarily* be foreign to the purposes of those same redactors.

If Carlson's arguments for an exilic D-group are not entirely convincing, at least he, more than other scholars, sees an important tension existing between the core of the complex, which predicates everything on David's righteousness, and the framework of chs. 21 and 24 with their portrayal of David's perfidy and God's mercy. From the standpoint of the present study, this tension introduces a complexity which makes the summarizing effect of these chapters all the more realistic and profound. Each chapter (21 and 24) provides an example of David's vulnerability to wickedness and guilt, then describes how he succeeds only by an appeal to God and by a final ability to take the right course of action. Hence, they lend depth materially *to the criteria of righteousness* stressed by David's final song and last words in 22 and 23:1–7.

The structure of the redaction in 2 Sam. 21–24 finds a close parallel in redaction of the epilogue to Qoheleth. Both assume a fixed body of literature with contradictory religious implications. While in the body of Qoheleth an unresolved tension exists between traditional wisdom and unbridled cynicism, there is similarly a vagueness within the Samuel traditions themselves about how one ought to evaluate David. Despite the obviously commendable acts of David in 1 Samuel and parts of 2 Samuel, K. Leimbach fairly describes 2 Sam. 11–20 as "David's sin and its consequences."[91] Carlson logically divides 2 Samuel into chs. 2–5 as "David under the Blessing (ברכה)" and chs. 9–24 as "David under the curse (קללה)."[92] Hertzberg, like von Rad, tries to find in each a common witness to divine grace. This solution attempts to solve the problem theologically by turning the negative reports on David's life into examples of his greatest dependence on the grace of God.

The solution offered by the redactor in 2 Sam. 21–24 moves in a different direction and parallels that found in the redaction of Qoheleth in two ways. First, the redactor speaks directly to this lack of a unified evaluation of the actions of David by *thematizing* the reports into two different types: one in terms of David's attaining success through righteous-

[91] Cited by Hertzberg, op. cit., p. 312.

[92] Carlson, op. cit., pp. 41 ff. and 131 ff.

ness (2 Sam. 22 and 23 : 1–7) and another, which brackets the first, concerned with David's guilt for wrong doing, repentance, punishment, and expiation (2 Sam. 21 : 1–14 and 24 : 1–25). By this means the tensions within the traditions were given a normative religious context which presents David as a model of the obedient life against the background of occasional failure and temporary punishment.

A second parallel with the redaction of Qoheleth and one which anticipates the studies in Sirach and Baruch lies in the redactor's understanding of what constitutes the norms for David's righteousness. The similar emphasis on David's righteousness in the song (2 Sam. 22) and the last words (23 : 1–7) contrasts with their dissimilar use of norms. On the one hand, between the repeated key phrase in 2 Sam. 22 that "the Lord rewarded me according to my righteousness," David elaborates, "For I have kept the ways of the Lord, and have not wickedly departed from my God. For all his ordinances were before me and from his statutes I did not turn aside" (vv. 22–23). This language recalls admonitions in the book of Deuteronomy and the required obedience to the Torah (e.g., Dt. 4 : 1–14; 7 : 12). On the other hand, the proverb in 2 Sam. 23 also declares David's righteousness but casts it in terms of Israel's wisdom traditions. Righteousness is identified with "the fear of God" in a manner common to Proverbs. So, with 2 Sam. 22 and 23 : 1–7 the commands of the Torah and the advice of wisdom appear to be complementary and the David stories illustrate the truth of both. True to the "conclusion of the matter" in Qoh. 12 : 14, David is portrayed as the righteous example who both "fears God *and* obeys his commandments."

Furthermore, the complex 21–24 with its core assessment of David's righteousness is not a free and independent estimate of David. Rather, it is grounded in an actual interpretation of the preceding narrative. For example, in 1 Sam. 24 : 17 David's surprise appearance before his enemy, Saul, results in the confession by Saul that "You are more righteous than I; for you have repaid me good, whereas I have repaid you evil." Consequently, his chief antagonist evaluates David's righteousness as superior to that of his own. In the redactional ending of 2 Sam. 22–23 : 1–7, what Saul has recognized in David at the dawn of his career continues to be considered the guiding virtue of his life. Moreover, when Saul repents for his anger against David in 1 Sam. 26 : 23 David's reply is axiomatic, "The Lord rewards every man for his righteousness and his faithfulness." The expression of "reward according to righteousness" is precisely the same as that in the key phrases of 2 Sam. 22 : 21, 25! On the basis of these attributes David accounts for his ambush of Saul and appeals to God for future deliverance from any tribulation (1 Sam. 26:23–24). Saul, then, blesses David and assures him, "You will do many things and will succeed in them" (v. 25). Finally, 2 Sam. 8:15 states matter-of-factly that David ruled over Israel and "administered justice [משפט] and equity [צדיקה] to all his people." These most obvious passages together with other related patterns in the narrative are evaluated together and epitomized by the redactional ending to the Samuel books.

Like the previous studies in Sirach and Baruch the narratives provide an occasion for moral judgement in terms of a distinction between wisdom and Torah. Similarly, the link between the interpretation and the texts being interpreted depends more on correspondence with key words or phrases than on full citations. Clearly, the implication for interpreting the narratives of 1–2 Samuel is similar to that recognized in the Sirach and Baruch studies. In Bar. 3:9ff. the narratives of the Torah and Prophets were used to show negative examples of how the wise and strong perished. They perished because they, unlike Israel, did not know "the way of wisdom." The redactor of 2 Sam. 21–24 invites the opposite assessment of the Davidic narratives with emphasis on David's success because of his obedience to the commandments of the Torah and the dictates of wisdom. Consequently, the narratives about David were set not only in the context of the book of Deuteronomy, but also within the shadow of the still undelimited sacred wisdom traditions.

In sum, the introduction of 23:1–7 invites a reading as prophecy with a vision for the future of the Davidic dynasty. Nevertheless, the use of a wisdom saying and its redactional position in context with 22 in the complex 21–24 discloses another, quite different function. It is combined with 22 to form a dual retrospective commentary on the previous narrative about David. By proverbializing the life of David, it evaluates fixed narrative literature in terms of the wisdom traditions. The minimal conclusion is that wisdom reminiscent of the biblical wisdom books now serves as one of the hermeneutical rubrics under which the books of Samuel have been interpreted redactionally. Once again, in the context of the earliest Scripture no unbridgeable gulf exists between the sacred historical narrative and the ideals of sacred wisdom. Wisdom in Scripture provides more than an anthropological point of view but a major theological evaluation of religious and moral reality. Therefore, the readers of Scripture are invited to see in David a model of the obedient life in the manner of the biblical wisdom tradition.[93]

[93] In this respect, Whybray's study of the Succession Narrative, like that of von Rad on the Joseph Narrative and Talmon on Esther, demonstrates the adaptability of the literature

Conclusion to the OT Studies

The preceding OT studies present a series of secondary redactions which interpret non-wisdom traditions in terms of wisdom. However, the distinctions used here between wisdom and non-wisdom traditions do not depend chiefly on an historical or form critical definition of wisdom in ancient Israel. In a strict sense, the search for wisdom's definition and religious significance is a part of the process of canonization which selected and shaped traditions into sacred biblical books and collections. Even as the five-book Torah was assigned to Moses, there was a tendency to delimit wisdom according to those books assigned to Solomon. The epilogue to Qoheleth demonstrates a concern for holistic integrity within this contextual definition of wisdom. Moreover, the OT redactions which were studied suggest that wisdom was assumed to have a hermeneutical function in the context of the canon and that it offered a model for the interpretation of other biblical narrative, prophetic, and hymnic texts as a guide to the obedient life. Unfortunately, this tendency of the redactions to generalize upon historical traditions for purposes of moral reflection makes them, like most wisdom sayings, very hard to date. At a minimum, this series of secondary redactions exercise a similar literary function. Furthermore, the redactions may be called "canon conscious" in the sense that they participate intentionally in a larger search for the definition and role of wisdom in the context of fixed traditions.

Although the late redaction history of the OT sharpened the definition of wisdom in the context of the canon, it also left many important issues unresolved. It established a tension between Torah and wisdom which other generations would seek to resolve. For example, in 2 Sam. 22–23, David predicates his righteousness on two separate grounds, obedience to the statutes of Mosaic law and obedience to a proverb describing the rule of a righteous king. While the complementarity between these two competing guides to righteousness is implied, the logical connection between them is left open. So, also, the advice in the epilogue to Qoheleth that one should "fear God *and* obey his commandments" links Torah and wisdom together without thoroughly exploring what that relationship might mean. Perhaps a parallel to this problem exists even in

---

to sophisticated wisdom interpretation. That these narratives were composed with this potential may be more a witness to one of the functions that classical or epical literature was expected to perform rather than to their unique status as representatives of a special didactic genre (see, pp. 14–16). Certainly this readiness of the literature was seized upon and amplified in the early religious usage of these texts as a resource for moral admonition.

contemporary debates over the relation of prescriptive to relational ethics. In any case, this tension, fixed in the context of the OT, sets the stage for the many later confrontations over the nature of righteousness within Judaism and Christianity.

The responses to this challenge which appear in Sirach and Baruch illustrate an aspect of the discussion in the second century B.C. On the one hand, their exegesis, like that of the selected OT redactions, chose a specific direction by which to explore the relation between Torah and wisdom. In contrast to much later Jewish interpretation they often chose to sapientalize the Torah rather than to find in wisdom literature a veiled reference to the law. On the other hand, the complexity of the book of the Torah itself helped create new possibilities for relating wisdom and Torah. The book of the Torah contains both legal codes and prosaic narratives, and it was precisely the narratives, not the legal codes, which provided the ideal medium for wisdom interpretation in Sirach and Baruch. Likewise, the brief hints at an historical biography for wisdom in Job 28 and in Prov. 8 offered a point of intersection with the story of Israel. By imitating Prov. 8 and by a didactic lesson on the way of wisdom, Sir. 24 and Bar. 3:9–4:4 offer an impressive, if not entirely satisfying, solution to the problem. At the very least, they recognized fully how the biblical description of righteousness had been both deepened and complicated by the call to "fear God and obey his commandments."

Bibliography

Albright, W.F. *Archaeology and the Religion of Israel*. Baltimore: Anchor Books, 1946.

Alonso-Schökel, L. "Sapiential and Covenant Themes in Genesis 2–3," *TDig*, 13 (1965): 3–10.

Barthélemy, D., and Rickenbacker, O. *Konkordanz zum Hebräischen Sirach*. Göttingen: Vandenhoeck & Ruprecht, 1973.

Barton, G.A. *The Book of Ecclesiastes*. The International Critical Commentary. New York: Charles Scribners, 1908.

Battistone, J.J. An Examination of the Literary and Theological Background of the Wisdom Passage in the Book of Baruch. Ph. D. dissertation, Duke University, 1968.

Bauckmann, E.G. "Die Proverbien und die Sprüche des Jesus Sirach," *ZAW*, 72 (1960): 33–63.

Baumgartner, W. "Die israelitische Weisheitsliteratur," *ThR*, 5 (1933): 259–88.

–. "Die literarischen Gattungen in der Weisheit des Jesus Sirach," *ZAW*, 34 (1914): 168–98.

Becker, J. *Gottesfurcht im Alten Testament*. Rome: Päpstliches Bibelinstitut, 1965.

Bloch, Renée. "Midrash." In *Dictionnaire de La Bible: Supplément*. Edited by Henry Cazelles. Vol. 5. Paris: Libraire Letouzey et Ané, 1957.

Bonnard, P.E. *La Sagesse en Personne annoncée et venue: Jésus Christ*. Paris: Les Editions du Cerf, 1966.

Boston, J.R. "The Wisdom Influence Upon the Song of Moses," *JBL*, 87 (1968): 198–202.

Box, G.G., and Oesterley, W.O.W. "The Book of Sirach." In *The Apocrypha and Pseudepigrapha of the OT in English*. Edited by R.H. Charles. Vol. 1. Oxford: Oxford Press, 1913.

Brockelmann, C. *Hebräische Syntax*. Neukirchen Kreis Moers: Verlag der Buchhandlung des Erziehungsvereins, 1956.

–. *Lexicon Syriacum*. Berlin: Verlag von Reuther & Reichard, 1895.

Brownlee, W.H. "Biblical Interpretation Among the Sectaries of the Dead Sea Scrolls," *BA*, 14 (1951): 54–76.

–. "Psalms 1–2 as a Coronation Liturgy," *Bib*, 52 (1971): 321–36.

Bruce, F.F. "The Earliest Old Testament Interpretation," *OTS*, 17 (1972): 44–52.

Bryce, Glendon E. "Omen Wisdom in Ancient Israel," *JBL*, 94 (1975): 19–37.

Budde, Karl. *Die Bücher Samuel Erklärt*. Kurzer Hand-Commentar zum Alten Testament, vol. 8. Tübingen: Verlag von J.C.B. Mohr, 1902.

Carlson, R.A. *David the Chosen King*. Stockholm: Almqvist & Wiksell, 1964.

Carmichael, Calum M. *The Laws of Deuteronomy*. Ithaca: Cornell University Press, 1974.

Charles, R.H. "The Book of Baruch." In *The Apocrypha and Pseudepigrapha of the Old Testament*. Edited by R.H. Charles. Vol. 2. Oxford: Clarendon Press, 1913.

–. "The Book of Jubilees." In *The Apocrypha and Pseudepigrapha of the Old Testament*. Edited by R.H. Charles. Vol. 2. Oxford: Clarendon Press, 1913.

Childs, B.S. "Psalm Titles and Midrashic Exegesis," *JSS*, 16 (1971): 137–50.

Clark, W. Malcolm. "A Legal Background to the Yahwist's Use of 'Good and Evil' in Genesis 2–3," *JBL*, 88 (1969): 266–78.

Conzelmann, Hans: "Die Mutter der Weisheit." In *Zeit und Geschichte*, pp. 226–34. Edited by Erich Dinkler. Tübingen: J.C.B. Mohr (Paul Siebeck), 1964.

Crenshaw, James L. "Method in Determining Wisdom Influence Upon 'Historical' Literature," *JBL*, 88 (1969): 129–42.

–. "Prolegomenon." In *Studies in Ancient Israelite Wisdom*, pp. 1–21. Edited by James L. Crenshaw. New York: KTAV Publishing House, 1976.

Cross, F.M., Jr., and Freedman, D.N. "A Royal Song of Thanksgiving: II Samuel 22 = Psalm 18," *JBL*, 72 (1953): 15–34.

De Boer, P.A.H. "Texte et Tradution des Paroles attribuées à David en 2 Samuel xxiii 1–7," *SVT*, 4 (1957): 46–56.

Deissmann, Adolf. *Licht vom Osten*, 4th ed., rev. Tübingen: J.C.B. Mohr, 1923.

Denton, R.C. "The Literary Affinities of Exodus xxxiv 6f," *VT*, 13 (1963): 34–51.

Descamps, A. "Pour un classement littéraire des psaumes." In *Mélanges Bibliques Rédigés en L'honneur de André Robert*, pp. 187–96. Paris: Bloud & Gay, 1957.

Driver, S.R. *Notes on the Hebrew Text and the Topography of the Books of Samuel*. Oxford: Clarendon Press, 1913.

Duesberg, H., and Fransen, I. *Les Scribes Inspirés*, rev. ed. Maredsous, Belgium: Editions de Maredsous, 1966.

Eichrodt, W. *Theology of the Old Testament*. Translated by J.A. Baker. 2 vols. Philadelphia: Westminster Press, 1961.

Erman, A. "Das Weisheitsbuch des Amen-em-ope," *OLZ*, 27 (1924): 241–52.

Festugiere, A.J. "A propos des Aretalogies d'Isis," *HTR*, 42 (1949): 290–334.

Fichtner, J. *Die altorientalische Weisheit in ihrer isr.-jüd. Ausprägung, BZAW*, 62 (1933).

–. "Jesaja unter den Weisen," *ThLZ*, 74 (1949): 75–80.

Fohrer, G. "Remarks on Modern Interpretation of the Prophets," *JBL*, 80 (1961): 309–19.

Forman, Charles C. "Koheleth's Use of Genesis," *JSS*, 5 (1960): 256–63.

Freedman, D.N. "The Law and The Prophets," *SVT*, 9 (1962): 250–65.

Fritzsche, Otto F. *Die Weisheit Jesus-Sirach's erklärt*, 5th ed., rev. Kurzgefaßtes Exegetisches Handbuch zu den Apokryphen des Alten Testament, vol. 5. Leipzig: Verlag von S. Hirzel, 1859.

Galling, K. *Die Fünf Megilloth*, 2nd ed. Handbuch zum Alten Testament, vol. 18. Tübingen: J.C.B. Mohr, 1969.

–. "Koheleth-Studien," *ZAW*, 50 (1932): 276–99.

Gasser, Johann K. *Das althebräische Spruchbuch und die Sprüche Jesu Ben Sira*. Gütersloh: C. Bertelsmann, 1903.

Gerleman, Gillis. *Ruth–Das Hohelied*. Biblischer Kommentar: Altes Testament, vol. 18. Neukirchen-Vluyn: Neukirchener Verlag, 1965.

Gerstenberger, E. "Covenant and Commandment," *JBL*, 15 (1965): 38–51.

–. "Psalms." In *Old Testament Form Criticism*. Edited by John H. Hayes. San Antonio: Trinity University Press, 1974.

–. *Wesen und Herkunft des sogenannten "Apodictischen Rechts," WMANT*, 20 (1961).

Goslinga, C.J. *Het Tweede Boek Samuel*. Kampen: N. V. Uitgeversmaatschappij J.H. Kok, 1962.

Gunkel, H. *Die Psalmen*. Göttingen: Vandenhoeck & Ruprecht, 1926.

Guthrie, Harvey H. *Wisdom and Canon: Meanings of the Law and the Prophets*. Seabury: Seabury-Western Theological Seminary, 1966.

Hartwell, R.R. *The Principal Versions of Baruch*. New Haven: Yale University Press, 1915.

Haspecker, Joseph. *Gottesfurcht bei Jesus Sirach*. Rome: Päpstliches Bibelinstitut, 1967.

Haupt, P. *Koheleth oder Weltschmerz in der Bibel*. Leipzig: J.C. Henrich's Buchhandlung, 1908.

Hengel, M. *Judentum und Hellenismus*. Tübingen: J.C.B. Mohr, 1969.

Hertzberg, H.W. *Der Prediger*. Kommentar zum Alten Testament, vol. 17. Gerd Mohn: Gütersloher Verlagshaus, 1963.

–. *Die Samuelbücher*. Das Alte Testament Deutsch, vol. 10. Göttingen: Vandenhoeck & Ruprecht, 1956.

Higger, M., ed. *Tractate Sopherim*. New York: Bloch Publishing Co., 1937.

Hitzig, F. *Der Prediger Solomon's*. Kurzgefaßtes exegetisches Handbuch zum Alten Testament, vol. 7. Leipzig: Weidmann'sche Buchhandlung, 1847.

Hruby, K. "Gesetz und Gnade in der rabbinischen Überlieferung," *Judaica*, 25 (1969): 30–63.

–. "La Torah Identifiée à la Sagesse et L'Activite du 'Sage' dans la Tradition Rabbinique," *BVC*, 76 (1967): 65–78.

Jacob, Edmund. "L'historie d'Israël vue par Ben Sira." In *Mélanges Bibliques Rédigés en L'honneur de André Robert*. Paris: Bloud & Gay, 1957.

Jansen, H. Ludin. *Die Spätjüdische Psalmendichtung, ihr Entstehungskreis und ihr 'Sitz im Leben'*. Oslo: Kimmisjon hos Jacob Dybwad, 1937.

Jastrow, M., Jr. *A Gentile Cynic*. Philadelphia: J.B. Lippencott Co., 1919.

Jensen, J. *The Use of Tora by Isaiah, CBQMS*, 3 (1973).

Kayatz, Christa. *Studien zu Proverbien 1–9*. Neukirchen-Vluyn: Neukirchener Verlag, 1966.

Koch, K. *The Rediscovery of Apocalyptic*. Translated by Margaret Kohl. London: S.C. M. Press, 1973.

Koehler, L., and Baumgartner, W. *Lexicon in Veteris Testamenti Libreos*. Leiden: E.J. Brill, 1953.

Kneucker, J.J. *Das Buch Baruch*. Leipzig: F.A. Brockhaus, 1879.

Knox, W.L. "The Divine Wisdom," *JThS*, 38 (1937): 230–37.

Kraus, Hans-Joachim. *Psalmen*. Biblischer Kommentar: Altes Testament, vol. 15. Neukirchen-Vluyn: Neukirchener Verlag, 1960.

Kutsch, E. "Gesetz und Gnade," *ZAW*, 79 (1967): 18–35.

Labuschagne, C.J. "The Song of Moses: Its Framework and Structure." In *De Fructu Oris Sui*, pp. 85–98. Edited by I.H. Eybers, et al. Leiden: E.J. Brill, 1971.

Lebram, J.C.H. "Aspekte der Alttestamentlichen Kanonbildung," *VT*, 18 (1968): 173–89.

Leiman, Sid Z. *The Canonization of Hebrew Scripture: The Talmudic and Midrashic Evidence*. Hamden, Connecticut: Archon Books, 1976.

L'Hour, J. "Les Interdits To'ebah dans le Deuternome," *RB*, 71 (1964): 481–503.

Lidell, Henry George, and Scott, Robert. *A Greek-English Lexicon*, 9th ed., rev. Oxford: Clarendon Press, 1940.

Löw, Immanuel. "Oil." In *The Jewish Encyclopedia*. Edited by I. Singer, et al. Vol. 9. New York: KTAV Publishing House, 1912.

McKane, W. *Prophets and Wise Men*. Naperville: Alec R. Allenson, 1965.

McKay, J.W. "Man's Love for God in Deuteronomy and the Father/Teacher–Son/Pupil Relationship," *VT*, 22 (1972): 426–35.

McKenzie, John. "Reflections on Wisdom," *JBL*, 86 (1967): 1–9.

McNeile, A.H. *An Introduction to Ecclesiastes*. Cambridge: Cambridge University Press, 1904.

Malfroy, J. "Sagesse et Loi dans le Dtn. Études," *VT*, 15 (1965): 49–65.

Marböck, J. "Sirachliteratur seit 1966. Ein Überblick," *TRev*, 71 (1975): 178–83.

–. *Weisheit im Wandel: Untersuchungen zur Weisheitstheologie bei Ben Sira, BBB*, 37 (1971).

Mays, James L. *Hosea*. Old Testament Library. Philadelphia: Westminster Press, 1969.

Middendorp, Th. *Die Stellung Jesu Ben Siras zwischen Judentum und Hellenismus*. Leiden: E.J. Brill, 1973.

Mowinckel, S. " 'Die letzten Worte Davids' II Sam. 23 : 1–7," *ZAW*, 45 (1927): 30–58.

–. *Psalmenstudien*. 6 vols. Kristiania: Jacob Dybwad, 1924.

–. "Psalms and Wisdom." In *Wisdom in Israel and in the Ancient Near East*, pp. 204–24. *SVT*, 3 (1955).

Murmelstein, B. "Adam, ein Beitrag zur Messiaslehre," *WZKM*, 35 (1928): 242–75.

Murphy, R.E. "A Consideration of the Classification, 'Wisdom Psalms'," *SVT*, 9 (1963): 156–57.

–. "Assumptions and Problems in Old Testament Research," *CBQ*, 29 (1967): 407–18.

–. "Ecclesiastes (Qoheleth)." In *The Jerome Biblical Commentary*. Edited by Raymond E. Brown, et al. New York: Prentice-Hall, 1968.

Pedersen, J. "Wisdom and Immortality (Gen. 1–3)" In *Wisdom in Israel and in the Ancient Near East*, pp. 238–46. *SVT*, 3 (1955).

Peters, N. *Das Buch Jesus Sirach oder Ecclesiasticus übersetzt und erklärt*. Exegetisches Handbuch zum Alten Testament, vol. 25. Münster: Druck der Aschendorffschen Buchdruckerei, 1913.

Pfeiffer, R.H. "A Non-Israelite Source of the Book of Genesis," *ZAW*, 48 (1930): 66–73.

–. "Edomite Wisdom," *ZAW*, 3 (1926): 13–25.

–. "Wisdom and Vision in the Old Testament," *ZAW*, 52 (1943): 93–102.

Philo. *Quis Rerum Divinarum Heres*. § 42, LCL, Vol. 4.

Podechard, E. *L'Ecclesiaste*. Paris: Libraire Victor Lecoffre, 1912.

Priest, J.E. "Where is Wisdom to be Placed?" *JBR*, 31 (1963): 275–82.

Procksch, O. "Die letzten Worte Davids (2 Sam. 23 : 1–7)," *BZAW*, 13 (1913): 112–25.

Rad, G. von. "Der Anfang der Geschichtsschreibung im alten Israel," *AK*, 32 (1944): 1–42.

–. *Deuteronomy*. Translated by Dorothea M. Barton. Philadelphia: Westminster Press, 1966.

–. "Die ältere Weisheit Israels," *KerDo*, 2 (1956): 54–72.

–. "Die Weisheit des Jesus Sirach," *EvTh*, 29 (1969): 113–33.

–. *Old Testament Theology*. Translated by D.M.G. Stalker. 2 vols. New York: Harper Row, 1965.

–. "The Joseph Narrative and Ancient Wisdom." Translated by E.W. Trueman Dicken. In *The Problem of the Hexateuch and Other Essays*. London: Oliver E. Boyd, 1965.

–. *Wisdom in Israel*. Translated by James D. Marton. Nashville: Abingdon Press, 1972.

Redford, D.B. "A Study of the Biblical Story of Joseph," *SVT*, 20 (1970): 100–5.

Reusch, F.H. *Erklärung des Buches Baruch*. Freiburg: Herder'sche Verlagshandlung, 1853.

Rickenbacher, Otto. *Weisheitsperikopen bei Ben Sira.* Göttingen: Vandenhoeck & Ruprecht, 1973.

Ringgren, Helmer. *Word and Wisdom.* Lund: H. Ohlssons Boktr., 1947.

Robert, A. A. "Littéraires (Genres)." In *Dictionnaire de La Bible: Supplément.* Edited by Henry Cazelles. Vol. 5. Paris: Librairie Letouzey et Ané, 1957.

Rohde, J. *Rediscovering the Teaching of the Evangelists.* Translated by Dorothea M. Barton. Philadelphia: Westminster Press, 1968.

Rost, L. *Die Überlieferung von der Thronnachfolge Davids.* Stuttgart: Verlag von W. Kohlhammer, 1926.

Rudolph, Wilhelm. *Hosea.* Kommentar zum Alten Testament, vol. 13. Gütersloh: Gütersloher Verlagshaus, 1966.

Rylaarsdam, J. Coert. *Revelation in Jewish Wisdom Literature.* Chicago: University of Chicago Press, 1946.

Ryssel, V. "Baruch." In *Die Apocryphen und Pseudepigraphen des Alten Testament.* Edited by E. Kautzsch. Vol. 1. Tübingen: Verlag von J. C. B. Mohr (Paul Siebeck), 1900.

Scheol, C. "Die 32 wunderbaren Wege der Weisheit und das Buch Deuteronomium," *TPQ,* 116 (1968): 229–37.

Schmidt, H. *Die Thronfahrt Jahves.* Tübingen: J. C. B. Mohr, 1927.

Scott, R. B. Y. *Proverbs.* The Anchor Bible, vol. 18. Garden City: Doubleday & Co., 1965.

–. "The Study of the Wisdom Literature," *Inter,* 24 (1970): 20–45.

Seeligmann, I. L. "Voraussetzungen der Midrashexegese," *SVT,* 1 (1953): 150–81.

Segal, M. H. ספר בן סירא השלם . Jerusalem: Bialit Institute, 1953.

–. "Studies in the Books of Samuel," *JQR,* 5 (1914–15): 201–31.

Smend, R. *Griechisch-syrisch-hebräischer Index zur Weisheit des Jesus Sirach.* Berlin: Gerog Reimer, 1907.

–. *Die Weisheit des Jesus Sirach, erklärt.* Berlin: Verlag von Georg Reimer, 1906.

Snaith, J. G. "Biblical Quotations in the Hebrew of Ecclesiasticus," *JTS,* 18 (1967): 1–12.

Sundberg, Albert C. "The Old Testament of the Early Church: A Study in Canon," *HTR,* 51 (1958): 205–26.

Sutcliffe, E. F. "The Clouds as Water-Carriers in Hebrew Thought," *VT,* 3 (1953): 99–103.

Spicq, C. *L'Ecclesiastique.* La Sainte Bible, vol. 6. Paris: Letouzey et Ané, 1946.

Staerk, W. *Die Erlösererwartung in den östlichen Religionen.* Berlin: W. Kohlhammer, 1938.

Talmon, S. "Wisdom in the Book of Esther," *VT,* 13 (1963): 419–55.

Tov, E. *The Book of Baruch.* Missoula, Montana: Scholars Press, 1975.

Vattioni, Francesco. *Ecclesiastico: Testo ebraico con apparato critico e versioni greca, latina e siriaca.* Napoli, 1968.

Walter, Nikolaus. *Der Thoraausleger Aristobulos, TUGAL,* 86 (1964).

Weinfeld, Moshe. *Deuteronomy and the Deuteronomic School.* Oxford: Clarendon Press, 1972.

–. "Deuteronomy–The Present State of Inquiry," *JBL,* 86 (1967): 249–62.

–. "The Dependence of Deuteronomy upon Wisdom Literature" (hb). In *Y. Kaufmann Jubilee Volume,* pp. 89–109. Edited by M. Haran. Jerusalem, 1960.

Westermann, Claus. *Genesis.* Biblischer Kommentar: Altes Testament, vol. 2. Neukirchen-Vluyn: Neukirchener Verlag, 1970.

–. *The Praise of God in the Psalms.* Translated by Keith R. Crim. Richmond: John Knox Press, 1965.

–. "Zur Sammlung des Psalters." In *Forschungen am Alten Testament*, pp. 336–43. München: Chr. Kaiser Verlag, 1964.

Whedbee, William J. *Isaiah and Wisdom*. New York: Abingdon Press, 1971.

Whybray, R. N. *The Intellectual Tradition in Israel*, *BZAW*, 27 (1974).

–. *The Succession Narrative: A Study of II Samuel 9–20; I Kings 1 and 2*. Naperville: Alec R. Allenson, 1968.

Wildeboer, D. G. *Die Fünf Megillot*. Tübingen: J. C. B. Mohr, 1898.

Wilken, Robert L., ed. *Aspects of Wisdom in Judaism and Early Christianity*. Notre Dame: University of Notre Dame Press, 1975.

Wilkens, U. *Weisheit und Torheit*. Tübingen: J. C. B. Mohr, 1959.

Williams, R. J. *Hebrew Syntax: An Outline*. Toronto: University of Toronto Press, 1967.

Willi-Plein, Ina. *Vorformen der Schriftexegese innerhalb des Alten Testaments*, *BZAW*, 123 (1971).

Wolff, Hans Walter. *Dodekapropheton: Hosea*. Biblischer Kommentar: Altes Testament, vol. 14., 2nd. ed., rev. Neukirchen-Vluyn: Neukirchener Verlag, 1965.

Wright, A. G. "The Riddle of the Sphinx: The Structure of the Book of Qoheleth," *CBQ*, 30 (1968): 313–34.

Ziegler, J. *Ieremia. Baruch. Threni. Epistula Ieremiae*. Septuaginta: Vetus Testamentum Graecum, vol. 15. Göttingen: Vandenhoeck & Ruprecht, 1957.

Zimmerli, W. *Prediger*. Das Alte Testament Deutsch, vol. 16, 2nd ed. Göttingen: Vandenhoeck & Ruprecht, 1967.

Authors Index

Scripture Index

A. Hebrew Scripture

1 Samuel

2 Samuel

1 Kings

2 Kings

1 Chronicles

2 Chronicles

Nehemiah

Job

B. *The Apocrypha*

C. *Pseudepigrapha*

D. *Mishnah*

E. *Tosefta*

F. *Babylonian Talmud*

G. *Jerusalem Talmud*

H. *Midrash*

I. *The New Testament*